KURT

A Guide to the Big Game Hunt of Your Dreams,

And How It Will Change Your Life.

I HOPE THE FEELING OF
ANTICIPATION & ADRENILINE
NEVER FADES!

A compilation of the lessons I learned about myself and others as I pursued big game animals. This guide proves that anyone can plan for and be successful on big game hunt.

I hope to inspire your dreams.

Follow me for more information at.

www.willndiscipline.com

Facebook - Will n Discipline

Instagram - willndiscipline

Table of Contents

Pushing Myself Past My Limits is What I am Most Proud of. 316

About the Author 317

Acknowledgements

I would not have been able to experience any of this without the support of my kids, Britni and Devon. They have always been my biggest fans. From peering out the front window as we pulled up with deer in the truck, to bundling up and tagging along with me, to loving the taste of wild game and hearing my stories repeatedly. They have always been excited about what I do.

If I accomplish nothing else with this effort, I will have documented my hunting career for my grandson's Caden, Riley and any other grandchildren that may follow. Passing the hunting tradition down has become more and more difficult to do, and my hope is this will inspire him as much as it did my kids.

Ironically, the women in my life did not last, but each one of them played a role in this adventure. They all thought it was cool and all supported me. I think most of all they appreciated how happy it made me, and the person it allowed me to become.

My brother-in-law Randy brought hunting into our family. Without that, I don't think any of this would have happened. We spent hours learning and shooting archery together and years chasing whitetail on Dad's farms. I know he appreciates what I have done.

Of course, my brothers picked up on hunting first, while I was just a little kid. The comradery hunting with all their friends drew in my nephews and me. You did not want to miss the opening-day parties and the stories told around the deer hanging in the barn. And my brother Bob was the one who handed me my first guns and took me to buy my first shotgun. I remember that trip as if it was yesterday.

All the rest of my family have been great listeners to my stories and have encouraged my writing. I cannot wait for them to read this book. They have heard some of this, but there are still surprises they did not know.

Dean kept me focused and into it, because hell, he was coming to hunt anyway. Tuna and Digger are two of the best deer hunters I know and I learned a lot from them—even how to party and have a good time. My cousin Steve taught me how to be humble and laugh at my hunting mistakes because he could make any tragedy into a funny story.

Lastly, I appreciate every outfitter and guide that has graciously taken me hunting. I left most of them feeling like I gained another brother. We always built a trust that allowed them to tell me stories that most might not tell their clients. Many of those stories sparked some of the topics in this book. If you return from a hunt, even one where no animal was taken, and did not have the absolute best time of your life, then you did it wrong.

My hope is you read this book, pick up a few pointers, and find the will and discipline to pursue that dream, that hunt of a lifetime, and come back with a smile and a mind full of memories.

Preface

Oh! Where do I start?

I have been thinking about writing this book for a very long time. It is funny, now that I put words on paper, the very reason I want to write this book is to prove to others there is no reason not to pursue your dreams and ambitions. Yet, here I am procrastinating about writing a book—an ambition I have been thinking about for a very long time.

I have had a great hunting career. The cherished memories that bounce around in my head are as vivid and real as the day they happened. I can never lose that feeling. Many of those times I have been able to put my thoughts on paper, documenting my story for others to enjoy. People often tell me, "You should write a book." So here I am, writing that book.

Most hunting stories, videos, and TV shows focus mainly on the kill, or "harvest" if you want a softer term. I will use "kill" because that is exactly what we do and we should not take that lightly. A handful of these so-called professional hunters will touch on the emotion of the hunt. Sadly, many hunters out there don't ever get to know the emotional side of a hunt, and I find that terribly sad. There is so much more to hunting, and many miss the subtle points.

Here is where I have struggled in writing this book. Most of you are doing it wrong and some of you will be so offended by the thoughts relayed here that you won't finish this book. Hunting is an ego-driven sport, and sometimes ego prevents people from learning new things. In all reality, I should come to grips with the fact that many of you will react this way. I can tell you though: I will touch on those feelings in this book and I hope that once you read it you will start to understand the lessons here apply to way more than just hunting. My goal is to change your focus so you have a lasting and more enjoyable experience.

These words are based on my experiences and my perspective, which is of course a male one. When I started, this was a predominantly male-dominated sport. Thankfully, as time passes, the role of women in hunting has grown. I am thankful for that for two reasons. I believe women get the emotion and the spirituality of a hunt right from the start. But more importantly, I believe that the growing number of women who take up hunting will be the savior of our sport. Hunting used to be an excuse for the man to get away from work and the family, but women will be bringing the family along with them. Their appreciation of the total experience will spread like wildfire. Seeing a woman experience a successful hunt, seeing a daughter get to spend time with her dad, and seeing excitement of a child who put in the effort to be successful will be the catalyst that makes our sport grow.

 I am very thankful that my hunting career spanned the best hunting times in history. I am very excited that I might help inspire anyone and everyone to pursue the love of the hunt.
Hunting can change your life. It can change your life in so many ways, if you pay attention and appreciate all the steps you are going through. I will prove to you that hunting adventure parallels other aspects of your life. That never-give-up attitude you have pursuing a trophy animal can be used everywhere else: your job, your marriage, your family, and your dreams. It really comes down to what drives you, what you choose to focus on, and what summons the will and discipline needed to be successful.

I will illustrate to you just how my life has changed because of hunting. I will tell you how it has made me a better person. I am healthier and stronger, both physically and mentally because of hunting. I am more confident knowing there is nothing I cannot do because of hunting. Hunting has made me appreciate so many things in my life outside of the hunting experience. I have a new appreciation of Mother Nature's beauty. I have been humbled many times by the stars in the universe, the violence that has made this planet, the awe of the Northern Lights, and how all this relates to how humans exist on this planet.

In ways it has made me more cynical. I am more aware of the selfish nature of some people. I have a lower tolerance for people who fail to appreciate the things they have. I am less tolerant of the people who claim to be champions of the animals but have no clue how best to protect them. Most of all, my heart aches for the people who think they cannot pursue their dreams and ambitions. I hope to show you how hunting when done right can change your life. I want you all to have the same warm glow that radiates from my heart when I remember the things that I have done.

This book will feature my hunting stories. I hope they will capture your imagination and the emotion from them will light a fire in your soul. My last trip, by far the biggest, was to Russia for moose. I kept a diary of everything I did and every thought I had during the preparation of the trip. I want this to be a how-to book of sorts, a book that guides you through the entire process. I am a firm believer that unknown costs and stress can ruin hunts, taking away from the little things that can make them special. If I can guide you through the process, eliminating the bad things that can pop up, you can enjoy yourself so much more.

I then want to stress all the things that hunting and the process of hunting have done to improve my life. Human beings tend to act and do the same things over and over. These are the exact things that prevent us from doing something, anything that might make us happy. I am no psychologist, but I am interested and aware of how certain things have changed me. I am also very aware of the things that stop me from doing new things—for a while, they stopped me from starting this book. Those same issues are keeping you from your dream hunt, or any dream you choose to pursue. I hope to help you fight through that. I hope to show you not only why hunting can change your life but how it does, and most importantly, how it can change other aspects of your life for the better.

Introduction

It was time to start building my firewood pile for next winter. I use a lot of wood and it seems to be a daunting task when I am in procrastination mode. My brother just had his woods logged and there were treetops everywhere, ready to be cut. As I drove the tractor into the woods, I wondered where the best place to start was. With tree limbs scattered everywhere and visions in my head of the size of the pile I needed, I struggled getting started.

I have been studying self-defense lately. I believe in the Second Amendment and the right to protect ourselves. I am also keenly aware that a gun is not the magic answer to every self-defense situation. If you don't know some sort of hand-to-hand combative, you are falling way short. Maybe that is a topic for my next book, but there is relevance here. Let me explain further. I am six feet tall and weigh over two hundred pounds. I am in pretty good shape. I am not any easy target, what is called a soft target. Being a hard target means the typical thug won't choose to screw with you. Multiple thugs might just decide they want to torment a guy my size. I won't get into the details, but my mindset in this situation is this: I am going to wad up the first guy so violently that I hope at least two thugs decide they are better off running away. Then I will deal with the second person, if needed.

As I drove the tractor into the woods, I thought to just attack the first pile of wood I saw and then move on to the next. Prioritize and execute, knocking one thing off the list at a time. Ironically, procrastination was getting the best of me. But by the end of the weekend I had one hell of a pile of wood. You know what? I felt damn good with what I accomplished. Ironically, I do this at work all the time, deciding on the top-priority task and getting it done. If I cannot yet see the priority, I pick something and get it done. This works every time and I am always satisfied with what I get done, but procrastination often still gets the best of me. Even though I know better, it is hard. I often think about this story my Dad told me about a farm hand he had.

Tink was an uneducated farm hand. Tink probably could not be formally educated, so no one ever tried. Tink was an unkempt man even for 1950s standards. I dare say the only time he could be called clean was after cooling off in a farm pond.

I did see him clean once, some thirty years later as he walked into my father's funeral. When my brother told me who he was I was in awe. Here stood a man that everyone stepped away from, yet ultimately taught me one of the most important lessons of my life.

As I was whining about doing the dreaded chore of the day, Dad stopped me from my hissy fit and told me the story of Tink.

Dad was headed off to town one day and in those days going to town was a significant event. The 1942 pickup truck didn't go all that fast on the rutted dirt road. He had two chores for Tink to work on while he was gone. One was to get the tractor out and mow the fields. Mowing was great job to do on a bright sunny day. The other job was to shovel the cow shit out of the barn. Mind you, in those days, this was all by hand and with a wheelbarrow. Neither job could be finished before dad got home. Dad drove off toward town thinking he would come home to find Tink riding that tractor in his shorts and no shirt, leaving the shitty job to others.

So, Dad told me that when he got home, there was no tractor in the field and no grass had been cut. He made his way to the basement of the barn, and there was Tink, shoveling away covered head to toe in sweat and, well you know, cow shit. Farmers luck would say that the tractor wouldn't start, or the mower was broke. Dad stopped Tink, asking him what was wrong, why he was cleaning the barn first.

Tink's answer was this: "I thought about mowing cause it is such a beautiful day. But, if I mowed, all I would be thinking about is having to shovel that shit when I got done. The only way to make the mowing job fun is to get the shit job done first."

Many times in my career people have made this comment to me. "You really must like work, because you seem to do a lot of it." Every time I laugh and think about Tink and say, "No, I hate work, but I found the best way to get out of doing it, is to just get it done."

They never get it!

There are so many things in life that seem more difficult than they are because human nature gets in the way. Dieting, exercising, walking, running, climbing a mountain, doing tasks at work, or planning a hunt often feel like daunting tasks with no end in sight. I hope to prove to you in this book that if you pick off things one by one and simply get after it the results will come.

You don't run a marathon before you run a mile first. Instead of saying you want to lose twenty pounds, say you want to lose a pound this week. Instead of worrying about the whole pile of firewood, let's just get a trailer load. Instead of saying you cannot afford to go on a hunt of a lifetime, start by saving one step at a time.

The Pinnacle of My Hunting Career

Facebook post from my Russian sick bed, December 8, 2015

I wrote this on Facebook on December 15, 2015. I was lying in bed in Moscow, sick, remembering what I went through and accomplished.

I am the first one up this morning. I drink instant coffee in the dining cabin, with my ass by the roaring fireplace. I am feeling pretty emotional as I sip my coffee in the dark. I got my ass beat yesterday, beat badly. I was pounded on that sled, I was frozen to the point of severe pain, but I kept going and I would not quit. We only stopped the sled once all day, and I peeled my frozen solid gloves off and put new warm ones on. We got within a mile of camp, almost pitch dark. The guide stopped and pointed to camp, then to the swamp on the left. I pointed to the swamp. I can see so I still want to go. My fingers did not like that decision so much. When we finally arrived at camp, I shook my guide's hand, patted him on the shoulder and said, "Tomorrow." I wanted him to know I was not done. I was going out to do it all over again even though the odds were starting to stack against me.

We were warned that if you didn't get your moose in three days, they would head to the mountain to get away from the snowmobiles. Every track I saw yesterday headed toward the mountain.

We rode so hard because I think Albert either wanted me to get a moose bad, or he wanted to beat me into quitting. Either way, I knew that he knew that it was getting impossibly hard to get in front of the moose.

I was having a hard time, feeling sorry for myself for wanting a "trophy," after all the hardship I had seen on the trip to camp. I felt ashamed to even feel bad about it. Plus, it is such a tough thing to come home empty handed. People shun you, like you did something stupid. "How could you spend all that money and not get anything," some say. Those people never really get why I do this. In contrast, the other hunters in camp were only focused on a rack. I hated their uniquely American attitude.

What I could say was this: I was leaving everything I had out there in that negative 30 degrees Celsius temperature. Every now and then I would yell, "I am hunting in Russia" and I would suck it up. I knew one thing for sure, I was probably never coming back here, and I am not going home regretting not doing everything I could. The only thing that was going to stop me was a moose on the ground or me being pushed into that Russian army truck to go home.

On the other hand, I am fully aware how blessed and lucky I am. I never take that for granted. The greatest benefit of a trip like this is renewing my appreciation for my family back home and my life.

So, as I drank my coffee, I became very content with the fact that I would likely go home without a moose.

I was proud of what I had put into it over the 5 days of travel and 4 days of hunting. You'll never take away what is in my head, and I am very grateful for that.

An hour and a half later our cabin door was kicked in by my Russian guide, toothbrush in his mouth, spewing Russian and throwing his hands up like a giant moose rack. He saw a bull a half mile away while brushing his teeth. So, out the door I went.

Luckily, I had already put my hunting pants on. I expected to shoot from camp, so I threw on my untied sneakers, grabbed my coat and on the way out grabbed my frozen gun sitting outside.

Standing by the shitter he tried to get me to see the moose. When I finally picked it out and got the scope on it, I could see that it was a million miles away.

So off we went, running through the frozen swamp. This was a bitch, because it was covered with little snow-covered moguls. I slipped and staggered and fell many times. I lost my damn untied sneaker once and had to dig it out of the snow. We ran over a quarter-mile, stopping and trying to see if I should shoot. I had no idea the range, since my rangefinder binoculars were still in the cabin. Then I saw Albert come to a small creek and wade right through it in his rubber boots. Well, no turning back now. In the water I went, with my sneakers on.

We finally get to the last spruce tree as cover. Like a Charlie Brown Christmas tree, it was not hiding much. Time to shoot. Now I was hot and sweaty, and trying hard not to fog up my glasses or the scope. I had nothing to rest my gun on. The moose was feeding, so at first, I couldn't even tell what way it was facing. Finally, its head came up. The first shot did nothing and I was not surprised. You put electrical tape on your barrel to keep the snow out, and it usually blows off. It was rock hard and I am sure it deformed the first bullet. Shots two and three went off, and still nothing. When I let shot four go, I had squatted down to use my knee, but still nothing. Did I ruin my scope? Did I suck? I wanted to go home!

Then it hit me: that animal is a lot farther away than I think. I raised the scope up over its back, pulled the trigger and he dropped. It was over in seconds. One shot from my 7mm shut off a 1500-pound animal, like that!

We finished the half-mile run. Once I saw it on the ground I was psyched and relieved and thankful. A giant, eight- or nine-year-old animal with a 57" wide rack was going back to America with me.

The rest of the crew came by snow machine. They kept making camera motions, but mine was back in camp. I kept showing them my wet, untied sneaker to get them to understand that I needed to go back and get dressed. No hat, no gloves, missing my bibs, and another three layers under my jacket, it was still -30 C, my hair was soaked from sweat and I was starting to freeze. They finally caught on and we all went back for tea.

That is hunting, hours and hours of nothing but patience and torture for a few minutes of adrenaline rushed excitement. I love it. Sometimes it is better to be lucky than good. I am a lucky man.

At dinner, we celebrated the Russian way with nine shots of vodka. You see, it is bad luck not to do shots in groups of three!

The short story you just read was the end of a long journey that I started on February 10, 2014. Although the climax of the hunt was 19 months later, on December 8 of 2015, the story does not truly end until June of 2016, when the rack and cape showed up at my door. The mount was finally done and moved to its rightful place in my house in March of 2017. The quest to hunt a giant Russian moose was three years in the making.

The Russian Moose hunt was the accumulation of my hunting career that has spanned 17 years and taken me to 14 different places, including 8 US states, 5 Canadian Provinces, and one foreign country. Those trips allowed me to bring home 11 big game animals. Throughout that period, if I include hunting back home in New York, I have taken 73 big-game animals, 29 with a bow. I am proud of what I have accomplished and cherish every memory that resides in my head. My hope is that this book inspires you to also pursue your hunting dreams. I set out to prove that anyone can do what I have done.

How the Hunting Passion Started for Me.

I am a gun guy and I always have been, dating all the way back to when I was a wee little man. Hoss and Little Joe from Bonanza had me wanting to be a rootin' tootin' six-shooter kind of kid. An air rifle given to me as a present for being the ring bearer in a wedding brought me into the big leagues. The air rifle was a lever action that made a loud pop and some smoke rolled form the barrel when I fired it. A few years later, I conned my mom into getting me this sweet wooden toy gun with a working bolt action. Damn, that was about as real as you could get for a little boy.

Then one day in my early teens, for some reason my brother handed me a M1 carbine of my own. My Dad was not a gun guy. My mom did not really like guns. So out of respect and wanting to keep my gun, I learned and practiced gun safety to a tee.

My brother-in-law was the first hunter in the family. He introduced the family to hunting through the trials and tribulations of him and his friends, creating some pretty funny hunting stories. My parents were farmers and owned two decent-sized pieces of land. So eventually my two brothers got interested in chasing deer on the hillside. I was just the little runt kid who got to tag along and "drive" once in a while. That all changed at sixteen when I saved to buy my own shotgun, a Remington 1100, and my hunting career started. I cannot tell you I was any good at it; I was really into it just to have a reason to carry my gun with a purpose.

The hunting bug started the day my high school girlfriend gave me my first bow. I was still in the looking-cool stage, and the bow was an Oneida Eagle. A black, space-aged-looking, Rambo-style bow that threw tree-trunk-sized arrows. I was hooked on archery. For a few years I shot a lot of warning shots at deer, then one day a little six-point decided to stop on my twenty-yard marker and look the other way. I felt like it was a gift from God and the arrow flew true, for once! I got my first deer with the bow.

The Day I Became Possessed.

One warm and sunny morning I sat in a handmade wooden ladder stand at the top of our field. Immediately below me was a large ditch, then a large open field. I was sitting in the stand with legs dangling over the edge, waiting for deer to pass by. This was a good spot and the deer activity at that time was tremendous. There was no doubt I would see deer, but would they step into my twenty-yard range? I would cut pine boughs off the trees and lay them out in a twenty-yard circle. There was no such thing as a range finder back then. Bows weren't that great at the time either. Twenty yards was the maximum range I would dare shoot because the arc of those giant arrows was like throwing a Hail Mary pass in a football game.

To my left was what we called the "triangle pines." It was a pine grove that was thick, nasty and the deer loved to hide in there. After an hour or so of sitting I heard a rustle in the pines. Out popped a doe heading straight at me. Behind her was the biggest buck I have ever seen on the hoof, even as I write this today, I remember was a drop tine on its right side. My heart jumped into my throat as the doe came toward me at a fast pace.

The doe came into my range then immediately turned and ran straight down the hill, crossing the wide-open field, with this magnificent buck right on her tail. My heart sank as they ran straight away from me. I remember thinking, "I wish she would turn around and come back," knowing that the buck would follow. At that moment, she did! She turned 180 degrees and came straight back up the hill. Amazingly, she ran by me, passing right over my twenty-yard marker. The buck would soon do the same. I drew my bow and aimed at the spot, leaning over my left knee. As this giant buck stepped on my pine bough, I let an arrow fly. This was a shot I made a million times in the back yard. I spent winters competing in an indoor range. I was about to put an arrow in a buck of a lifetime.

The Oneida Eagle was a compound recurve bow. It has characteristics of both compound and recurve bow. The unique thing was that the recurve limbs folded as you drew back. I let the arrow fly and I immediately felt a tremendous slap on my left thigh, as the arrow harmlessly fell at the feet of the deer. The loud slap spooked them and they both ran to the other side of the field. The bottom limb had hit me knee! I blew it!

As I gathered my thoughts, trying to figure out what just happened, I looked over to see the deer. At the other side of the field about 250 yards away, the doe had stopped. The giant-racked, drop-tined buck mounted and bred her as I watched. This is no shit! When he was done, he climbed off her, stepped out from around her like a cocky tough guy, and stared directly at me. I could almost hear him say, "Ha! You missed me and I still got what I wanted."

I shook so violently that I could not get out of the stand for quite some time. The adrenaline of that moment was the most intense thing I had ever felt. Most people would have been pissed that they missed, but I for some reason was giddy with excitement. It was such a pleasure to be in the presence of such an animal, and on our own land. I had just gotten to experience something very few people ever get to see. I was just schooled by a wild animal and I knew that he knew he got one up on me that day. Best of all, I knew an animal of that caliber existed and I would hunt every second I could for another chance at him. I became possessed on that sunny morning and officially became a hunter.

Later, as I told this story repeatedly with the same feeling and excitement of that moment, I started to realize what hunting was all about. Sure, if I killed that buck that day, I would have had a great story. But looking back on it, the story of the miss was so much better and way more memorable, and most importantly it changed my life for the better. That miss led to a lifelong passion that has done so much for me.

That big-racked, drop-tine buck forced me to study and learn. I ramped up my shooting practice and eventually upgraded to a higher-end bow. I learned about scents and calls. I studied stand placement and wind. I became a student of hunting. I thought about it year-round and prepared to be a better hunter the next chance I would get. It worked and I started to become a successful New York deer hunter.

How My Story Contrasts from the Many Others I See

So many times, I have seen young hunters go out and be successful on the first try, or first season. We old guys call it beginner luck. Many of those lucky beginners end up quitting hunting. They often think it is easy, then a couple hard seasons go by and they get frustrated. Because those lucky hunters kill quickly, they have not paid their dues. They didn't get in enough time to start to see the other cool things that go along with hunting. Their tag is filled so they go home, while the other hunters spend days chasing deer, telling stories and enjoying their time together.

What many would have called a failure turned out to be a huge success for me. I gained a passion I did not know I could have. I gained knowledge of hunting and of animals that has served me well. All those hours in the stand or the field have gained for me an appreciation for the little gift's nature provides. The smell of the autumn leaves on a warm sunny day. The freshness of a crisp, frosty morning as the sun rises over the hills. The smell of a rutting buck as it passes up wind of you. The subtle noise in the leaves as your brain hones in on the fact that it is a deer creeping toward you. The comedy of the squirrels; who does not love the squirrels?

I know. I know that you all hate squirrels, but If reincarnation is real then I want to come back as a squirrel. I love being in a tree so much, and the best part would be that you get to screw with hunters!

I have one quick squirrel story. I am in a wooden ladder stand at the end of a heavily used trail. The deer use this trail to come out in the field on a regular basis. If they use the trail, they pretty much will walk right under me past the ladder and into the field to feed. Again, it is a warm, sunny day and I have been sitting there for a while. Leaves covered the trail, so there was no way a deer would come through without me hearing it. All the sudden there is running behind me, the unmistakable sound of a deer being chased through the woods. I snatch up my bow and ready it on my knee, expecting a doe to run by me and a buck to follow. As the rustle in the leaves grows closer, all the sudden I feel the ladder shake. Doe being chased by bucks do wild things. I think, "That damn deer just ran into my stand." A few seconds later I feel something on my leg, then up onto my bow climbs this one confused and curious squirrel. He hangs onto the side of my bow, chewing me out for being there, then off he jumps to a tree limb for safety. The look on that squirrel's face still makes me laugh. He is probable saying the same thing about the look on my face.

Lesson – Embrace your failures since they are just minor setbacks.

We all hate to fail but the truth is our failures are what make us grow. The people that embrace their failures and put the work in to prevent them from ever happening again are the ones who gain the most appreciation in their journey. Like it or not we learn from our mistakes.

I don't care what you all think, but the missed opportunities and blown shots make the best and funniest hunting stories. The deer suddenly appeared, I let my arrow fly and he dropped 75 yards away. Whoopie, what a tale that is! Compare it to this. The giant-racked buck walked into my range. My heart rate spiked and I gasped for air, choking on my tongue. As I raised my bow, it was shaking violently to the point the arrow jumped off the rest. In my haste to put the arrow back on, it came off the string, hitting every step of the ladder on the way down. Ting, ting, ting, as the big buck turned looking at me in shock, but then stared at me in confidence. He would live to breed another doe. I would go home and lick my wounds. Yep. True story, just another day in the woods.

Lesson – What are you good at?

What are you good at? Take a few moments and think about that. If there was one thing you were or are good at, identify it now.

Are you good at your job? Are you a good parent? Are you good at golf or another sport? Whatever it is that you are good at, there is a reason. Whatever traits you possess to be good at one thing can be used on anything else, but we humans often seem to fail to realize that. If you can plan major projects at work, why wouldn't you be able to plan the hunt of your dreams? If you have the will and discipline to practice and be great at a sport, why can't you put that effort into your dreams? Parenting is the toughest job on the planet. Have you ever once thought about putting parenting off for a few months because you have other things to do? Hell no! Dreams are important, and you should put as much effort into them as anything else you are good at.

A Dream Started Burning Inside Me

The moment I shot that first arrow from my Oneida Eagle bow, I thought about taking a brown bear with the bow. Even in my teenage years, I started envisioning one day making this happen. The challenge intrigued me, the adventure called at me, and the danger summoned something that burned inside me.

For nearly twenty-five years that dream was smoldering in the back of my mind. I talked about it many times. I approached outfitters and researched archery bear hunts on and off for years. The cost just seemed prohibitive. A costly divorce and a costly aftermath of that divorce taught me by force what I really required financially to live on. When that passed I was in my early forties. One day, I simply made up my mind that I was going to do it, one way or another I would hunt grizzly with a bow before I turned fifty years old.

For the ten years prior to the divorce, I thought bear hunting with a bow was out of my league financially. I spent a ton of time searching, collecting web addresses for outfitters and animals all over the states, Canada, and the world. If you don't focus on only a few animals you can literally drive yourself crazy with choices. Finally, I decided it was all too much and focused on only five animals. My top five animals became Grizzly / Brown bear, Mountain Lion, Wolf, Mountain Goat, and Moose. At the time, out of those five, Mountain lion seemed like the only one I could ever really think of affording.

Diary February 10, 2014 – An email that poured gas on a smouldering flame.

A random email from Denny Geurink of Outdoor Adventures came in.

Dear Bear Hunting Enthusiasts!

Guess what? I just got my business back from the guy I sold it to 3 years ago. He was having a hard time keeping up with it as he has so many other frying pans in the fire. Didn't really want to come out of retirement all that bad but decided if the Beach Boys could do a Reunion Tour and Cher can do a Farewell tour, I guess I can too! Going to give it one last blast and am contacting all the clients who had fun over in Russia to see if they want to go. "One More Time." I would love to have you join me and some of my friends on one more hunt. We always had a blast together! Anyhow, let me know if you would like to join me on a reunion blast. One more time for old time's sake!

The last hunt was only a few months back, but the fire was already starting to burn inside me. I had learned that I am a much happier person when I have something planned for the future. Denny and I had talked many times because the thought of giant brown bears was always stuck in my head. This email just ramped up my need to decide and plan a hunt.

The Elephant in The Room

No, I am not talking about a giant elephant mount in your trophy room. The elephant in the room that needs to be discussed is the fact that most people make a huge assumption when they learn about my hunting or anyone else that has been able to hunt multiple places for multiple species.

"You must be rich."

I have heard that so many times, and it really pisses me off. Granted there are a lot of "rich" people out there that have been able to fill trophy rooms. These people exist in all aspects of life, but we cannot let our jealousy, or envy of these people get the best of us. There are even more hard-working, self-sacrificing people that have been able to fill trophy rooms. We need to focus on what they do to be successful hunters, especially focusing on what drives their passion.

No, I am not rich! I am an electrical engineer that manages a small satellite engineering office. I supported a wife, then a divorce, as I supported my two kids. I do live in the country where the cost of living is probably less than some, but that is my only real advantage over most folks. So, how does a guy like me get to hunt multiple places and take multiple species of game? This is the first and foremost thing that you need to come to grips with before you can hunt, be successful, and thoroughly enjoy what you have done.

Lesson – Make your priorities, and then have the will and discipline to stick to them.

I have a magazine clipping Scotch-taped to my laptop. It says this: "**Disciple** the art of discipline really boils down to priorities and execution – figuring out what really matters to you and paying the price to achieve it." This little piece of paper has always reminded me of what I wanted and what I needed to do to get it.

When I say set your priorities, I don't mean quit feeding your kids so you can save money for hunting. That sounds dumb, but I bet there are those out there that do it. I am talking about taking a hard look at your life and a hard look at where you spend your money. Once you have done that, now think about the joy those things bring you versus the joy and memories that a "hunt of a lifetime" might bring.

Allow me to digress a minute and rant about the phrase "hunt of a lifetime." I feel that this phrase stops many people from believing they can successfully go on a big-game hunt. It feels like you must spend your life savings, hunt once, and then boom, your life is over. People say it like you just won the lottery and the chances of them winning or doing the same thing is null. However, if you want to use that phrase positively, by describing the amount of dedication, effort, planning and memories you will obtain, then I am all for it.

Here are the priorities that I changed in my life that allowed me, in my own head, to believe I could save money for a big-game hunt. I quit bar hopping on the weekends. I could easily drop a $100 a night going out to the bars. For one, I am an idiot and tend to buy people drinks. But $100 is not hard to do on any given party night. Do that both Friday and Saturday and you have spent a chunk of change. $100 a week for 52 weeks is $5200. Double that and you are pushing $10,000. I did not party that much, but you can see how habits add up fast.

My second sacrifice is that I burn wood to heat my New York home in the winter. I refuse to turn the LP gas furnace on. I figure that is worth $4000 - $5000 a year. Cutting and chopping wood is hard work, but I consider it my part-time job that supports my hunting passion.

The third big thing is the fact that I refuse to go out to eat lunch when I am at work. It takes too much time and it costs too much money. I eat way too much, which is a topic for another chapter. Drop $10-$15 per day over the workdays per year and you are spending $2400 - $3600 just on lunch. My answer was a bag of bagels and a jar of peanut butter in my desk drawer. Yep, I have eaten that for over thirteen years.

Ego and envy rear their ugly heads when you tell big-game hunting stories. I usually get told I must be rich by the guy who spends two nights a weekend in the bar, buys a twelve-pack of beer every weeknight, and smokes a pack of cigarettes a day. That person will give me attitude about me being rich, about how he couldn't ever afford to do what I do, but he drops thousands of dollars on beer and cigarettes. Don't get me wrong, you can do what you want. I am all for freedom! Just don't put your jealous issues on me because of the choices you make.

What else have I done? I drive a pickup. Oh yeah, those big-ass, fuel-guzzling, powerful trucks are nice, but the extra cost of the truck and the huge dollars dropped at the pump don't add any value to my life. My little Toyota Tacoma was $10,000 cheaper, gets better gas mileage, and does everything I need on a daily basis.

Another big one that adds up in a hurry is the urge to stop and grab a convenient store drink. A $2 soda, coffee, or bottle of water (Really, spend money on water?) adds up to $700 a year if you stop once per day.

Look at the cost of going out to dinner on a regular basis. I love to do it and I treat every time as if it were special, but it is special because I don't do it all the time. Going out to eat should be a treat not a way to feed you. I am not even going to try to add up how much people spend a year eating out. If you treat food as fuel for your body, you tend to worry less about an awesome meal you need. Most days I eat to fuel the body, and then on occasion I will splurge and eat to really enjoy myself. Oh, and a side benefit of this is that you will eat way healthier doing this.

Am I perfect? Not on your life, but you can start to see how I can pile up a pretty nice pile of money over a year or two's time. Once you have identified the items you are willing to sacrifice, then you need the will and discipline to stick to it. I literally pick up a soda and think, that is $2.50 I can put toward hunting and I set it back down. Once this mindset sets in, it becomes easier and easier. Once the pile of money starts to grow, it gets even easier. Once you successfully complete a hunt and locked those memories away in your head, it then becomes very easy to have the discipline to save money.

Lesson – Track what you waste your money on

For many of you, just reading what I have done to save money probably is enough push to get you to sacrifice things on your own. If you find it harder than that, then I would suggest you start writing things down. For a month, keep track of everything you spend money on. Then at the end of the month categorize it, add it up, and stare at it. For each item, ask yourself what long-lasting joy you got out of it. Damn that meal at Red Lobster was awesome, but how does that compare to tagging that bull elk you have always dreamed of? My everyday Starbucks coffee is so good, but the coffee at work is free and I bet you would rather go hunting. "But Pete, I have to have my beer when I get home." No problem, if that brings you joy then you should keep doing it. But maybe two beers versus a six-pack is enough to get you over that long, hard day at work.

One trick I heard that people do to quit smoking was to physically put the money they would have spent on a pack of cigarettes in a jar. That way you can see how quickly the jar fills up. A cool little trick that quickly shows you what it means to reach your goals, and one that could easily be applied to other superfluous habits and vices.

I sat on a hill, overlooking a lake that only a handful of people had ever seen before. I was in Quebec, Canada, on my first-ever big-game hunt. We were after Caribou. I had taken a nice bull with my bow the day before and today I was just out scouting the land to see where I might get a chance to fill my second tag. The Sunshine was warm and the skies were bright blue. There was not an excess noise to be heard. A young Caribou walked up the hill and heard me as I snapped his picture. He looked at me with curiosity, cocking his head like a puppy, having never seen a human before.

I spent forty-five minutes with that Caribou bull, watching him eat just a few yards from me. I have been many places since and I have been very close to many different animals, but the time he and I shared that beautiful day was one of the greatest experiences of my life. Not once did I say, damn I wish I didn't save all that money by eating bagels and peanut butter.

Lesson – I will do it when I retire. Really?

Some of you are already big money savers. I know many people who work their asses off and collect money. Watching it pile up in some sort of investment fund. They always say something about "saving for a rainy day," or "When I retire I am going to…" It is not me to judge what you do. But I will throw out a few comments to think about. What these people are saying is that when they get older they plan to do all these things, or when they get older something bad might happen and they will need money. The keys words there are "getting older." Will you be healthy and in shape enough to go on that hunting trip when you are older? I know the truth and fully admit that when I get older I will have slowed down, and slowing down takes less money. When I am old, I would much rather have a brain full of memories than a huge pile of money and a failing body that keeps me from using it.

Lesson – Be cautious of your obsession

Passion can lead to obsession and obsession can lead to addiction. If anything has a negative effect on your life, family or friends, then you are addicted. I have had the privilege to learn from an addictive person and I have seen and felt the destruction that comes with that. Chasing your dreams, and refocusing your finances to meet those dreams, is a healthy change. Taking away from your family and building debt is not what I am suggesting here. Please be careful and mindful of you approach.

Lesson – People hate change

One of the most prevalent traits of human beings is that they resist change. Any little change to their routine and the grumpiness takes over. People hate change so much they will continue to do the very things that ruin their lives even if it might just require a subtle adjustment. You must look in the mirror and become aware of what holds you back. That admission is the very first step. The second is having the faith and courage to step outside your little box, outside your comfort zone. I have often been scared, but I have never regretted the times I stepped out of my comfort zone. As a matter of fact, I relish those occasions because they are the ones that engraved amazing memories in my head.

How Can I Plan That Far in Advance?

In the previous lesson I talked about all the ways you can pile up money for a hunt. $2, $10, $50 a day or week can be saved just by making some conscious decisions to change how you prioritize your spending. I know what some of you are thinking though, "Damn, Pete, this is going to take years to get enough money to hunt. Yep! But when it comes to big-game hunts you have the time, because it takes time to plan a hunt.

The first thing you need to get past is your *I need it now* attitude. Trying to get immediate satisfaction is not going to work in this case, but that is okay. I will show you why this is okay and all the benefits that go along with it. This is not easy, but you must summon the will and discipline required to make it happen. Yeah, I throw that term "Will and discipline" around a lot, because it is important throughout this entire process. You need to identify what it is you really want and have the discipline needed to achieve it.

We need to talk about the timeline required to plan a hunt. You should expect to go on a big game hunt in two years, that is, if you start right now planning and saving. The main reason for this is twofold. Any good guiding operation is booked at least a year in advance. Secondly, you will need all this time to get ready. The good news is two years will give you all the time you need to save money. Do you think you can you save the money you need in two years? Considering how much time you have, now go back to the previous chapter on spending priorities and do some math. I bet my life that this is starting to look like it can really happen.

Sure, you could get a loan, or throw it on a credit card and accelerate the process. I don't advise that. You want the memories of this hunt to be something great. You cannot have the stigma of a credit card debt or loan hanging over your head. That would just tarnish all the good memories each time you make a payment. Plus, I doubt it will ever work out to go on a second hunt. Trust me, as soon as the first hunt is done successfully, you are going to want to start work on the next. Having lingering bills to pay is not going to allow that to happen. My way will work, if you have the will and discipline to make it happen.

Maybe you already know what your dream animal to hunt is. If so, that is awesome. But do you know you can afford it? Do you know where you can go? Do you know if tags are obtained over the counter or by a draw? The decision stage can be time consuming, but fun nevertheless. I suggest visiting outdoor shows to gather information on what is out there to choose from. The internet has a wealth of information and many outfitters have web pages, but don't forget how many are so remote that internet access is less than desirable. So, finding outfitters that don't use internet, although they exist, are harder to contact. The States Department of Natural Resources websites may have information that leads to outfitters. There are companies such as Cabela's that sell hunts and help you handle the tag-draw process. Each Canadian Provence has an Outfitter Association that publishes a list of outfitters, easily mailed to you. Word of mouth is a great way to start your hunting career. One of my favorite things about hunting is that you can strike up a conversation anytime, anywhere with a hunter.

Speaking of the camaraderie of hunting, there is that urge to want to hunt with a friend or a group of friends. I will have a separate section on this topic. It is not as easy as you might think.

It takes a few months just to gather information, look it all over, and start to make decisions on where to hunt. Once you have an idea and a few outfitting businesses in mind, you will need to start the process of talking to each outfitter. I will get a lot of flak for this statement, but some outfitters are like strippers. If you have money to spend they will be your best friend. But they are there to sell hunts, and you should keep that in mind when talking to them. There are bad outfitters out there and there are ways to weed them out. In another section I will tell you what questions I ask them, and how I feel about their responses. I have been lucky and my outfitters and guides have all been great, to the point I consider them family. It can be done if you are cautious.

The outfitters will typically give you a list of references. You will want to take time to contact them. Again, there will be a section reviewing my thoughts on what information you can get from a reference.

Once you have whittled it down to an outfitter or two, you should do one last financial check. You will now have a hunt date, spring or fall, or a target month and year. You will have an idea of the cost to book the hunt. This is the money you will pay the outfitter directly. He will want a deposit and probably want progress payments, so you must write down when you need to send him money. There are always costs outside of that outfitter payment. In another section I will outline what some of these might be.

My thoughts on hidden cost are this: if you are not honest with yourself and don't take fully into account what out-of-pocket costs there might be that are above and beyond the outfitter costs, your hunt will likely be ruined. I see so many people plan for the outfitter cost and end up having to skimp on the travel and surprise charges. They always get pissed off and it always leaves a bad experience in their minds. Plan on saving enough for the hunt, plus the extra costs you know about, and a good financial cushion for the unexpected. That way you can enjoy your experience without worrying about money. If you don't spend your slush-fund money, then guess what, you already have a deposit on your next hunt, or your taxidermy bill!

Doing a final check on the math, you should know the rate you think you can save money. You will know when payments are due the outfitter and you should be able to estimate the extra costs needed during the hunt, plus a slush fund. If you schedule all this out and something falls in the negative column then you are not ready to hunt the year you planned. Believe me: you will be happy just postponing it one more year to make sure you truly can afford this trip.

Lesson – A Typical Savings / Payment Schedule

Here is a mock savings plan for a typical $7500 hunt, with overall costs coming in at $10,500. You researched it for about a year and booked it over a year in advance. Considering a tax return and a bonus, you only needed to save $125 per month.

	Money saved	Money Spent	Total	Notes
January	$125		$125	
February	$125		$250	
February	$1,200		$1,450	Tax return
March	$125		$1,575	
April	$125		$1,700	
May	$125		$1,825	
June	$125		$1,950	
July	$125		$2,075	
August	$125		$2,200	
September	$125		$2,325	
October	$125		$2,450	
November	$125		$2,575	
December	$125		$2,700	
December	$1,000		$3,700	Bonus
January	$125		$3,825	
February	$125		$3,950	
February	$1,200		$5,150	Tax return
March	$125	-$1,500	$3,775	Hunt deposit - You booked a hunt!!!
April	$125		$3,900	
May	$125		$4,025	
June	$125		$4,150	
July	$125		$4,275	
August	$125		$4,400	

Month	Deposit	Withdrawal	Balance	Note
September	$125		$4,525	
October	$125		$4,650	
November	$125		$4,775	
December	$125		$4,900	
December	$1,000		$5,900	Bonus
January	$125	-$3,000	$3,025	2nd payment
February	$125		$3,150	
February	$1,200		$4,350	Tax return
March	$125	-$600	$3,875	Airfare
April	$125		$4,000	
May	$125		$4,125	
June	$125		$4,250	
July	$125		$4,375	
August	$125	-$3,000	$1,500	Final payment
September	$125		$1,625	Hunt date
September		-$500	$1,125	Hunt License and Tags
September		-$600	$1,025	Tip money for cooks and guide
September		-$500	$525	Misc. travel cash
September		-$300	$225	Shipping
October	$125		$350	
November	$125		$475	
December	$125		$600	
December	$1,000		$1,600	Bonus
December		-$500	$1,100	Taxidermy down payment
$125		$7,500		Total hunt cost
		-		
		$10,500		Total Money spent on the hunt

Your adrenaline starts to pump. You have an outfitter all lined up. You have done the math and can save the money when you need it to do this hunt. This feeling of excitement is exactly like the night before opening day. You are going on your dream hunt!

Congratulations, you have just experienced the first of many adrenaline rushes.

Lesson – Saving money gets easier once the hunt is booked

It becomes much easier to focus on saving money once you have made the decision to book a hunt. It is much like the phenomenon of a car loan. Once you get a car loan, you deal with the payment, usually with little thought. Then that last payment finally comes and you are excited, knowing you now have all that extra money per month. A couple months go by and there is no extra money. What happened? You didn't have that artificial thing to focus you so you pissed away your money. The same thing will happen when you book a hunt. Once the hunt is booked, you will scrutinize all you are spending and make better decisions. Just like making a car payment, once you establish a schedule it will become second nature to save.

Embrace the Anticipation

What are you going to do with yourself over the next few months waiting for this hunt to come? I say enjoy the anticipation. Hunting is all about anticipation. Give it some thought. The kill or harvest of the animal usually takes seconds. It is simply the culmination of all the anticipation you went through to get to that point. I guarantee you won't sleep well for a few nights once you have mailed that deposit check for a hunt. You will have that warm, glowing feeling as the adrenaline continues to seep through your veins. You will dream of the animal and the stalk. Your anxiety will peak, wondering if you are in shape enough or if you have practiced enough to make the shot. You will question your hunting gear, wondering how well it will work.

You have been practicing your shooting every night for weeks. You have washed your hunting clothes in scent-free soap and hung them outside to dry in the fresh air. Your hunting license and all your gadgets are neatly packed in your bag. It is the day before hunting seasons and your friends and family start to arrive. The stories start to be told. The hunt camp food tastes so good and the cold beer washed it all down. You won't sleep well tonight because of the excitement of opening morning. This is the feeling you can have for the next few months if you allow yourself to enjoy the entire hunting experience. You remember that feeling as a little kid on Christmas Eve. We all love that feeling of anticipation.

Anticipation, The Gift of a Lifetime

It hit me out of nowhere; suddenly it all made sense to me. I've sat and wondered why other people can't seem to get hooked on hunting like I am. Then you read articles about the number of hunters dropping, and the average age of a hunter going up. The fact is, the younger generation is not getting interested in our sport. Hunting is awesome! My adrenalin goes up even when I'm simply planning a hunting trip, and I couldn't for the life of me understand why this doesn't happen to everyone. Why aren't others feeling like I am? I wondered where this feeling that drove me came from and then one day it all made sense.

Over Thanksgiving we went to Illinois, hunting big Pope and Young whitetail. We were taking our chance for a buck of a lifetime. It could possibly be the worst week of hunting in history. Out of five days, the wind blew hard once, and it was a downpour for three. The day that it was decent weather, we saw no deer at all. After sitting in a tree for hours on end I would come back to the cabin miserable, cold, and wet. Then the fire would warm me up and the fire inside me would rekindle once again. I couldn't sleep, waiting and wondering if I would see my buck of a lifetime while sitting in the next day's rain. I had a blast on this hunt. The anticipation of what could happen was the greatest feeling, driving me to try again and again.

My wife came home from work the other day with five "paper angels" and a handful of money. Paper Angels are the names of little kids — written on a paper angel — who won't have much of a Christmas unless people pitch in and buy them something. The people where she works all pitched in money and they originally chose to buy for two of them, until one man stepped up with one hundred dollars and told her make sure all five children had presents for Christmas.

I lay in bed that next morning, the morning we planned on doing our Christmas shopping for our two kids, and now five children we knew nothing about. As I lay there I wondered, what do poor little kids do Christmas night? As I did when I was a kid, they must be full of anticipation, not being able to sleep, wondering what Christmas morning might bring. What happens to these little minds when they wake up to a simple little present that was bought by someone who doesn't even know them? Worst of all, what if they wake up to nothing at all?

Then terror raced through my heart as I wondered what their parents or parent might be thinking when there is nothing at all. What hell must that person be going through on that Christmas Eve night? If someone did step up and buy that "Paper Angel" a gift, what a feeling of relief and joy must it be for that parent? It really isn't a gift for a little kid; it turns out to be a gift for a family, making multiple people's dreams come true. I know that feeling of anticipation as a parent, not for the presents I might get, but for the look on my kids' faces as they wake up and see the presents under the tree. Lord knows people must thrive on the anticipation, because in a matter of a half an hour, the presents are opened and the rest of the day is spent climbing through rubble, installing batteries and assembling toys.

As I got choked up with the thought that this might be the Christmas of a lifetime for these kids, we decided to make sure it was. We matched that hundred-dollar donation and bought stockings stuffed with trinkets and candy. We bought sleds, because every kid needs a sled. Each got more than one wrapped present plus gloves and hats. To top it all off, we put in an extra wrapped gift that was labeled "to mommy" from each little kid, because sometimes it's the giving that makes the little ones the happiest.

Most are wondering what this has to do with hunting, but bear with me; I am building up to my point. Shopping for these kids was easy. I had a terrible time shopping for my own kids. They each had a list. When I was a kid it was a called a wish list, today if seems like a "must have" list. You feel like a failure if you can't find what they want. Why? Because they expect it and they will be disappointed if they don't get it. I saw time and time again a distraught parent running to a store employee just to find out the specific toy they are looking for is sold out. Then, to top it all off, you must be careful not to buy one of your kids more presents than the other. Quantity is the issue, not quality.

So, as I stewed about this issue, I thought back to my childhood. I'm sure I got more of what I asked for, but I could only remember one thing that I really wanted and I got it. Mom must have been excited about it too, because I got it in my stocking, no less. See, she let me open the stocking while all my older brothers and sisters slept in. It was one of the new top-of-the-line, handheld video games called Merlin. No one else had one, but I got mine. As I look back on it, that must have been real tough for mom to buy such an expensive toy. I wanted this game, wondered if I would get it, but never really expected it. I wouldn't have been disappointed, because I would have gotten cool stuff and I was excited to find out what that stuff might be.

So, as I think back on this, I realize that it was the buildup, the anticipation of Christmas morning that got me excited. I didn't expect to get what I wanted, but I wondered if I would. If I didn't, what would I get for a present? As I came down off my shopping tantrum, my mind jumped to deer season and that big buck that we have hunted so hard for. I was planning on hunting the next morning. Would I get the buck I have wished for? Maybe I'd get a different one, or maybe even a big doe? The anticipation was getting me all pumped up. It hit me like a snowball upside the head. All this feels like Christmas Eve. The fun part is not what we get; it is the thoughts of what we *might* get.

Have we ruined our kids by letting them make lists we pay close attention to? Have we lost the excitement of not really knowing what is in store for us? Is disappointment really a bad thing, or does it make you a better person, one who gets excited about what he might get, and appreciates what they do get? Maybe the older generation of hunters is still clinging to this feeling, while the kids of today, the ones that get what they want, don't really know what they are missing. If you have the "I want it now" attitude, hunting is not for you. I think we need to teach our kids that part of the fun is the adrenaline rush of wishing, hoping, wanting, and working hard for what we want. We can offer hunting to the younger generation, but we cannot make them hunters. I think that part of them has to be engrained in their minds long before they have the chance to hunt.

You know what is going to be on my future Christmas list? I want to take a kid hunting that on a past Christmas day was one of those "paper angels." They can become lifelong hunters, because in their hearts they will remember, after such an anticipated wait, how sweet it was to finally get that "present of a lifetime."

Lesson – It isn't about the trophy.

It isn't about the trophy. The kill is mere seconds of a journey that might be months long. Yes, that trophy on your wall is important, but it is only a trigger for all the memories stored in your head. Don't miss out on the thoughts, memories, and especially the anticipation as you prepare for a hunt of a lifetime.

Ride the Adrenaline

Hunting is often described as hours upon hours of boredom for a few seconds of excitement. Many might think the same thing about planning a hunt a year or two in advance. We are a society of people who want it now; we want instant gratification. What you should think about is: what do I miss along the way? So yes, sitting in the deer stand for hours for that split-second chance of a big racked buck walking into range might be boring, but the sights, the smells, and the solitude are an added benefit. The anticipation is what keeps you in that stand. Now contrast that to turkey or elk hunt, or even a giant moose in the rut. The difference is the feedback you get from the animal. Instead of a few seconds of rush, the adrenaline trickles into your body the whole time you hear that animal respond. Remember that feeling? If you open your mind and allow the planning stage of a hunt to take you over, you get that trickle of adrenaline the entire time you wait for your hunt date to come.

I haven't slept much these last few nights. The adrenaline is still taking over my body like a drug. It feels so good and I am so excited. All I can picture in my head is my trophy animal slowly walking in. He seems timid, knowing something is wrong, but I am so still he cannot make me out. He turns perfectly broadside, just like in the textbooks. My mind races as I walk through the mental checklist I have practiced a million times. Draw back the arrow. I did it; he did not see me. Check my anchor, bend at the waist, check my peep, pick a spot, breathe, squeeze the shot, and follow through. The arrow flashes through the giant beast's lungs. I immediately know he has less than fifteen seconds to live. The sequence repeats over and over in my head, keeping me from sleeping most of the night.

The anxiety starts to kick in. Am I a good enough shot to make this hunt a success? I need to start shooting; I need to make sure my gear is in working order. I need to dedicate time every night and shoot at least a few arrows. Am I in good enough shape? I need to start to work out. I hate working out! But I need to work out. I cannot fail if I am sucking wind and cannot make the shot. I will work out!

I see hunting videos and TV shows differently now. Instead of just waiting for the kill shot, I start to notice the steep hill they are climbing. I start to notice how they dress, taking off and putting on layers as they go. Man, they seem to be glassing a lot. There is an animal. Would I shoot it? Is it big enough? How do I judge the rack size? Do I shoot it on the first day, or wait? The hunter makes the shot, look at him shaking; look how the emotion has overtaken him. He pushed himself so hard and he made the perfect shot. As they say, "now the hard work starts." But they all have smiles on their faces. The hunting guide, giddiness on his face, looks like he is the one who shot the trophy animal.

Everything you see or read will start to mean so much more to you. You will start to feel what they feel. Believe me: that will get better when you get back from your hunt. You are joining the big leagues; you are stepping up your hunting game. Whatever hunting you have done before suddenly gets more intense and you become better at it. Those two hours in the morning deer stand before the thought of breakfast pulls you away suddenly becomes lunch, then before you know it they're all-day sits. You start to push yourself and realize that you can do it. You can be a better hunter.

You will wear out the pages of the Cabela's and Bass Pro catalogs, wondering if the clothes you have are good enough, or should you upgrade. My advice to you is this: buy the best clothes you can afford and maybe push your budget a little bit to get the best. Better clothes will make you a better hunter at home. Better clothes are instrumental to your comfort and success on a big-game adventure. Cold and wet can get in your head really fast and you don't need that.

You will reassess all your hunting gadgets. You will hear about the importance of binoculars and you should listen. A good set of binoculars is crucial and if taken care of properly will last forever. I use the Bushnell range-finding binoculars. They are a good compromise in glass quality and the built-in rangefinder means you carry two devices in one. But most of all get a good binocular harness. The normal binocular strap will kill your neck in a short time.

As far as other gadgets, we hunters love them, at least until we try to carry them up a mountain. You will go leaner and meaner on every hunt you do. I probably won't be able to convince you what to leave home, but you will figure it out. I will share my hunting list and you can see what I take, and what I no longer carry. Today's airlines suck, making you keep your bag at fifty pounds or less. Your rifle or bow case will be your second bag and will already cost you extra money, so keeping your bag at fifty pounds is crucial. I wear heavy items like hunting boots on the plane. Even though it is hot and uncomfortable, it gives me more room to pack. Don't buy a bag with wheels. The frame and wheels weigh pounds and you need those extra pounds for gear. Buy an archery scale and take it with you. One extra pound will cost you money, so being sure you packed right only makes sense. It sounds stupid, but I practice packing weeks ahead of time. You never know what you might need to buy at the last minute so you may have to leave something else out.

Target practice becomes a whole lot more fun now that you have a purpose. Learn your weapon inside and out and be able to fix things in the field. Striving for perfection takes time. Out of respect for the animal and your guide, striving for perfection is important. Push yourself, making shots from weird positions and at weird angles. Get your heart racing and your breathing rate up, and then try to shoot. I took a ten-yard shot on a mountain lion. Sounds easy, right? She was probably fifty feet straight up in a spruce tree, almost completely covered with branches. But I had spent time hoisting a target up a tree and shooting through its branches. I knew exactly how to do it and more importantly how the arc of my arrow would fly. A branch covered her heart, but I knew my arrow flight would skim over it if I aimed right at it. The lion was dead before it hit the ground. My hunting partner had not practiced that way. The result was a gut-shot lion, a hurt lion dog, and a follow-up chase using a handgun to finish it off. The results of that could have been a lot worse. Push yourself. Get outside your comfort zone.

Take the time to Google everything you can think of about your hunt. Know the animal you are hunting and how they live in the area you are going. If you don't have realistic expectations, you will make a bad decision, or end up disappointed. We all talk about 170-class whitetails and they do exist in places. They might exist where you are going, but the chances of seeing and shooting one is like winning the lottery. A 130-class animal might be more prevalent and a more realistic expectation.

If you don't know how to judge the animal, you might be disappointed. Remember: a guide's job is to get you a shot opportunity, not necessarily the animal of your dreams. Know how to decide for yourself, but always, always consider what your guide is saying. He is weighing your ability to move around, the weather, the population of the animals and many other factors when he suggests shooting. I will talk about communicating with your guide in another section but remember this. He might just want to get it over with too; the quicker you shoot the less hiking he must do. The moral is, do your homework ahead of time.

Do some research on the places you will be and the people that live there. Learning the culture of the people you will be with is fun and sometimes necessary. Learning how they live might change your mind in how you prepare or pack. Obviously preparing for an Arctic hunt is much different than a Texas hunt. Prepare yourself for the food you might eat; things are a little different in other countries. If time allows, knowing some of the sights nearby will allow you to take in even more culture. An overnight stay in Moscow and a quick subway ride to Red Square was an amazing addition to my Russian moose hunt. Seeing Lenin's tomb with the Lenin's body preserved in glass was an awe-inspiring experience.

The more you know and the more you prepare both physically and mentally the greater the odds of your success. It was quite evident that the two hunters in the Russian moose camp had not done any of this. I am sure they could not point to where we were on a globe and hunting on the fringes of Siberia was one of the great things about the trip. Needless to say, they complained about all their hunts and their success rate, in their words, "sucked." My success rate has been great because I leave no stone unturned in studying for my trip. I am mentally and physically prepared to do what I should to be successful. More importantly I have realistic expectations. I am hunting and an animal is not guaranteed, therefore I never rely on getting an animal as my measure of success. I enjoy the planning and the anticipation and the trip getting to that point. If I take an animal, it is icing on the cake, and I have had my share of icing!

Lesson – Wait for sales to buy hunting clothes

All the big outdoor gear chains have huge sales during the off-season. My advice is to visit these stores and make a list of the styles and the brands you would buy if money was no object. Then watch for those off-season's sales. Joining their buyers' clubs can get you discounts and random coupons to use. Using a store credit card that builds up points can amount to dollars off that lessen the sting of the purchase price. I always order Cabela's products when I have a discount or free shipping and points on my credit card. Many times, the gear you want might be cheaper because they are changing camo patterns or have excess stock. Camo is for human eyes; the animals don't give a shit, so saving some cash on an old camo pattern is a smart choice.

Envisioning Your Success, aka The Power of Visualization

I am an electrical engineer and I help build large automated systems that produce things in factories. My superpower, the thing that makes me good at my job, is the fact that I can visualize the entire thing in my head. Doing this allows me to plan the job, prioritize the work, and create a system that meets production's needs.

This same skill manifests itself into the dreams I have about hunting. The first hunt, the one for caribou, I would have this vision of a caribou walking in, perfectly broadside; I would raise my bow and go through my mental checklist, releasing the arrow and watching it soar through the lungs of the beast. My first caribou bull was shot exactly that way.

I know, you think I am batshit crazy! But let me finish.

For some reason, I always dreamt or envisioned shooting two wolves, one after another. This was farfetched, since I was given a 25-percent chance of seeing a wolf and a 10-percent chance of shooting one. Each time this vision was in my head, I remember being very nervous, thinking I would screw up the first shot. Many hunters miss their first shot, because they are already thinking of the second. You hear it every gun deer season; Bang, then a slight pause, the bang, bang, bang and you know the deer is running across the field, not harmed the least bit.

My nerves would spike in my dream and I always talk my way through: "Make this first shot count," I would tell myself. The first wolf would drop in its tracks, allowing me to move to the second and make a quick shot to bag number two. This happened repeatedly as the months passed by, waiting for my hunt. It was vivid and real and I had no control over the ridiculous notion of taking two wolves. The hunt happened exactly how I envisioned it.

Lesson – Visualization can be used in all aspect of your life

When you take the time to use the powers of visualization, you put yourself into real-world scenarios. It is more than a dream at that point. You can practice the perfect execution of each step in your head. It breeds confidence in your abilities and your preparation. You have the ability to slow it all down and see the whole process as it unfolds to perfection.

This is vitally important when hunting dangerous game. You need to control your emotions and your fear. Visualization is one way to practice putting yourself in that situation repeatedly. Visualizing success over and over again will bring you success in the field. On the other hand, if you visualize failure, you will fail. You are not in this to fail, so if those thoughts enter in your mind, you quickly need to refocus those thoughts on positive outcomes. There is no room for doubt in this game because chances are few and you must capitalize on them when you can.

Self-defense is another passion of mine. The people who refuse to admit that evil exists and more importantly refuse to visualize what they would do when evil chooses to attack them will likely lose. You only rise to the level of your training. When your stress level spikes and the adrenaline rushes into your head, your mind loses the ability to reason, resorting to the memories filed away in your subconscious thought. If all you have filed in your subconscious is failure, you will fail. Using the power of visualization pre-programs your subconscious with a winning strategy. This is a very powerful tool.

Shooting arrows at dots on targets is much needed practice, but with the power of visualization, you can practice perfect form, thinking and follow through in real life situations. Once you are confident with the textbook broadside shot, start to play the "what if" game in your head. Visualize scenarios where the conditions are not quite perfect, but you still manage to react and make the perfect shot. Extra practice in the comforts of your bed or easy chair gets you mentally prepared for the field.

Quebec Caribou, The Hunt That Started It All

I am writing this book to help you plan your first hunt the most successful way possible, but my first hunt didn't happen that way. What I learned and am writing in this book is based on an evolution of my experiences over multiple hunts. My goal and hope is that you can capitalize on my experience and fulfill your dreams successfully and happily on the first try. This is not to say my first hunt went bad, but I did learn a lot. I could easily see how it could have gone the other way. It sure did spark a passion in me to pursue bigger and better dreams. Like many of you, I was reluctant to go on a hunting trip. It was too expensive. I could not save all that money. I had all the hunting fun I needed chasing whitetail deer around our land. Why do I need to go anywhere else?

I worked on and off on projects with another electrical engineer, named Bill, who owned a company in Syracuse. He knew of my work ethic and wanted to hire me multiple times. He was a big game hunter and his pictures lined his office walls. We often debated how the engineering business should be run, then the talks got frustrating and he would switch gears and try to convince me to go hunting with him. I never would bite on either, the job or the hunting. He would get frustrated and we would part ways until another time. This happened multiple times and it never worked out, the job or the hunt. I did tip him off to my friend Dean who was a perfect candidate for the job and also liked to hunt. Dean had become a regular in one of my tree stands when he moved to New York. Years passed and Bill and I did the same old dance time and time again. Coming home from work one day, I decided to stop at my brother's business to chat. He told me that the local funeral director, a serious big-game hunter in my hometown, had been over and asked him to go on a caribou hunt. He was trying to book a bunch of hunters to go with him. It was an easy decision for me: if my brother wanted to go, I would go.

As with anything else, I also wanted to include others that might be interested, so I reached out to my friends Dean and Bill and told them about the hunt. They both were interested. Bill being Bill, he immediately researched the hunt and thought it was a good choice. But Bill was not going to wait two years to go; he wanted to book now. Because my brother grew timid of the proposition, Dean, Bill, and I ended up booking that hunt a year earlier than the other group would go.

Man do I wish hunting trips only would cost $3000 now, but damn that was a lot of money then. We would get two Caribou tags each and hunt them in the far north of Quebec. We would carry both rifle and bows, hoping to never have to take out the gun. My rag-tag New York deer-hunting gear would have to do, even though there were some mighty tempting high-end hunting suits for sale at Cabela's.

I spent hours shooting my Hoyt bow. Two weeks before the hunt date, I was practicing in my garage and the arrow all the sudden would not hit the bull's-eye. I looked at the bow noticing that the fiberglass limbs had started to separate. I rushed to the bow shop to find a fix; they had nothing there for parts. A call to Hoyt got a new bow shipped overnight and in a few days, I was back to shooting again. I am extremely grateful and loyal to Hoyt for that service.

What follows is the second story I put on paper, but the first and only to be published in a major printed magazine. *Big Game Hunters* out of Canada was a nicely published magazine that used the stories from everyday hunters like me. They picked up my article and put it in their publication. My fifteen minutes of fame.

Here is the original text that I sent them. They did some major editing for the story that made print in their summer, 2005 issue.

So, How Close Can You Get to a Caribou?

After booking a Caribou hunt in Quebec, I started doing my homework. Before this I really had no idea caribou even existed, or what they were all about. All these years of waiting for Santa Claus on Christmas Eve and I didn't know that reindeer and caribou were basically the same thing. As I read magazine articles and watched videos, I began to wonder if I could get close enough to a caribou to take him with a bow. My previous archery-hunting experience was from a tree stand, trying to get a shot at the elusive and extremely wary whitetail. Being on the ground, wide-open ground at that, left me with doubts on how close I could get to a caribou.

The Otter floated up to the dock as the past week's hunters and guides waited to greet us. They had smiles from ear to ear. They had all tagged out, two caribou per person, and were excited for us. The migration was in full force and there were caribou everywhere! We swapped hunting stories as we swapped out a planeload of gear, and soon they were taking off from the cold, crisp water. As we watched them fly away our guides told us, "Lunch was ready, so get your gear around and we will hunt as soon as we are done with lunch."

We hurried to unpack and organize our gear, then went to the main cabin to swallow some food. Before I knew it, I was in the bow of a small aluminum boat heading out to hunt caribou. My guide was skeptical about getting close enough to take an archery shot. I had brought the rifle as backup and he would have preferred I used it. I really wanted to hunt with my bow though, and I would accept going home empty handed if I couldn't get close enough for a bow shot.

As the boat rounded the point, it was evident that getting close to caribou was not going to be an issue. There in front of us were three bulls swimming the lake. The guide sped toward them, yelling for us to get ready to shoot. I had been at hunting camp for only an hour and a half, and we were already racing in a boat to shoot the first Caribou bull I had ever seen. I got an arrow knocked as the boat pulled up alongside the bulls. Only a couple yards of choppy water separated us. I was uncomfortable, but had previously told myself to listen to the guide; after all, they know the game. I drew back as the boat circled the frightened animals, but I could not let the arrow go. I let the bow down, turned to my guide, and told him to take me to shore; we were going to have a talk!

The talk was a bit one sided, because I was a bit upset. I explained that I wouldn't hunt that way. I would take my chances on land. I could live with myself if I ended up going home empty handed, but I couldn't hunt that way. I asked to be dropped off at shore and left alone; if need be I could follow the lake shore back to camp.

He reluctantly dropped me off at the rocky shore and motored away with the other hunter. The migration would carry more caribou across the lake. It was just a matter of where they would come ashore. Moments after the boat hummed away, I saw a herd of caribou entering the water on the other side, just 300 yards away. As they swam toward me I prepared my gear. Hiding by a skinny spruce tree I waited as they got closer to shore. The shore was lined with moss-covered rocks, with a many large boulders mixed in. I drew my bow and waited as each caribou found footing on the rocky lake bottom. One at a time the caribou walked onto the rocks, then quickly leaped up the hill into the thickening spruce and brush. They passed by me just fifteen yards away but never hesitated long enough to give me a shot. I must say I was a bit perplexed by their size, both body and antler. In less than two hours I had been up close and personal with multiple caribou.

I decided my ambush spot was not the best and decided to investigate what was up the hill. I made my way through the brush and entered an opening seventy-five yards up the hill. In the center of the opening was a cluster of spruce, with about fifty yards of clear shooting in either direction—a perfect ambush spot if more caribou happened to migrate the same way. I went back to the shore to watch the other side of the lake. Within moments another herd entered the water. I could see some real nice bulls, with one topping them all. I watched as long as I dared, then ran up the hill to my chosen spot, hoping they would continue the same path as the others.

It didn't take long before I could hear their hooves as they stepped up on the rocks. The clicking sound was loud and unmistakable; they were on their way up the hill. The brush rattled as the big-racked bulls pushed their way through, but I still couldn't tell what side they would pass. Then to my right the first bull appeared, about forty-five yards away. It was the biggest rack of the bunch and looking back on it, it was easily a Pope and Young caribou. As I turned and drew the bow, he froze looking at me. The sight started to settle on his chest when another bull stepped in the way. Then another, and another, until five Caribou bulls stood side by side staring at me. The big one, being the farthest away, started to walk up the hill. I probably could have made the shot, but the closest bull, not twenty-five yards away, was a more comfortable choice. I swung the bow in his direction and released the arrow. Thwack, the arrow went through his chest and then twanged off the rocks behind him. As he disappeared into the thickening brush, I could see his fur turning crimson red. It was a perfect shot. I had taken my first caribou, with the bow, only two and a half hours into the hunt.

As my blood pressure started to drop, I heard my guide yell, "I heard it hit. I can't believe it. I could hear it hit!" He had seen the caribou swimming in my direction and had floated the boat back down the lake. He asked me what direction it ran. As I pointed down the shore I could see a giant rack sticking out of the water and the rocks. The caribou had tried to escape back to the water, but didn't make it. My guide was as excited as I was; a bow hunter had taken a caribou. We took pictures and dressed the animal. As we worked we talked about what transpired earlier. He told me that many of his hunters would have been glad to shoot the bulls in the water. They would then spend the rest of the week in camp, drinking beer and playing cards. Now he knew I wanted to hunt, and we would spend the rest of the week hunting for my second caribou. We were both excited about what the next week of hunting would bring.

The next morning signaled another glorious day. The sun was up and warm and the sky was clear. This is not typical weather for this part of Quebec. As the owner of camp said, "If the sun shines, take a picture." The weather could change in an instant, usually for the worse. We headed up the hill behind camp for a day of spot and stalk. I carried the rifle, having no intentions of shooting my second bull on this day. I wanted to scout for a good ambush spot for another try with the bow. We had bear tags and I hoped I might get a crack at a bruin as we walked the land. Blueberries were ripe and the previous weeks caribou remains meant there was bear food everywhere, and winter was just a couple weeks away.

Scraggily spruce trees struggle to grow fifteen feet high as they cling to the soil between the rocks. The white moss and red brush give the landscape a Christmas-like atmosphere. From the air this land seems flat and desolate, but on the ground, you'll find subtle peaks and valleys, often a pile of boulders to walk around. The ground is like sponge, like walking across an endless trampoline—that is, until you break through, sinking past the knee, and you're glad you listened to the outfitter and brought knee-high rubber boots.

Bill, the other hunter with us that day, had not taken a caribou yet, so I was left on a rock overlooking a valley and two new lakes. After a couple of hours and a few caribou walking by, I decided to meander and see where else I might try to hunt with the bow. I peaked at the top of the hill, overlooking the lake our camp was perched on. From here I could see the one end of the seventeen-mile-long lake. From this vantage point I could see numerous lines of caribou snaking down the bank on the other side making their way on their 5000-kilometer journey.

I spotted a lone bull a couple of draws away. I decided to have some fun and see how close I could get to him. Off I went, running when I could, being careful not to slip on the moss-covered rocks. As I started down the bank of the second draw, there he was making his way out of the brush-filled bottom. I got down behind a small rock and took off my pack to get my camera. As I unzipped the pack the bull heard me and stopped and looked my direction. The bull was a young one, with less of a rack than the one I had taken the day before. As I took his picture his curiosity peaked and he started coming my way. He got to within twenty yards of me as I stood up, taking my final picture. He cocked his head back and forth like a small puppy, trying to figure out what I was. I talked to him, but it didn't seem to bother him. He was not afraid. I was the first human he had ever seen. I sat back down on the rock and watched him as he nibbled on the white caribou moss and slowly meandered away. That was a pretty special moment for me; to spend that much time with him and be close to such a great animal was a wonderful experience. I think of him often when the hectic days of work get to me, because it brings serenity to my day. It takes me back to the moment when neither of us had a care in the world.

I walked back to the top of the hill, overlooking our lake. It was lunchtime so I sat on a rock in the warm sun, eating my lunch and watching caribou swim the lake. I enjoyed the quiet of the wilderness, not a sound to be heard. The sun was warm, it was an extraordinary day. As I finished my lunch I saw a string of caribou entering the water directly on the other side of the lake. I noticed that the draw I was standing on would surely funnel these caribou toward me. I made my way to the bottom where I found a rock wall with a flat rock floor at the base. In the very center was a lone spruce tree. On either side of the draw the banks slowly gained altitude, out to about 100 yards. A perfect ambush spot with the camera—the bulls were sure to pass here.

I knelt behind the spruce and sat my rifle to my right. I got the camera out of my backpack, getting ready to shoot some great photos. I could hear the distance clicks of their hoofs on the rocks as the caribou came out of the water. They came up the steep hill quickly, brush snapping as they plowed through. The lead bull appeared below me, just on the other side of the lone spruce. It was an awesome bull, not a big rack, but it had character. It had all the features of a caribou rack: great tops with unique back points, a good shovel and nice bezels. My wife and I had watched many videos and both agreed on the size and shape we liked for the living-room wall. This chocolate colored Caribou was exactly the trophy I wanted to hang on that wall.

Now I had a dilemma on my hands: do I shoot this Caribou with the rifle, or take pictures and let him pass? I really wanted to try again with the bow, but on the other hand this was the exact Caribou I came for. I had to have this Caribou, so I hastily snapped a quick picture and sat the camera down on the moss. I reached back to my right to grab my rifle. As I turned, I was nose to nose—not six feet away—with another caribou bull. He was going to walk between the base of the ledge and the lone spruce, a five-foot-wide path that I sat in the middle of. We both froze, him staring at my wide eyes, me staring up his huge cow-like nostrils. I knew that when he spooked, my chances for a shot on my dream caribou would vanish. I wondered if I could grab the camera and take a quick picture. All I might get in the frame would be his nose, but that would tell the story. I reached for the camera and he bolted the other way, scaring the rest of the caribou into frenzy.

I grabbed the rifle with hopes of finding my chocolate-colored caribou. There he was sneaking into the cover of some trees, hiding from the unknown danger. Because he was the lead bull, the others did not run away, they just bounced around not knowing what to do. I thought if I could only take a couple steps out, I might squeeze a shot into the trees. As I stepped out I saw something out of the corner of my eye. Three caribou were standing there staring at me. I slowly stepped back as if they would forget they saw me. They finally had enough: lead bull or not they were getting out of there, and they took off up the hill.

With his friends leaving him, the lead bull came out of the trees and headed up the hill. I tried to get the crosshairs on him as he weaved in and out of the spruce, boulders, and piles of brush. At 150 yards I finally found an opening and let a shot go. He froze as if startled by the gun's report. I racked in another shell and brought the scope back on him. As I aimed, his rack started to weave, his rack grew heavy, and he toppled. I had taken my dream Caribou, The trophy for my living-room wall.

In a little more than twenty-four hours, I had taken two magnificent caribou bulls and been within spitting distance of many more. I guess you can get close to caribou! I cleaned, caped, and quartered my caribou, using what I'd learned from watching my guide the previous day. With the loins in my pack and the rack and cape on my back, I proudly made the two-mile walk back to camp. At the day's end my guide Stephan made his way back to camp, a little bit worried that he had lost me. Once he saw my bull, a smile came across his face; he was now sure I had come to camp as a hunter. Off we went to pack out the rest of the caribou meat.

Because the entire camp tagged out in two days, we spent the next five days fishing and hiking to spot more caribou, ptarmigan, snow owls, and maybe a wolf or a bear. Stephan, my guide, had his own tags to fill so we hunted more, taking a huge bull with a fifty-inch-wide rack to fill his freezer. It was a great time spent on the lake, searching for caribou on the shore. The pressure was off for me; this was even more fun, an added bonus to hunt with a new friend.

We spent the evenings sitting around a campfire on the lakeshore. The skies were so clear; it seemed as if there were a thousand times more stars than I had ever seen before. So clear that you could see the reflection off of satellites as they streaked across the sky. Then to top off our evening's enjoyment the Northern lights would dance their mystical dance, sending chills up our spines. A double rainbow capped of our week, as if it was a sign that "this is the best I can give you."

It was a somber morning as we tried to figure out exactly how we got all that gear in that bag. We wanted to go home, to see our families and share our stories, but we didn't want to leave such a wonderful place. The silence was broken as what sounded like a huge Harley Davidson flew overhead. The Otter had returned to take us on the first leg of our 995-mile journey home. The thousand-horsepower plane swooped at the water like a snow skier coming off the long jump. The plane floated to the dock, and the peering eyes of the next week's hunters stared out the windows, wondering what to expect but excited to see the pile of bone we had collected for our trophies. They were the now the ones filled with anticipation and excitement and we were the jealous, envious veterans who knew what lay in their future.

Loaded into the plane, the huge engine popped as the pilot did circles in the lake, creating a chop that would allow the pontoons to break the suction-like hold of the ice-cold water. In moments we were airborne, watching our paradise disappear behind us. A tear came to my eye as I thought of my little buddy Caribou, now miles away on his journey. I wondered if I would see him again and what a trophy he would be when I did. If we crossed paths again, I would know him, I was sure. Again, I would let him pass, trophy rack and all, because he is my link to that great wilderness and I could not take him away from such a place. He trusted me not to hurt him once and I would not betray that trust.

Once my guide Stephan and I understood each other, we became pretty good friends. I had proved to both of us that you could get close to caribou. We kept in touch over the years. Stephan really wanted to hunt turkey, but bear season would not allow him to come to New York in the spring. I had promised that I would hunt with him for my first black bear, but it just never was the right time. Then one day I learned that he had died suddenly of a brain aneurysm. He was in his early forties. He had left the high-paced, high-stress, long-hour world that we deal with every day to become a full-time guide. He told us at camp one day, while we were complaining about having to go back to work, that "he had the life." It is too bad it wasn't a little bit longer.

Lesson – Sometimes you just know

Your heart will tell you what to do and I highly suggest you listen to it. Many times when you are hunting, you just get sucked up into the moment, and you begin to act instinctually. All the plans you made in your head and the smack talk you said to your friends melts away and you know, in your heart, this is the animal you were destined to take. Picking up the rifle to take that caribou was one of those moments, and I have no regrets.

In Buffalo County, Wisconsin, I sat in an archery deer stand at the top of a draw. Early that morning, I knew deer were passing by me in the dark. As daylight grew I could hear chaos in the neighboring cornfield. At about 9:30 that sunny, cool morning this large buck started walking toward me. He barely could keep his nose from dragging in the leaves. His tongue hung outside his mouth. As he grew closer, he was obviously on a crash course to pass me at twenty yards. His rack was wide and thick, but had shorter tines; it would not have met the 130-inch limit put on by the outfitter. His face was old and gray and the fact that he had chased does all night made him look like he was making his last walk back to bed. Anyway, the rack didn't meet the standard that I or the outfitter had in mind. I passed on this buck. I regret that decision still today. He was an old monarch of a beast and the rack was obviously on the downhill slide. He was still trying and still fighting like he did when he was young, but the truth is, this was likely his last year. I should have honored that warrior by taking him home and proudly placing him on my wall for eternity. I will say this: it was an honor to be in the presence of a deer of that age.

Building a Relationship With Your Guide

What went down between Stephan, my Caribou guide, and me that day was a lesson I took very seriously on subsequent hunts. The guide knows nothing about you and will make assumptions based only on past clients. You know nothing about what your guide will assume and if you don't talk to him it could be a recipe for disaster. It can very easily tarnish your hunt.

It isn't a stretch for a guide to think that most hunters want to drink beer and play cards in camp. I have done it, enjoyed the hell out of it, but that was a different time and place. If that is what you spent your money to do, be honest about it. Hunting camp for some is the place you go to get away from your wife. Although that might be an added benefit, I am not sure the hunt camps I am talking about are that place. If you came to hike and hunt and put in any effort required for a good animal, your guide will likely be highly motivated.

Understand that your guide lives through your success. He is the scout, the strategist, and the hunter, and you are a mechanism that he uses to take an animal. Guiding you to a great kill is as much a thrill to him as it is for you when pulling the trigger.

Many hunters come to camp in poor health or at the very least cannot put in the effort needed to get very far away from camp. The guide must assume this and plan for an easy kill at an even easier distance away from camp. On the flip side, if you have not gotten yourself into proper hunting shape, you cannot have a guide that outruns and leaves you, or he'll be miserable all day that you cannot keep up.

Remember, their sole purpose is to get you a chance at an animal. In most cases, once you get a chance they'll feel like their job is complete. Granted, there is a little more to it than that, but without proper communications, it can easily end up being that simple. The only way to insure you both are on the same page and have the same expectations is to communicate, then communicate some more.

With that said, if you piss off your guide or outfitter because you are just an asshole, you will be marched all over that countryside and never see an animal. They know where the animals are and they also know where they aren't, and they can easily make sure you don't ever see an animal. My advice is to be friendly, honest, and humble, making sure your guide knows how you feel. And for God's sake, listen to your guide. He lives this land. He has done your scouting for you. He knows what is there, the quantity and quality of game and he knows what your best chance is.

Listen to him.

I prefer to use email as my main communications to the outfitter. I will first ask him questions to make sure I have a good feel for what a realistic goal is. Once you book the hunt, you should get him out of salesman mode and make it clear that you want to know the truth. Some outfitters fear telling the truth will make you back out. I hope after reading this you are a better, more secure person than that.

Nearing the hunt date, I will send an email stating my goals and my level of preparedness. They don't give a shit about your hunting resumes so keep those details to yourself. They have heard more bullshit hunting stories and they will immediately think you are a liar. I tell them that I am willing to go home empty handed, but I am there to take a reasonable representation of the species. If a Boone and Crocket-caliber animal shows up I will take a crack at him, but I want a decent animal. I will say I need my guide's help to make that call.

I then discuss what I have done to practice shooting. Again, don't be the ass that brags about 700-yard shots. For rifle, I have practiced shooting long ranges often. Even though I can shoot long distances, I would prefer to shoot the animal at bow range. I carry a 7mm Remington Magnum and I love the gun as much as it loves me. I am confident with it. If I am archery hunting I also talk about how much I practice and that I practice long yardage, but would prefer a 20-30-yard shot. They will always be skeptical, because many hunters have let them down. You have no idea how many stories I have heard about hunters showing up with brand-new, magnum-caliber rifles that have never been shot.

Then I talk about the fact I will do what it takes to be successful. I have exercised to the point where I believe I can do the work required of me. I am here for the adventure and am willing to be pushed outside my comfort zone. Of course, the key is to make sure this is actually true; you can push on even with tired and sore muscles, but you cannot recover from mentally giving up.

I ask the outfitter to share this with the guide head of time, and state I will also have a conversation with him early on at camp. You will be able to tell if it was communicated correctly when you get there. There is always one guide that hates sitting at camp and wants to hunt, and hopefully, you were paired with him. Likewise, if you want to stay in camp, there is always that guide that masters the hunting story and loves doing camp chores. Either can be a fun experience, if it matches up with your expectations.

In Russian camp, I felt like I was the last kid picked for the kickball game. The lead guide took one hunter, the big burly Russian kid took the next, and I got the camp driver. I was a little pissed when my guide dumped me off the wooden sled, he and the snowmobile continuing out of sight. I felt like I drew the short straw.

We were told that many moose were shot from camp, or close to camp. But the snow conditions were wrong; there was little snow. We also never expected the temperature to be -30 degrees Celsius. The moose now had the advantage, because they could outrun the snowmobiles. I soon realized that the guides wanted at least one or both the other hunters to score early and be done. Listening to these hunters talk, it was evident that they expected giant racks, but the minus-30-degree Celsius temperature was coaxing them to stay close to the woodstove. It was obvious they would shoot quickly to get it over with, but because I communicated, they knew I would put the time and work in to do whatever it took. They know they could count on me to be patient and work hard. I would be the one they would spend the time hunting with, because I communicated with them long beforehand.

Lesson – Communication with your guide

Communicating with your guide is a huge key to success. Without it someone is likely to be disappointed and that someone is you, the hunter. The guide needs to know your expectations, so he can help you with split-second decisions on the size and quality of game. He needs to know your physical abilities and more importantly your willingness to put in the extra effort. You have to be honest with yourself and the guide. His job is to make your hunt a success and if taking an easier route is what you need, he will be happy to oblige.

Diary, August 19, 2015: Communicating With Your Guide

The following is an email sent to Denny to pass on to my guide.

Denny,
One thing I have learned in the hunting trips I have gone on is that communication is key and having everyone know my expectations makes for a great hunt.
With that said, would you please pass this on to the Outfitter and if possible the guide that will guide me.
I spend a lot of time planning and thinking about my trips. I enjoy the planning, and I believe I have had my fun well before I get on that plane, so I treat every aspect of the trip as "icing on the cake."
The last animal on my bucket list is a giant moose and that is why I am coming. I usually strive for a reasonable representative of the species, but in this case, I really want to push hard for a giant. If we pass up a great moose with thoughts of bigger later, and I go home empty handed, I will live with that. I have learned long ago that the adventure is hunting the animal, not taking the animal.
I will put my trust in the guide's judgment whether to shoot or pass and I will not second-guess it.

My guide can expect that I will be in top shape. I consider this a partnership and I will work hard to carry my share of the workload. I will know my gun and have practiced many shots before I come. This rifle is like an extension of me. I will do my very best to make the first shot count. I will work hard, be patient and hunt as hard as we need to get the job done. I don't mind getting pushed outside my comfort zone, but we all need to get back home safe. My hope is that my guide tells stories about how I hunted and he wishes all his hunters would hunt like me.

I am an archery hunter at heart. If I had my way, we would be taking 20-30 yard shots. I will be able to make a long shot if needed, but my preference is the closer the better.

I hope to have a guide that enjoys the hunt as much as I do, and isn't looking to just get it over with. I would also appreciate taking time out to enjoy the wilderness and understand some of the culture.

To most this sounds pretty obvious, but I have seen many guides get excited to find out their client is a hunter (willing to do what it takes) versus a harvester (The one who wants to shoot the first animal they see).

Hopefully this helps get us off on the right foot. I cannot wait to see how it all plays out.

Pete Forman

Check Your Ego

Hunting is a bragging man's sport. We all love to tell and hear the great stories of giant trophy animals and the adventures that only a few seem to be able to take. Sometimes ego turns story telling into bragging and that never goes over well. There are five stages of a hunter's career and our ego will act differently in each stage. Be conscious of where you are in your hunting career, and especially be aware that you may be in a different place and time than the people around you and even your guide. I talked about communicating and being honest with yourself and your guide; part of that is leaving your ego at the door. Treat this as a completely new experience that you can learn from, enjoy immensely, and walk away from as a better hunter.

Shooter Stage: Hunters at this stage simply want to do a lot of shooting.

If you are in the shooter stage then you aren't ready for a big-game hunt. First off, throwing lead is irresponsible and dangerous. In my opinion, you need to have the goal in mind of one shot, one kill, before you take on this kind of adventure. This stage is typically for young hunters anyway, so I doubt it really comes into play, unless Dad is loaded with money and he takes his son or daughter on a hunt long before they are ready.

If you do take a young hunter along, let them shoot what they want. Don't put pressure on them to take giant animals. You might be in the trophy stage, but they still have four stages to work through. They want to get an animal, any animal, and have a story to tell their friends.

Limiting-Out Stage: Hunters at this stage simply want to take a lot of game.

We all want to fill out tags, or limit out. I don't think there is anything wrong with this expectation. The need to fill every tag you can at this stage is okay. You bought the tag, and you can do what you want with it.

But, I remember my Caribou outfitter telling, a story of a guy who was completely smashed on vodka the night before the float plane arrived, explaining loudly how he was going to blast everything he saw and pick out the biggest to take home. Well that attitude was not something the outfitter would deal with in a remote camp, and that hunter was not allowed on the float plane the next morning.

1. **Trophy Stage**: Hunters at this stage are interested in the quality of game, not the quantity.

The trophy stage is where some egos can really get out of control. My attitude is that I am happy for anyone who takes an animal and very happy for anyone who bags a trophy or even one bigger than mine. For me, part of the hunting-camp experience is enjoying the success of other hunters. If that success is my friend or better yet my family, I am over the top with joy.

This is not the way with some people. Some people are not happy unless they get the biggest animal. I was told the story of a hunter after big whitetail in Saskatchewan. He had hunted with this outfitter the year before and shot a giant buck. He had told his friends that he was coming back to get another one, even bigger. In Saskatchewan, you sit all day over bait, usually an alfalfa bail, waiting for a big buck to come in and feed. When the guide got there that night he noticed a blood trail and human footprints heading away from the bail. When he got to the stand, maybe 100 yards away, he asked the hunter what he got. The hunter said strongly, "I didn't see a deer all day." The guide dragged him out of the stand and they followed the blood trail and footprints to a deer that was buried in the snow. It turns out that the hunter shot a buck much smaller than one he had bragged he would get, and chose to try to break the law to cover it up. Needless to say, that hunter is now banned from ever hunting in Canada again.

Trust me: ego is a hard thing to control. You cannot let an opportunity to rib your friends go by if yours was the biggest or you took the best shot. There is a huge difference in poking fun and just being a giant dick about it. When you are poking fun, you should remember that you can be humbled at any moment. This hunting thing is hard and we all make mistakes. That is what makes it challenging and fun.

I got humbled really badly in Manitoba on a black bear hunt with my sixteen-year-old son. This hunt was meant to be all about him, and he scored on the first night on a nice, probably 200-pound black bear. He was on cloud nine and I was one proud father. I heard the single rifle shot just before dark and I knew that was him. It was good that he got one early because it was ninety-five degrees out and bear sightings were next to nothing. It was so hot that we stripped down to our underwear in the stands to stay cool. Thank you to the person who invented the Thermocell; they work like a champ keeping the mosquitos at bay. I hunted very hard, and even hunted a few cooler mornings, but saw nothing but mosquitos.

After a few days with zero sightings, we decided to hunt our way out of the bush that night and try another area later in the week. Now remember, I have a pretty good hunting resume now, and I should have known what I was doing. A bear came into my bait. I had a ton of time to look this bear over. I did not want to trump my son's bear by getting a bigger one; I preferred one just a little smaller, so he could have the bragging rights. I knew hunting was still going to be hard because the temperature was showing no signs of cooling off. Maybe I was getting a little tired. Do you feel all the excuses I am throwing at you to justify the ground shrinkage after I shot this bear? I dropped him right on the spot, climbed down to give him a look over, and he was smaller even than I had thought. Climbing back into the stand to sit until way after dark for the guide to pick me up, I spent the time licking my wounds and it was very hard to deal with. The outfitter and guide knew my history well and they expected better, I imagined. My son was just going to laugh, or cry in embarrassment. It was a huge shot to my ego, but I sucked it up. Being humbled makes you grow, and I grew a lot that evening. I can laugh at it now — a little!

Method Stage : Hunters in this stage are focused on one method only.

You all know how egos go when we start talking the weapons we use. Your caliber is for wimps! My gun is way better than yours. If you shoot anything but Mathews, you are an idiot. I stay out of this little game. Many think my rifle caliber is too small being a 7mm Remington Magnum and not one of the 30-caliber Magnums. It works for me and my rifle and I are one when it comes to hunting. I have yet to see an animal that had access to the ballistics charts before I put one in the engine compartment. Shot placement is the key!

The method thing can get out of control especially when we talk about things like "over bait" and "high fence." I am not going to start a debate here because I could give a shit what you do. My favorite line to use is this: "It is your tag and you can use it any way you choose." Hunting is a sport, it is supposed to be fun, and how and where you do it is all up to you. In my mind the more people who take up hunting and enjoy it the better; the adrenaline rush is always the same.

Sportsman Stage: The hunter begins to place the emphasis on the total hunting experience.

This book is more tailored to the sportsman stage. Hopefully something you read here will help you progress through these stages to the point where you begin to enjoy the whole adventure of the hunt. I hunt as an excuse to see the world, push myself to be better mentally and physically, and find places that are spiritual to me.

I like to hope that at this stage we have learned to leave the ego at home. If you haven't yet, I think it is clouding your vision of everything good that is around you. When you can spend money on a hunt, then fail to take the animal, but still come home with a giant smile and a head full of memories, you have won. Welcome to the hunting big leagues!

Some Unexpected Benefits of My Hunting Trip

You are probably wondering if I am going to talk about how to convince the family, especially your significant other, that your hunting trip is something you should sacrifice for. I won't lie, I am very lucky in the fact that my family has always supported my hunting passion. My kids Britni and Devon have always been my biggest fans.

During this time, I travelled a lot for work, so being away from family was not abnormal. The caribou hunt was the first time I was away for that long, only ten days, but without any way of calling home. That was hard for all of us. Today technology exists that makes this a non-issue.

Diary, April 7: InReach

I am looking at ways to communicate. It is going to be a long time away. The SPOT communicator does not do what I want to do. I have seen satellite phones not work, plus there is no way for people to call me. I wouldn't be able to leave it powered up. I just found the DeLorme InReach. This looks like it has some merit. I need to research it better.

I came home with two big caribou racks, three boxes of meat, and a giant-ass smile on my face. The unexpected surprise was the house being decorated with the welcome-home signs of my then two- and eight-year-old kids. That was the highlight of my whole trip. A couple weeks later I remember my wife suggesting I book another hunt. With a shocked look on my face I wondered why. She said, "If hunting makes you this happy, then you need to keep doing it."

The thought of booking a hunt two years in advance is simply a burden to most people. Me, I get two years of fun out of the planning process and preparation. I always tell my guide that I have already had my fun; any success we have during the hunt is just icing on the cake. But even after the hunt is over, the glow you have telling your stories and sharing your pictures lasts for months. If you choose to have your trophy mounted, all the stories start again when the truck pulls up to deliver a big crate containing your mount. The best part of all is what resides in your head. I can close my eyes and go back, seeing every detail, feeling the sun on my back, the sweat on my forehead and the smells of nature. Much of that is what I have been able to write down, but there are still things in my head that I can never convey. I am not sure I want to; those memories are all mine.

Lesson – You need to break away from your life to rejuvenate

Some women like to go on spa days. Some people like sitting on a beach. Some love to go to amusement parks. Hunters like to get close to animals and become one with nature. I believe we all need a favorite place to get away. Family time is important, but everyone should venture out on their own to chase their dream. It is okay to want to spend time away from others. "Absence helps the heart grow fonder," it's been said, and it is so very true. Finding yourself, pushing yourself, and appreciating nature can only make you appreciate all the things you have back home even more.

Oh, and you should put as much passion in encouraging your family to chase dreams as you do your own. Maybe buy them their own copy of this book!

Hunting Back Home With the Family

The effort I put into preparing for the caribou trip directly translated to a hugely successful archery and shotgun season back home in New York. Somehow, I had magically been promoted to the level of good hunter. It made me a better all-around hunter. I could stay in the stand longer, I made multiple one-shot kills, and I was easily finding ways to dedicate time in the field. My kids were much more interested in my hunting too. The highlight of my deer season was taking Britni, then eight years old, out for her first sit with me. This is our story of that morning.

Britni's First Hunt

We sat side by side on the twelve-foot-high platform named "Christi's Stand." Twilight from the rising sun started to illuminate the sky, silhouetting the trees and brush, and brightening the open pasture. Rustling of hand warmers in her little hands told me this would be a short day. I could only hope the cock pheasant would walk in, so Britni could see the morning sun flash off the brilliant colors of his plumage.

It had been a great hunting season for me. A fantastic Quebec Caribou trip had started it all off. Then back home, on our land, I had the opportunity to fill a few deer tags. Britni had wanted to go hunting with me, but my drive to bag more deer kept me putting her off. The season was coming to an end, and I only had one more chance to take her on her first deer hunt with dad.

I had prepared for this day by spending the summer building towers with large platforms and big solid legs. I wanted a safe and comfortable spot for my wife and kids to hunt. That Friday night I broke the news that tomorrow morning would be our day to hunt. We would go to Christi's stand, a tower that I built for my wife. Immediately the ribbing started. "You'd better not shoot a buck out of my stand," Christi said.

The late season morning was cold, so we packed Britni in as many warm clothes as we could. So many in fact that I'm not sure how she made the long walk to the stand. I put a hand warmer in each of her pockets and off we went to a stand in the edge of a thicket, overlooking the open field.

My greatest hope was for Britni to experience the sunrise as it brings nature to life. I had sat in this stand before and a cock pheasant had walked by. Seeing that majestic bird would be a real treat. It was much too cold to expect much more than this. Fifteen minutes of dark started to fade as the sun came up over the hill. Time was of the essence, fidgeting was starting and I could hear the rustle of hand warmers.

I leaned over and whispered for her to try real hard to be quiet; this was the best time of the day. I told her to listen to the silence, because very soon the birds would be waking up. As I sat back up in my chair, I saw a silhouette of a deer at the edge of the field. I had tags for a buck or a doe, so I planned on shooting at any deer that happened along. I pointed and she saw the deer, and I whispered to plug her ears. The shotgun roared as the muzzle blast blinded us.

As my eyes began to focus again, there was nothing to be seen in the field. "Great," I thought, "I just missed my first deer with my daughter." Just then a flicker of white caught my eye; it was the tail flicking off the ground. Waving like a surrender flag, it told me our deer was down. I told Britni to stay there as I ran to the deer. As I got to the deer, all I saw was horns. I had taken the biggest buck of my life, on my first hunt with my daughter. I ran back to the stand, yelling that we had just got a big buck. She beamed from ear to ear as we ran back to the downed deer.

We ran back to the truck and drove home to get the camera. Christi wondered why we were home so soon; I assume she figured it was because Britni couldn't handle the cold. The emotion overwhelmed me as I waited for Britni to break the news. She nervously told her mother that we had just got a big buck from her stand.

I'm quite sure we will have many great moments together as father and daughter, but this one will always rank near the top. If any of the future things that we do together make us feel like we did that morning, we have a lot to look forward to. The buck now sits in our living room, and someday will sit in Britni's new home.

The Day Britni Took Control of the Shotgun

Jumping ahead a few years, when Britni was now sixteen, she put in the work to complete her hunter's safety course in which she aced the final test. It was now time to hand the shotgun over to her and take her on her first spring turkey hunt.

We live in a valley with the house on one side facing the rest of the land on the other. The advantage is that we can watch the wildlife from the house, which means we can usually see if the turkeys will roost in the large pines at the top of my field. I had two ground blinds set up. One blind was set in the open field where the birds would likely pass later in the morning. The other was at the foot of the large pines.

That morning, way before sunrise, Britni and I headed across the valley. I told her the advantages and disadvantages of each blind. The field blind was a safer choice in that there was no way we would spook any turkeys fumbling our way into it, in the dark. I was pretty sure the gobblers had roosted in the pines; if we went to that blind we risked spooking them. The choice was up to Britni and she chose the blind in the pines.

We did manage to get into the blinds quietly with no issue. It just started to lighten up and I whispered to Britni that turkeys could be in the trees above us. It wasn't a few seconds later and a gobbler let loose, right above our heads. We could peak up through the porthole of the blind and see the silhouette of a turkey roosting on the branch.

As the sun rose, so did the turkey chatter; each time we stared at each other with these silly, shocked looks on our faces. As the woods started to brighten, we heard turkeys hitting the ground one after another. For an animal that sleeps on a branch, they sure do hit the ground with an uncontrolled ruckus. Now it was just a matter of which direction they would go.

A few minutes passed and the gobbling competition started. One gobbled, and then another and the sounds grew closer and closer by the second. If they came to the field, they would likely go through a deep ditch by the blind. I peeked out and saw four gobblers in perfect line heading our way; each taking turns out gobbling the other. With their fans spread, they walked with that tough-guy swagger, each trying to outdo the other birds in line.

I got Britni situated at the small porthole opening toward the ditch. Like a shooting gallery, these birds would walk the bank on the other side, not fifteen yards away. I could no longer see out of the blind, so I watched Britni's finger on the trigger as she took aim. Her little finger quivered as the adrenaline raced through her veins. I was beside myself waiting for her to squeeze that trigger. The gobblers were egging her on with one gobble after another.

It seemed like I had been staring at her trembling finger for fifteen minutes or more. I did not know what she was seeing or even if the birds were still in sight. I whispered in her ear, asking what was going on. She replied, "They have been gone for a while, I hope you're not mad that I didn't shoot." I took the gun from her shaking hands and explained to her that it was her decision to shoot or not. I then stressed that that was the best day of turkey hunting I had ever had.

She decided at that moment that even though she will eat any game I bring home, she does not want to shoot it herself. I am just glad she tried it first, got to experience turkeys gobbling that close and was brave enough to make her own decisions. Those two hunts with her are very special to me. Yet another gift from hunting.

It Doesn't Have to be a Big Hunt

It doesn't have to be a big, long, and expensive hunt to be a memorable experience. Those two hunts with my daughter took all of four hours of time. A weekend trip to a buddy's house or another state can ramp up your game with different challenges and more fun. There are still a lot of places to hunt out there that are cost effective and won't break the bank.

We have a family pig roast every year. I need to buy a pig anyway, so I booked a day at a high fenced operation in Pennsylvania. I took a bow and my brother brought the video camera, and we chased wild boars around the land all morning. I was fortunate to arrow a nice boar from a tree stand as the herd of hogs ran by. I think my brother's story was better since he had to sit on the ground amongst the hogs as he videoed me shooting the boar. This put him way out of his comfort zone. The hog turned out to be a pretty big and ugly boar with nice sharp teeth. For the hell of it, I decided to get a mount done. It makes a cool conversation piece as he hangs on my wall. So, for a couple extra hundred bucks I got to take a hog with my bow and gained some fun memories in the process.

A Thirteen-year-old, a 30-06, and a Boar

My son Devon was all in when it came to hunting. He shot the 30-06 for the first time when he was eight years old. He was ready to hunt critters, but New York State says you must wait until you are sixteen. So, what is a father to do? I bought Devon a boar hunt in a preserve in Pennsylvania for Christmas.

The anticipation for the little guy was intense as we planned the hunt and the days grew closer. He practiced with his trusty 30-06, shooting from shooting sticks to increase his odds of success. We would spend the day chasing boars, but the trick was to get set up for a good humane shot. A lot of training and thought went into our preparation.

The day we went was cold, bitter cold. The thermometer stuck at zero and the wind felt like needles on our faces. These were not the greatest conditions for a fun and relaxing hunt, but we were determined to give it a go. In the fence were other animals, such as rams and fallow deer. When a big elk walked in, Devon's eyes grew wide. He kind of wanted to shoot one of them, but Dad's wallet wouldn't allow it.

The guide was hurrying us around, trying to get positioned on the group of hogs. Not spooking them or moving them was a challenge, and when they did finally stay still, we had to wait for a good one to position itself correctly without others standing in the bullet's path. It took a few tries over two or three hours, but then three good ones broke from the herd.

We got the shooting sticks up and Devon got the gun aligned on the boar. I was nervous, not wanting him to rush the shot. There was no need to be nervous with Devon behind the gun. A squeezed trigger and down that boar dropped, cold in his tracks. Well you can imagine the excitement for both of us. Even the guide was giddy, telling everyone how well the kid could handle a 30-06. Some nice trophy pictures and some pork for the freezer; all in all it was a pretty fun day and a very cool Christmas present. Some bragging rights for school as the trophy picture got hung up on the woodshop trophy board. And of course, the story got told over and over again with every little detail, like no one other than Devon can.

Start them young and let them shoot a big gun.

The Quest for Mountain Lion

The mountain lion was one of my top-five animals to hunt. In 2001 it was the only one that I thought I might be able to afford, so my focus shifted to finding a place to hunt cougar. There are many places to hunt mountain lion, one lead led to another, and somehow I got the name of rancher in Arizona who was apparently pretty good at it. The internet was new at the time, strangely; I had to email his girlfriend in Prescott, Arizona, and she would talk to him when he visited on the weekends.

For lion hunting, you want tracking snow. That does not happen in Southern Arizona. When driving through Skull Valley on the way to the ranch it became clear that it was hot and dry and would stay that way. Dry-ground lion hunting is special, but this rancher was confident and he had a history of taking a lot of lions. The final selling point for me was that my mother had relatives in Prescott, and I was going to treat her to a trip out to see them.

Back home in New York a large farm might be 400 acres. The driveway to this ranch was nine miles long and passed through three creek beds, which I am not sure the rental-car company would appreciate. I came to find out it covered a measly 22,000 acres. Stephen was a six-foot-six-inch-tall cowboy with the hat, vest, and giant mustache that went along with it. He had a ranch hand, like Festus of the old *Gun Smoke* days. He was an old hired hand that you had to hide any alcohol from, but this man could tell stories all night long. Sneak this old cowboy a beer and he would do anything for you.

This would be a horseback hunt. At 4:00 AM we were out by the barn saddling up horses for the day. Stephen asked me if I had experience on a horse. I smiled and said, "Yes, about five minutes' worth." He laughed out loud and stated, "You sound like my dad. I took him to Montana for a mountain elk hunt. I told him he should get out and walk to get in shape. He told me bluntly, 'Why do I want to get sore twice?'"

Lesson – Physical or Mental Preparation?

There is a lot to say about being as physically prepared as you can be for a hunt. In other areas of this book I will talk about the other advantages of having something to train for, a goal. But don't underestimate how much your attitude plays a role in all of this. I knew that not having horse experience was a risk, but I had made up my mind to deal with whatever happened and I did. Sure, I was way out of my comfort zone, but I refused to let any fear gain control of me. It also helped that I was keenly aware that if I was afraid, the horse would sense it and would have a negative reaction.

If you are a parent you have had those times when you were scared to death, but you had to "suck it the fuck up" so your kids did not get scared. You've done it before and can do it again, if you get your mind right. Never have I regretted getting out of my box, my comfort zone. The week on that horse was such an amazing and educational experience; I now have so much respect for those animals. The blisters on my ass made the flight home a bitch, but other than that I enjoyed every minute of the saddle.

My horse, Diamond M, was an old animal that didn't really care anything about walking too far. For the most part this big walking couch just followed the lead horse. I did have to coax him to go straight every now and then because he tended to want to veer off in a different direction. I had my GPS strapped to my arm. Stephen picked on me and asked if I didn't trust that he would get me back. I commented that something could happen to him and I might end up alone. He laughed and said, "Just kick Diamond M and tell him to go to the ranch. He knows the way. That is why he keeps veering off the trail, he knows where the ranch is and he wants to go home." No shit, at the end of the day we decided to head back. Diamond M passed the lead horse and led the way. Finally, he was getting his way.

Diamond M and I got along just fine, except when he tried to scrape me off his back with a tree limb. I know he did it on purpose to test my mettle. I stayed on, so I guess I passed his test. I gained a new perspective on horses that trip. We rode up to the edge of a canyon; I was thinking we were just looking over the edge for lions sunning on the rocks. Stephen kicked his horse and over the edge he went. The sure-footed horse was in total control, while I just hung on for life. Many times, it was so steep that I just lay back on his rump to stay on. In places he would put all four feet together in a little square and rotate his whole body to turn. Once he firmly set his feet on top of a huge boulder, and then slid off the side, jumping at just the right time. When we got to the bottom Stephen asked me, "Did you ever think you would ride a horse over something like that?" I responded as I caught my breath, "No, I wouldn't even have tried to walk down that."

Arizona is dry and hot, so who knew I would pick the week it rained nearly all week. I am not a fan of rushing water; a little phobia kicks in. The first swollen creek crossing on Diamond M was terrifying. We tried a similar crossing later in the week on a four-wheeler and, well, they float down the creek. We got a little wet on that one. I will take a horse ride through the water any day.

The dogs hunting on dry ground have a hard time picking up a track. It cannot be done when the scent is washed away with pouring rain. We did see tracks and signs where a male would mark his territory, but nothing the dogs could track. On the very last afternoon we did pick up a track. The cat climbed to the top of a mesa and was gone once hitting the flat ground. We could have run that animal down, but we wouldn't have made it back for me to leave and make our travel plans.

Remember, my mom was in Arizona with me and she wasn't keen on me chasing mountain lions. I couldn't be late; she would have been worried sick. Stephen was so dejected that he gave me half my money back. He had only failed one other client in his lion career. This one hurt.

When I got back to work people avoided me like the plague. They could not handle the thought of spending that kind of money and not getting an animal. I was a little shocked and dismayed with their attitude. I did amazing things. I saw amazing country. I got to take my mom on a trip and show her the Grand Canyon. I remember Stephen asking me if I was bored as we just plugged along on horseback, hour after hour. He figured the slow pace was killing me. I said, "You know I drive past a sunrise every day and seldom take the time to look at it, slowing down and actually experiencing it like this is amazing." To me the entire trip was a success. On the bright side, I had money in my pocket and I did not have to pay a taxidermist bill. I was well on my way to saving for the next hunt. Let the planning begin!

Lesson – Failure does not have to be final; it is just a change in direction.

People get really hung up on failure. But I had realistic expectations for hunting, so I did not see it as a failure at all. I focused on all the positive things that I experienced. With every failure there is a lesson. I used the lessons of this hunt to make future hunts better. My advice is to embrace failure for what it is: a temporary setback that you can learn from. Then shake it off and move forward.

Saskatchewan Color-Phased Black Bear

A black bear hunt is Saskatchewan in 2002 was the first time my two work buddies and I tried to hunt together. Those two and some friends of theirs were going black bear hunting and asked me if I wanted to go. I couldn't think of hunting without offering the chance to Dean, so I did and he said yes. Come to find out there was only room for one person in camp, but the week before had openings. Dean and I decided we would go together the week before and the others would follow the next week. So the idea of friends hunting together fell through really fast.

I was excited about this bear hunt because they have color-phase bears in Saskatchewan. A color phase black bear can be the color of chocolate, cinnamon or even blond. Hunting a black bear hadn't really tripped my trigger, but a chance at a color-phase black bear was exciting. It also gave us an opportunity to use our bows. Ironically, the outfitter was not real keen on archery hunters. He kept saying, "A lot of tracking and no skinning." In his experience archery hunters had taken poor or marginal shots, and because a bear has so much fur, the wound closes quickly and the blood trail can dry up fast.

We arrived at camp to find out there were two families who brought three teenage kids on their first hunts. One dad was a dentist and he and his wife had been on this hunt before. Their son and daughter would hunt bear for the first time. The other was a father-and-son combo, the father being a rough and grouchy man. He told the guide, "This is my first and only born. I am too old and too ugly to have more kids. You bring him back safe."

We talked of giant 300-pound bears. We heard stories of color-phased bears and one with a missing front paw. The dental parents told their kids to hold out for big bears only. They all seemed like very nice people and we were bound to have some bears on the ground the first night. You typically hunt bears in the late afternoon to dark. This gives you all day to pace back and forth with anticipation and excitement. That excitement peaks when you are told to fire up your four-wheeler for the trip to the stands.

From the cabin, a series of roads and trails lead in every direction. I drew a stand called "fender," named after the old car fender rusting at the trail head. My stand was the closest and it was a solid forty-five-minute ride away. Others rode for nearly two hours to get to their stand. We were covering a lot of ground.

We would hunt from mid-afternoon to dark. The stands were situated in dark, gloomy gullies or depressions and they used rotten beaver carcasses for bait. I remember vividly that first sit when all the sudden a black bear appeared at the base of my tree. I was amazed at how quiet it was; I did not hear him coming at all. His black form just appeared in my peripheral vision. The first bear I had ever seen. He was jet black with a gray snout and offered me a broadside shot for a very long time. I was there for color phase only, so I passed on that beautiful black bear. Plus, it was the first day, and I was sure to see more bear.

After dark settled in, we all made our way back to camp for a late, late dinner. Everyone had seen bear except for Dean. That poor guy went dry for days. The kids were all hyped up telling about the bears they saw. The dentist's teenage daughter really wanted to shoot her bear, but dad had said it was too small. I could tell she was frustrated. The dentist parents preached big bears or no bears, to the kids; they were only there to shoot giants.

The camp cook chimed in with words of wisdom I still use today. He said, "If it is big enough to take on the last day, it sure as hell should be big enough to take on the first." He wasn't appreciating the dentist's attitude. Quite often hunters will "settle" for a lesser animal to fill their tag on the last day, in order to take something home. The cook's point was, if you are willing to settle, then it should not matter the day. If you are holding out for a giant animal, then you should be willing to go home without one. Teenagers want to get a bear and show their friends, they should not be trophy hunting on their first real hunting trip. We also discussed color-phase bears. The cook simply said, "If you like the color, take it because they are here but they are still rare."

The second night I sat in the stand for a while and movement caught my eye. In ran a chocolate-phase bear, grabbing a beaver from the barrel and scurried off. That was cool; I got to see a color-phased bear. I knew he was close, because I could hear the crunching of the beaver bones as he chewed up the carcass. A few minutes later he snuck his way back in. I knew this bear was not 300 pounds. It was on the small side, but it was chocolate phase. The cook's comments echoed in the back of my head as I drew back my arrow and took that bear. He let out a loud growl and climbed straight up the tree beside me. About half way up he lost strength and grip and fell back hitting the ground dead. There would be no tracking this bear.

They weighed the bears at camp and he was just 100 pounds. I was surprised at the weight and said, "If you didn't have that scale, I know that bear was 200 pounds." Yes, hunters tend to round up, and guessing bear weights is nearly impossible. The son of the grumpy dad shot his black bear, weighing in at 120 pounds. The dentist's wife chided the boy for shooting a small bear. She made it known that her daughter was not to shoot a small bear. The poor girl had seen yet another bear deemed too small for her to shoot. I could see tears well in her eyes.

I was so fucking pissed at the comments this mother was making to her kids. I could do nothing about that, but I could talk about my bear; after all, I the big badass hunter chose to shoot the smallest bear so far. I made it clear to the kids why I made that choice and why I was really happy with my bear. I still am: today he is one of the smallest animals in my trophy room, but perfect for the expectation I set for myself on that hunt. Just to be clear, the biggest bear of the week was 200 pounds. I think the next week got a 250-pounder. It turns out these bears were typical size for the region.

The outfitter let me take my video camera to the stand on night three. In rushed three little cubs, one black, one cinnamon, and the third a very rare blond. Mom was a giant cinnamon bear. It was a blessing to be in their presence. They did not stay long, being driven off by a larger male who had breeding on his mind. It was awesome to watch them romp and play and eat the corn scattered on the ground. The video was yet another trophy of mine as well as the memories.

Back at camp, the poor girl had to pass up even more bears deemed too small. I think she started to hate her parents as much as I did. The outfitter watched my video and asked me to help him the next morning. Both adult bears were fair game. The cubs were two years old and as soon as mom was bred again, she would leave them on their own. We rode out to the Fender stand that morning and built a ground blind for the girl, fifteen yards from the bait. The outfitter smiled at me and said, "All bears look big from the ground, she will shoot one tonight." After all that girl had been through, I really hoped she would shoot one of those bears that coming night.

I stayed at camp reading magazines and having a beer as I heard four-wheelers return in the dark. The other grumpy father had volunteered to sit with the girl in the ground blind. A bear came in that looked big enough, but this dad knew he shouldn't care. She made a great shot on that bear, putting it down for good. Back in camp with her bear, she grinned from ear to ear. Mom and dad proved to be assholes and showed their disgust, while the rest of us helped her celebrate shooting her first bear, a whopping 120-pounder that she will remember forever. Dean finished off the hunt with one around 150 pounds. The "know it all" dentist parents went home with nothing. Justice I say!

Lesson – Attempting to get a group together to hunt is difficult.

Not thinking you can afford it and not thinking you can take the time to go on a hunt are the first two dream killers. The third issue is one very few people understand. We all want to hunt with our friends, but the chance of getting your friends' dreams and goals to align can be slim. We are all in a different place in life. One may have kids, one may be in a divorce, another one's job won't allow him to take vacation, the excuses are endless. Then add the challenge of deciding what to hunt and where to hunt it, and the chances grow slimmer. Finally, getting everyone to commit that much money and time is near impossible. Waiting to hunt with your friends often ends up being a futile effort. I decided to hunt alone and I don't regret it one bit.

Lesson – Shot placement is critical and it changes depending on the animal.

Bears' vitals are not in the same place as a deer. On a deer we usually aim just behind the elbow of the front leg as it is stepping forward. Attempting the same shot on a bear can lead to a wounded bear. On a bear, the rule is to split it in half, belly to back or halfway up the body. Then split the length in half and move your pin about four inches toward the head. This will seem too far back, but it is perfect shot placement for a double lung hit. If the bear is slightly quartering away, it is a perfect and deadly shot. As I say, he has fifteen seconds to live! The point is, be sure to research proper shot placement before you hunt, because it can drastically differ depending on the animal.

Lesson – Realistic Expectations

Outfitters make their living selling hunts. They will show you Boone and Crocket-sized animals all day long. I have had one admit that they posed with another outfitter's Booner whitetail, for the cover of their own brochure. On the other hand, I have hunted with two outfitters that looked me in the eye and told me the truth. Todd gave me a 25-percent chance of seeing a wolf and less than 10-percent chance of shooting one. Because of that honesty, I went and shot two! Jason Lambley publishes an excellent summary of his previous season, and it is always filled with honesty and cold hard facts. That honesty is why I took my son there for his first bear hunt.

But the responsibility really is on you to research the area and make sure you have realistic expectations. Yes, we all want that monster whitetail, gold-medal stag, or that eleven-foot brown bear, but they are rare. Not for nothing, the animals get that big because they are smart and I have often wondered if I was smart enough or good enough to outsmart one of them. Are you, really?

You cannot hunt Bonne and Crocket deer where Boone and Crocket deer don't live. You hear of the caribou migration with hordes of caribou running you over. Luckily, I hit the migration just right and that happened for me, but if the caribou where running our camp over, they weren't at the other camps. While someone is experiencing the hunt of a lifetime, another is just in the wrong place at the wrong time. Hunting mountain lions with the tracks washed away is impossible. The weather is always an unknown. Sure, there are 300-pound black bears in Saskatchewan, but they are smart, nocturnal, and rare. Saskatchewan gives you the best chance at a color phase, but they are still a small percentage of the population. Wolves circle a very large area, coming back maybe every seven days or even longer. How does the week you pick to hunt coincide with that? Mountain lions need to leave tracks, and you hope they just ate, full and lazy, or they will run your ass up and down every mountain. I hunted the area in British Columbia with the largest population of grizzlies there is. I was lucky to see four; they strongly hinted that I should not pass on another. Manitoba black bear don't get hungry in ninety-five-degree heat. You can't kill a mountain goat that isn't on the mountain. Who would have guessed the biggest black bear I would see was in New Jersey an hour away from New York City? If you do your own homework you can align your expectations up with reality. Sure, maybe you talk yourself out of going on a hunt, but that beats being disappointed. Just maybe the area you thought was good isn't the really the one that meets your expectations.

The greater benefit of having realistic expectations is that is gives you room to exceed them. If you shoot for the moon and miss you are disappointed. If you shoot for average, you have a 50/50 chance of getting something better than you expect. This in my mind is why many hunters come back with the attitude of sour grapes. They expected too much and feel like they let themselves down, that the outfitter failed them, or that their luck just sucks. They spent all that money and bragged to their friends of giant trophies, and then they are embarrassed to have taken a lesser animal or none at all. Please don't set yourself up for like this. There is so much else to enjoy on a hunt that can only be seen if you free yourself of the pressure of tagging the biggest and the best.

I had a guy show me his grizzly bear mount. He shot the bear as it charged down the hill after him, his guide, and the horses. As he opened the door to his trophy room he said, "It isn't a big grizzly." My response was simple: "It was charging you, you put it down, and not a soul around here has a grizzly in their house; I think it is big enough." His expectations will haunt him and I find that sad.

Lesson – Videoing your own hunt

I asked Ron, my Saskatchewan bear outfitter, what he thought of videotaping my bear hunt. He said this as he smiled and winked, "I have never seen a camera help a hunter kill a bear." Enough said. I left it in the pack.

Are you there for the experience you will gain or are you there to brag to your friends? I know video is awesome, but I don't want to screw up the possible memory in my head by making a mistake trying to run a camera. Quite frankly, no picture or video that I have ever taken has truly conveyed the beauty or feeling I had at that moment. I wish it did. I wish I were that good a camera man, but I am not. Concentrate on enjoying every little detail of the hunt and quit fucking with your camera.

Hunting Partners

Other than thinking you cannot afford to go on a hunting adventure, the need to hunt with your friends ranks high on my ways "to kill the hunting dream" list. When you are chasing whitetail at home, part of the fun of opening day is the gathering of your friends and family for the big hunt. Likely the pre-hunt ritual of food, beer, and stories is the only reason we attract new hunters to hunting. The kids watch us joke and laugh and want to be part of that tradition. This is especially true in asshole states like New York where the child must wait until he or she is sixteen to become a hunter. By the time they reach sixteen, school activities and friends have taken over and without that opening-day pre-hunt party, they may never have had a reason to become interested in hunting at all.

So, when you grow up hunting with others, it is normal to want to share your big hunt dreams with those same people. This need to hunt with your friends kills many of those dreams. This is because we are all at a different place and time in life, family, money and vacation time. You literally must line up all these things with someone for you both to agree to book a trip. It is nearly an impossible task. Plus, you must both have the same desire to hunt the same animal in the same place. Our dreams hardly ever match up.

There are so many species of animals to hunt and so many places and ways to hunt each of them. We all have our favorite. Everyone has a different animal that they dream about taking. Everyone has a different hunt that they would call their hunt of a lifetime. I have friends that I would love to hunt with and they have the finances to do it. About once a year we send emails saying we need to go. Then we all send emails on the animals each one of us wants to go after and they are all different. The momentum comes to a screeching halt and another year passes before we start the cycle over again. We will never hunt together. It is not in the cards.

Financially, getting someone else to commit that much money toward a hunt is near impossible. There are so many people that I would love to be with on their first hunt, but they are not in the same position I am financially. That is not to say I make more money than they do—often it is the opposite. But I have gone through the mental process to decide to sacrifice things so I can hunt. They have not. They buy boats and four-wheelers; I don't, so I can go hunting. We have different priorities. It is not in the cards.

Time is another big killer. Some jobs are seasonal and friends cannot pry themselves away during that time. Some people need to spend their limited vacation time with their families. There are a lot of people who simply freak out when they think about being away for ten days or more. I get that! Preparing for vacation and dealing with the workload after vacation can make it seem like it isn't worth going at all. Then add the unknown to it that you need to plan your life and work schedule a year or two ahead of time and most throw in the towel immediately.

If the planets do seem to align and you find a person who is financially ready, who has time available, and has the same animal and place in mind as you do, you still need to be cautious. The best way to find out if you like a person is to travel with them and be confined in a little space like a hotel, tent, or cabin for long periods of time. A hunt trip can end a relationship very quickly. That person might carry the thoughts of work with them the entire trip. They might not have the money they thought they would and now they have to skimp on spending throughout the trip. Then you fight about where to eat or where to stay, or even sights you might see on the journey. Family pressures can get to a person; the wife might not be too excited about this trip. We miss our families too; it can be hard to leave them behind. There are so many aspects of a trip that can make or break the experience. You must be careful, remembering this is a huge investment in time and money for you too; you deserve to get all the joy you can out of it.

Your hunting partner might be very uncomfortable hunting this animal or going to this place. It all sounds cool until you really must step up and do it. I had a pretty good hunting partner in Dean, but we grew apart. Some of the places I wanted to go, like Russia, were too big an adventure for him. I also grew very uncomfortable as I started hunting more dangerous game. I knew what I put into my practice and preparation, but I cannot control others. What if they weren't ready and something bad happened? I don't want that on my shoulders.

Dean was a great hunting partner for many trips. Dean moved to New York and we met at work. He liked to hunt and I offered him a tree stand to hunt for that first deer season. He never left and I never got to use my tree stand again. We started naming it "Dean's Stand." Dean was with me on the first Caribou hunt, the one that started the whole hunting passion for me. I still did some hunts on my own, but we linked up on a Saskatchewan bear trip. Harrisburg, Pennsylvania, has a huge outdoor show that became a favorite mid-winter weekend trip for us. I was interested in mountain lion, and we met Holly at the outdoor show. When we got home, Holly called and told me she liked talking to Dean and me, and was wondering if we would hunt with her if she dropped her price. I jumped at the deal. I remember sending Dean an email saying just this: "You are going to Montana in December for mountain lion." He responded back, "cool." Now that is how hunting partners should be! We were both lucky, but it is rare that it works out this way.

Even as well as we travelled together there are always little things that make it tough. Like I said, being trapped in small spaces for long periods of time can be difficult in any situation. The long hours of travel are tiring for everyone. One person is tired and the other wants to go sightseeing or grab a beer. These sound like little petty things, and they were. The good still outweighed the bad. But the more I travelled alone the more I appreciated the freedom to do what I wanted.

I know the thought of travelling alone is probably freaking you out right now. I know this because as soon as I say I am going somewhere alone, my friends and family cannot comprehend it. I enjoy it for many reasons. If it were for anything else but hunting I might freak out too. The great thing about hunting is that hunting stories are great icebreakers. I can strike up a conversation with anyone, anywhere, in any language when they are a hunter.

Yes, I said any language, and I don't speak other languages. For some reason, you can understand the passion behind a hunting story in another language without understanding the words. Jim Shockey has a TV show where he is in the Arctic with an elderly Inuit woman who sings a hunting song in her native language. It brings Jim to tears and he says, "I know exactly what she is singing about." I have felt that many times and it is simply an awesome experience. It is a bond that only true hunters have and it simply is an amazing connection.

Here are the main reasons I chose to hunt alone.

- It is very hard to spend someone else's money before they can afford it, or put a priority on saving it.

- Scheduling vacation time a year or two in advance is hard for one person, let alone two.

- I don't want the responsibility of someone else hunting dangerous game, or even going in what could be dangerous places.

- I want to choose the animal I hunt and the place I hunt it.

- I don't want the responsibility if they fail to get their trophy.

- Travel is easier to deal with on my own. I can suck up the hardships without worrying about others. I can eat what I want, sleep when I want, and make those decisions easier.

- What if one of us backs out at the last minute? I did this to Dean and it forced him to make a thirty-hour drive on his own. It was not good for either of us.

- With one-on-one guiding, you don't hunt with your buddy anyway. Much of time you spend with them is doing the mundane tasks.

If you can find a hunting partner and it all works, that is the sweetest way to do it. My point is, if you want something badly enough sometimes you need to go at it alone. It can be done and there are benefits to it. You can waste your time waiting for others to come around. Get after it. You won't regret it.

Lesson – That Final Decision to Shoot

Hopefully I have talked you into doing all the research you possibly can so you have realistic expectations regarding the quantity and quality of animal you are pursuing. I hope that you have communicated your goals with your outfitter and especially your guide, guaranteeing that you are all on the same page.

But there is still that moment of truth—the split second in which you are the one that ultimately decides to pull the trigger, or release that arrow. For me, this anxiety attack starts the night before we hunt. For months I have likely talked smack about holding out for a trophy, a monster buck or a giant bear. Then doubt creeps in and your mind starts playing those games. I don't care what anyone says; the thought of spending all this money and time and going home without an animal is crazy. Those who truly do it have way too much money and way too much time to hunt. I know I am not in that league and never will be. I want to take something home.

The thoughts of "settling" creep into your head. You start to feel a little guilty because of the all the smack you talked, the thoughts of settling for less hurts a little. What if I shoot the first day and see a bigger one later? Oh, that can happen! What if I pass one up and never see another animal, the weather turns bad, or I grow tired or get hurt? Your ego starts to take some punishment. If I don't get the biggest and best out of camp, have I let myself down? What will my friends back home say if my trophy is smaller than they imagined? All these questions start playing their little games in your head.

Then days of your hunt start to tick off. You have hunted hard and you are sore and tired. Maybe sitting in a tree all day is getting to you, or the lactic acid in your legs from climbing hills has you walking like a ninety-year-old man. Hunting for a week to ten days is hard, and most of us have never done it before. The pains in your body will start messing with your head.

Hopefully your will and discipline is such that you ward off all the negative vibes in your brain. Many of us, if not most of us, cannot keep away the demons. I listened to a caribou hunter brag, waiting for our Otter flight into camp, that he shot nothing but Boone and Crocket animals. Then he shot a cow caribou the first afternoon, and a small bull out of the boat the next day. He then spent the next few days playing his electronic football game in his bed, and then asked to be flown out early. Obviously, he was not prepared for any of that hunt and he let all those demons get into his head. I climbed over 7000 feet of mountain in search of mountain goats. As we enjoyed the majestic view from the top my guide told me I was the fourth person to attempt this climb this year and only one who made it that far. The other three were ten to fifteen years younger than me and one was an Olympic athlete. I could keep the demons out of my head and push on. I put the time in up front to prepare physically, but more importantly mentally. There were no goats to be seen, but it is still one of the greatest things I have done in my life.

When we got to Russian moose camp, the temperatures were an unexpected -30 degrees Celsius. That simple fact immediately got into the heads of the other two hunters in camp. One talked about shooting a moose on the first day, to get it over with, and he did. The other spent so much time staying warm that he missed multiple opportunities because he was not ready. He went home empty handed. I won't lie and tell you it didn't freak me out some and I was a little scared of the thoughts of frostbite, but I couldn't let any of that get in my head. I would yell, "I am hunting in Russia," as we streaked across the snow, me bouncing in a wooden sled. Sometimes you just have to "suck it the fuck up!" Having a mask on my face was an issue because when we stopped my glasses immediately fogged up. I could never take a quick shot like this. Sub-zero temperatures or not, I decided to ride without a mask, to suck it up and do what was necessary to be successful.

Sometimes you must read the conditions and make an educated guess. Could you make it back up that mountain tomorrow if you had to? Mother Nature has her hand in every hunt and can stop you cold in your tracks for days, so you must pay attention to that in your decision process. I have been bit by bad weather and blessed by some of the most beautiful days in the wild. You never know what card Mother Nature will deal.

During the British Columbia grizzly bear hunt, I saw four grizzlies. One ran across the highway in front of us on the way from the airport to camp. The first day in, we were going to hunt out of a tree stand along a salmon-run river. As my guide was halfway up the tree he stopped, shushed me, and pointed to the river. On the other side of the thicket not ten yards away was a grizzly looking for salmon. How the bear did not notice me, I will never know. I froze and waited for our eyes to meet. He could have had me in a flash. That afternoon another grizzly gave me an easy broadside bow shot at forty yards, but my guide told me he was too small. Back in camp, they all were amazed at the three bears I had seen. They made a point that many people have never seen a grizzly bear, let alone three. As the next three days ticked off with nothing to see but salmon, that comment started to sink in. When the next bear came out to fish, it was obvious it was a shooter. My guide whispered. "That is a nice bear; do you want your rifle?" If he turned left I would have had my bow shot somewhere within forty yards. The moment he turned right I set the bow down, grabbed the rifle and sunk him with one shot. My dream of shooting a grizzly with a bow was still fulfilled, in my head. I gave it my all. He is a beautiful bear and there are zero regrets with the decision I made.

Remember my motto: "It's your tag, you can do anything you want with it." Just don't bitch about it when you get home. This is not time to leave anything on the table and have something to regret the rest of your life. My point of all this is to illustrate that these decisions are hard. These decisions can also lead to the excitement of the hunt, and that should not be taken for granted. The best way to keep the bad things from creeping into your head is to think about and deal with them long before. Research, preparation, and visualization are keys to being mentally prepared.

Choosing an Outfitter

I have been within a stone's throw of animals that could and would love to eat me that scared me less than choosing an outfitter. Knock on wood, I have been very lucky with every outfitter I have had, but deciding who to book with sometimes feels like you are doing it on blind faith. You are usually making a long-term commitment, and let's face it: guys don't do commitment well. You must give them a significant amount of money up front, with little legal guarantee except a word document with some promises on it, called a contract. You hope they are good at their jobs. You hope they prepare accordingly and care about your hunt. There isn't anything smart about this transaction, but people do it successfully all the time. It does work, but I think that is because of the mutual love of the hunt more than anything else.

On the flip side, I bet outfitters would love to have a better screening process for their clients. We tend not to be able to shoot. We are often out of shape. We often lie to our wives about the cost and spending becomes an issue. We often underestimate the hunt and our abilities to do that hunt and need to be pampered.

My goal in every hunt is this: I want a chance at a reasonable representative of the species and I want to leave my outfitter and guide wishing that all their other hunters would be like me. I will be prepared, knowledgeable, work hard, be a team player, listen to their expertise, and make a safe, clean kill. Much of that starts with the first email I send to inquire about a hunt.

The very first thing to consider is that an outfitter makes his money selling hunts, not getting you an animal. He provides the best opportunity he can under the conditions available and it is your job to close the deal. I say this because there is a lot of "car salesman" in many outfitters; they will tell you what you want to hear to get you to book. Sadly, TV shows and magazine articles make it look like trophy deer or game, the record-book animals, are everywhere, but the reality is they are rare and you need to understand that. Trophy quality might be there, but then you must ask yourself if you have trophy-hunting skills. Big old animals got that way from being cagy and smart. You'll have to be smarter.

You can tell a lot about an outfitter by how he answers questions, and I have a bunch of questions. If it sounds like bragging, then the bullshit meter should go off. If he tries to lower my expectations to a realistic level, then I feel like I am getting the truth. I am a detail-oriented guy and the amount of effort they put into answering my questions says so much for me. If I can get a guy to type a long email back to me, I believe he cares. Now I know there are outfitters out there that live in the bush, and email is stupid, and typing is hard, and computers are dumb. I may miss a great hunting experience with them, but all I can tell you is how I do it.

Once you pick an animal and a place to hunt, you will find that there are more outfitters to choose from than you expect. I gather email addresses and ship the same list of questions to them all. I have developed the following list of questions over many hunts and I get a very good feel very quickly who is in the running. Two or three quickly rise to the top and I usually get a good feeling for at least one. Usually one will describe more about how he loves to hunt the animal and I love to hear that. You will always get one that immediately calls you and spews information. None of that information is ever in writing.

The following is the set of initial questions I would ask and the reasons I would ask them. If you get solid answers to these, then you have all the information you need to make a good decision. This is just the start of an incredible journey. You will feel an adrenaline spike as you get responses back. That is why I love the planning as much as I love the hunt.

Questions I Ask an Outfitter

You might easily come up with a list of twenty or more outfitters to contact. I prefer to do it over email so that I can ask the same questions of each of them, and compare answers. Here are the questions I would ask in the first email:

1. My first paragraph would explain the animal I am interested in. Be very specific, because that might not be the primary animal he outfits for. My Russian contact mainly focuses on brown bear, and I had to refocus him on the fact that I wanted to hunt moose.

2. **What hunt dates are available?** *Spring, fall or winter hunts have completely different things to consider, so you need to plan accordingly. Picking the correct hunt window can make or break the success of your hunt. Are you paying for the rut, pre-rut, normal feeding time? It all*

makes a huge difference. Lay out each window on your calendar and then plan travel around it. It took me five days to get to Russian moose camp and four to get back. That was a lot of vacation days. I made a mistake and hunted over one of my son's birthdays. I think he was okay with it, but I was haunted by this decision until I made my wife an ex-wife. Not my fault he was born during hunting season! Well, I guess it could have been partly my fault.

3. **Is this fully guided, one-on-one, or two-on-one?** *Two-on-one is two hunters per one guide, so one hunter gets to watch the other hunt. My time, vacation, and money is precious, so I will not do a two-on-one hunt and have to wait and watch another person take an animal. I would not even do that for a hunting buddy. But this decision is yours and your buddy's, I guess. I would be having a long hard talk ending in a solid agreement before I would book a two-on-one hunt with a friend. That friend you hang out with can become a different person in the bush, far away from home, having just spent more money than he should have. Be very cautious because the stress of a hunt can turn best buddies into assholes. I cannot even imagine doing a two-on-one hunt with a hunter who is a total stranger.*

4. **What is the cost of your hunt?** *As you will see, there is more to the total hunt cost than the advertised price.*

    a. **What deposit is required and when is it due?** *You will need to make a deposit to hold your hunting spot. That deposit will likely not be refundable for any reason. This is a big commitment and I hope this book helps you make it.*

    b. **What payment schedule do you require?** *Depending on the cost there typically is a payment schedule. More people than you know back out, so it is to the outfitter's best interest to get as much money he can out of you ahead of time. But you also need to plan these payments into your savings plan.*

    c. **When and how do you make the final payment?** *Typically, the final payment is due about ten seconds after you shake your outfitter's hand for the first time. They will typically want cash. You don't get to hunt until they confirm they really got all their money. Make sure you fully understand this final transaction and be prepared to travel with that much cash.*

5. **Describe the hunt.** *You may be a deer hunter from the East, but deer are hunted differently in the West. Don't magically assume you know how you will be hunting.*

    a. **Where will we hunt?** *You need to know where you hunt, so you can research the area and have a good idea what you can reasonably expect.*

    b. **What is the method of getting around?** *Have you ever walked fifteen miles in the bush? Have you ridden a horse? Can you drive a four-wheeler or snowmobile in rough terrain? You need to know about and prepare for what is expected of you.*

    c. **How physical is the hunt?** *This should go without saying, but most hunters fail because they are not fit enough to do what they need to when the moment counts. You might tree-stand hunt at home, but have you done it dark to dark for seven days straight? Can you climb a hill for an hour to get to a stand?*

6. **What are the accommodations?** *There is a lot to be said here and I go into in detail in another section. You need to know what to expect so you can properly plan.*

7. **What airport do I fly into?** *There are many things to consider here, like the cost of the flight, potential flight schedules, cost of hotels in the area.*

    a. **Do you pick me up at the airport? Do I need a rental car?**

    b. **When do you need me to be there for pick up?** *This is extremely important because other hunters will be coming in too. The outfitter is likely dropping hunters off at the airport to leave. If the camp is a long way from the airport, you don't want to make it a long day, getting there late at night.*

    c. **How do I get to camp?** *If they don't pick you up, then how do you get there?*

    d. **If I must stay overnight, what is a typical cost for a hotel?** *They might suggest a place to stay, but at the very least you can get a rough nightly rate so you can budget an overnight stay*

        i. I now fly a day early because that gives my luggage and my bow or rifle a chance to catch up to me. I can afford to lose my stuff on the way home, but going to camp without my gear is out of the question.

8. **What does the price of your hunt include?**

a. **Cost of the license and tags?** *These are costs taken right from the government website. Landowner tags can be pricey, so make sure you know what the costs are.*

b. **Transportation from the airport?** *If the outfitter does not get you, then there are costs for you to get there. Is there a bush plane or helicopter ride needed? Sometimes they are extra costs that need to be paid directly to the air carrier.*

c. **Accommodations and meals while hunting?** *In most cases your accommodations and meals are included during the hunting days. Sometimes the hotel and your meals are not included. Trust me when I say, you will be happy if someone is back at camp cooking for you. Cooking for yourself after a long day in the bush is hard to do.*

d. **Trophy care?** *Your guide will only help you so far in trophy preparation and meat care. They might cape the animal and cut the rack off, but do they prepare it for salting and salt the hide? (See the section on caping an animal.) Do they provide a container for shipping, or taking it on a plane?*

e. **Meat cutting and packaging for transportation?** *The cost of butchering and packing meat can be expensive. If you take your animal late in the week, what is the timing to get this work done? Packaging it so you can take it home, or on a plane can be expensive. Putting it on a plane can be very costly. You really need to do your homework on this based on their feedback.*

f. **Are there any government fees required?** *Canada is notorious for their taxes; there are two of them. They also have fees on taken animals. It cost me $1000 when I took the grizzly bear. Part of the taxes can be refundable depending on what it's for.*

9. **Are CITES permits required, if so do you handle that?** *CITES permits are permission to import an animal. That animal might be protected in the U.S. and you need proof where it was taken. The outfitter usually gets the Cites permit, but this means he keeps your stuff until it is legal to ship into the United States.*

10. **Who handles arranging shipment of trophies, racks and hides?** *This can be significant and can cost you some money. I will expand on this in this book, but you first need to know what your outfitter is willing to help you with. If he won't do it, have a plan ahead of time.*

11. **Are there any special hunter's safety-course requirements?** *Some Canadian Providences require you to prove you have taken a hunter's safety course. Most of us old guys from the United States took the course, turned the certificate in for our first license, and no longer have this proof. Make sure you know the requirements and give yourself the proper time to obtain the proof. You might just have to take a course over again.*

12. **Can I add any other animals to the hunt?** *What if you are successful on the first day? What do you do in camp now? Extra tags are a pretty cheap way to keep hunting. I suggest you get every tag you legally can.*

    a. **How much are tag fees for those animals?** *You want to know the tag fees, so you can plan. Think about the area you will be in and the possibility of success. Black bear and grizzlies don't get along, so a good area for one may be bad for the other. A high moose, elk, or deer population might mean a low population of predators. Do some research and weigh the cost versus the chance for success. You also need to think about when to take another animal. Taking a secondary choice on the way to hunt your first choice has consequences. A gunshot could spook other game. Recovering an animal could take time, even days of work. Make sure you think and plan just exactly what size animal is worth negatively impacting the dream animal you came for.*

    b. **Are other animals included in the price of the hunt?** *Sometimes the extra animals are included in the price. Black bear and wolf are often thrown in. But heed my advice from earlier, and make sure it does not degrade your hunt if you take one of these animals.*

    c. **If other animals are in season, but are not included in the price, what are the trophy fees if I am able to take an extra animal?** *You will want to know the exact trophy fee so you can have cash in hand. They don't carry credit card readers in the bush and they won't accept you saying, "The check is in the mail." Be prepared to pay for what you take, immediately.*

13. **Please list any possible unknown costs. I like to be aware of and prepare for anything I might need to spend money on.** *Usually, the outfitter starts providing things like accommodations and meals after they pick you up and during the hunting days only. Therefore, the time before and after the hunt can cost you extra. I have seen a lot of people get pissed about this. They barely could afford the hunt. They have a little*

cash for souvenirs. The extra cost puts them in a bind, leaving a bad taste in their mouth and ruining the hunt. In my opinion, if you cannot afford it, you should wait till you can. More importantly, if you plan for any possible cost, plus a little extra, you will be covered and probably bring a little cash home for the next hunt.

a. **Hotels in and out of camp.** *It often costs you for the stay before and after the hunt. Many times, if you are successful early, they might bring you back to town. If you come out early, you will have to pay for hotel nights or flight changes.*

b. **Transportation.** *Most will pick you up and drop you off at the airport. In some instances, you will have to rent a car and drive to a camp, or meeting spot. In Russia, we had to pay for the cab fare and chartered rides while we were in Moscow, because the hunt didn't start until we were on the other side of the country, nine time zones away.*

c. **Trophy fees.** *Most trophy-fee rates are a dollar value for the animal once taken. But beware when the trophy fee is based on the score of the rack, like Texas whitetail, African game, and New Zealand game. I don't know about you but I know I don't have the self-control to pass a monster in the heat of the moment. Communication with the guide can be sketchy when seconds count, so what if he says it is bigger than you can afford? You won't catch me putting myself in that position.*

d. **Fines for any reason.** *Fines can be levied if you shoot a buck with a rack that does not meet a minimum score, usually 130 inches. Beware that hitting, wounding, and losing an animal often ends your hunt. In some cases, you can pay a fine and hunt again, but you need to know that up front.*

e. **Beer, drinks, snacks or food for camp.** *They will feed you and keep you hydrated, but they won't spend much money on the comforts of home. Many outfitters would prefer you leave the alcohol at home. The risk is too great for them when people drink too much. But even soda, milk, coffee, or tea can be on your own. The same goes for your favorite snack. Make sure you know what they supply and make sure they will take you to a store on the way in to get what you want or need.*

14. **Will you provide references?** *I will give you my thoughts on references in a separate section. The willingness to give them is the key*

here. Two or three names does not mean much to me. His whole client list means he is confident. A list of hunters who failed to get their animals is awesome.

This is a lot for an outfitter to answer on the first communication. Their willingness to take the time to answer these questions fully is a big factor in whom I choose to hunt with. If I like the answers, I would follow up with a second email with further, more specific questions.

In the follow-up email, I would describe a little bit about me, how I would like to hunt, my physical stature and preparation and the fact that I am after a reasonable representative of the species. Remember, they are in sales mode and want to tell you about giant beasts. Somehow, you need to get down to realistic expectations.

1. **What is the population of the animal?** *Where I was in British Columbia has the highest population of interior grizzly bears on the planet. I was blessed to see four in a week and most see one if they are lucky. Caribou migration is an awesome spectacle, if you are lucky enough to be in their path at the exact moment they walk by you. Again, getting your expectations in order is crucial to a good hunting experience. Hunting a Boone and Crocket animal where Booners don't grow will never work.*

2. **Please describe the true trophy quality. What are some reasonable expectations for this hunt?** *I can tell you right now that no place on the planet has a huge number of record-book animals of any kind. 160-plus-inch deer, color-phase bears, 72-inch moose, 400-inch elk are all animals in the peak of their prime and they didn't get old by being stupid. Set your sights on an average animal and secretly hope to run into a monster and I guarantee your hunt will be more fulfilling. If an outfitter boasts about record-book animals but has no pictures to share, he is full of shit.*

3. **Is the tag mine, or do you sell multiple tags until your quota is filled?** *When the outfitter is on a quota basis, such as three grizzlies over five years he will book hunts until all three bear tags are filled. Think about this! He makes more money if hunters fail to get their bear over the first few years because that same bear tag can be sold multiple times until a hunter finally takes a bear.*

4. **I am willing to do this physically. How does that help or hinder the way we would hunt?** *Be honest with your physical abilities and*

the shape you are in. You are only hurting your own experience if you fail to communicate the shape you really are in. Consider your own fears. I have a phobia of rushing water, yet I have crossed rivers many times. Are you willing to stare down a dangerous animal with a bow and arrow in your hand? If you don't like heights, don't book a deer hunt where they put you up thirty feet in a stand.

5. **I might ask if he is willing to lower the price of the hunt and have the balance be on a trophy basis if I am successful.** *This puts the burden back on your outfitter. Remember, you are buying a chance to hunt, not an animal. If the outfitter readily agrees to a trophy-fee-basis hunt, that tells me he is confident in his ability to get you that animal.*

What I Think of References

All outfitters will send you references and it usually is a list of three to five names that you can call. I find this of little to no value, but I will still take the time to call anyway. For one, three to five names out of all the clients they have taken hunting is a small sample and there could be reasons for that. Outfitters typically don't share the names of failed hunters, but those are the ones I would really want to talk to. I want to know how much fun they had despite not getting a kill. I find most references will jump at the chance to tell their story to a new person, so it always gets me pumped up to hear their stories. I have never made anyone's reference list even when I have left as a friend. This is because they know I am a straight shooter and will tell both the good and the bad. I am the type of reference the hunter wants to talk to, but I don't make the list.

Lesson – Hunter's safety-course certificates

Some places are now requiring proof of hunter's safety courses. It used to be, if you had a past hunting license of any kind that was proof enough. In Manitoba, you must show the actual certificate. This is difficult for us old hunters because our hunter safety course was years and years ago. Make sure you know and listen to exactly what the requirements are.

Lesson – Trophy pictures on outfitter websites

I read a lot into the pictures I see on the outfitter's websites. Keeping a website up to date can be difficult for an outfitter that lives in the bush, but when the trophy pictures are very few, or from years ago, I begin to wonder. If they are all pictures of stud animals, then that makes me wonder too. Did no one shoot an average animal? Every hunter takes trophy pictures, so getting them to send a picture back is easy. Why guides and outfitters don't take their own pictures of every hunt make me wonder too. Truth is, not all hunters are successful, or shoot animals that make trophy standards. Think about these things when you are looking over outfitter websites.

Let's Talk About Money

The Cost of the Outfitter

Through your research and after the outfitters answers all your questions, you should have a pretty solid number that you will be required to pay the outfitter. Most outfitters will follow up with a contract to sign. If not, I always regurgitate what I believe I am getting for my money and have the outfitter respond back. You should also know the payment schedule. A down payment or deposit is the thing that usually finalizes it all, sealing the deal. Congratulations! When you make it to this point, it is an exciting milestone. Note that if you cancel, you likely won't get your deposit back. They use that money to discount the hunt to another hunter. Remember, if no hunters show up, they don't make any money. Depending on when you cancel, they may have already paid out a lot of money in licenses, leases, and hunt preparation.

With that said, a good way to save money is hold out for cancellation hunts, where you get the savings associated with the loss of the previous hunter's deposit. In my head, you miss out on all the planning phase, because you will have to mobilize in a few short weeks. If you are that person always looking for the deal, this is a good way to get hunts booked on the cheap.

Some outfitter-advertised prices might be negotiated depending on his circumstances. Just beware they have control over your hunt, and irritating them about cost may cost you an animal in the end. It is to the outfitter's best interest to book hunts, since they have costs invested whether or not a person hunts. But pushing them too hard can irritate them and they can get even. I know of one story where the guides kept the hunter far away from game because he was just an asshole. Don't be that guy.

I have had success in changing the cost structure from a single price to a reduced hunt fee with a trophy fee upon getting the animal. If they do their job and get you in front of an animal to take, they get their money anyway. If things go against you and you come home empty handed, at least you have a trophy fee in your pocket to go toward the next hunt. If they agree to this without hesitation, it is one more thing that brings me confidence in their ability to get me on game. If in their mind it does not matter knowing they will get you an animal anyway, that is great news for me the hunter.

I always get as many tags as I can, and agree on a trophy fee for each animal. That way if I get done early with my main goal, I can continue to hunt and only pay for what I get. Considering the costs and time of travel, bagging more than one animal is extremely cost effective. This is great for filling time if you get your primary animal early. It makes the trip that much more fun for you and the guide; he doesn't have to sit in camp staring at you for days. But beware, I advise you to have one goal and stick to it. Say you have a mountain caribou tag to go along with your grizzly hunt. Shooting that caribou could affect your grizzly hunt in a negative way. Human scent and noise could drive grizzlies out of your valley. Just be conscious of your decisions and keep your priorities in order.

Hidden Costs

You pick your outfitter and you have agreed on a price. This price is the amount of money that gets paid directly to the outfitter, usually in some form of payment schedule. You should be very careful that you fully understand what you are getting for your money. The bad news is there are always costs above and beyond that need to be considered. I will try to list the hidden costs so you can properly prepare.

Flying

If you are flying to get there the cost of your air travel is typically not included. The outfitter agrees to pick you up at a certain location, and typically the hunt starts there. Bush flights or helicopter rides to camp may or may not be included. These flights can be costly, so be sure you know the details ahead of time. Baggage and weight need to be considered and I will talk about the separately. Also, understand that weather can prevent you from getting out of camp on time. Having to change flights can come with significant costs.

Baggage
Getting bags on airplanes costs money: you might get one bag free, but it must be fifty pounds or less. Even one pound over and you will pay extra, maybe $50 or $100. I carry an electronic bow scale with me to verify the weight as I pack. Your second bag is going to be your gun or bow case, which is usually oversized and will almost always cost you. So, if you think you need another bag for clothes and gear, becoming your third bag, they won't guarantee they will take them. The fine print sometimes says that they reserve the right to not load your third bag if the plane is loaded. Baggage on bush planes is even more critical. Your body weight and baggage weight are calculated to see if the plane can even get off the ground and fly. In some cases, having big bags or gun cases cannot go, because they have to break them down. And fit them in all the little spaces they can find. It is wise to pack smaller bags inside your big one. There is a whole section in this book on packing for your trip.

Tips
The guide gets paid something for the week, but most of his income is from your tips. You made your money doing whatever it is you do and probably deserved it; this person is going to work his ass off for you and deserves to get paid too. Ten percent of the entire hunt cost is a good place to start. That can be a significant amount of money. If you bag your trophy early in the week, you are happy and might be happy to tip the guide well. Remember, if you hunt all week and go home empty handed, your guide worked hard for you all week, much harder than if you tagged out early. Keep that in mind when you tip.

Camp hands and cooks should get tipped too. Because all the hunters in camp pitch in, it can be less out of your pocket. They work very hard to make sure you are comfortable.

If your outfitter is your guide technically you don't need to tip him, but a thank-you tip is appreciated.

Hotels, food, and transportation before and after a hunt
The time between when you fly and when your hunt starts is usually on your own. If you have to stay overnight the hotel is on your dime. This would include travel to the hotel and any meals. Once the outfitter picks you up, he usually starts to pay. This is not cut and dry and some will hesitate and make you pay.

If you come out of camp early, you will have more days to stay waiting for your flight. You will have to pay for that.

Meat care and trophy shipping
If they take your meat to a processor, you usually have to pay for that. If it is done in camp, it might be included in the services. Flying meat home or shipping meat home is costly to the point of being prohibitive. I know that sucks for most of you, but the meat can go to the locals and they need it. Shipping racks, capes, or hides home has its own issues. Large racks might need to be split, or take large wooden boxes to be shipped whole. Split racks can no longer be scored for the record books. Depending on the animal, you might need a CITES permit. The outfitter usually takes care of this, but they must keep your trophy until the paperwork is complete. Once it is complete there are customs papers and shipping to pay for. A customs broker is needed to receive and help clear your shipment through customs. Add to that the final trucking from customs to your house. For trophies taken on hunts overseas, the hide needs to be dipped and dried by a taxidermist or tannery and the skull needs to be bleached. This keeps any bugs or diseases from reaching the U.S.

Beer or alcohol in camp
No outfitter will stock the beer coolers for you. They will often stop at a store and let you buy your beer, alcohol and soft drinks for the time at camp. I don't like to drink when I am hunting, but sure do appreciate a beer to celebrate after I score on the big one. In Russia, you cannot have enough vodka around.

If you eat or drink a lot of anything, consider packing your own. If you are coffee drinker and camp runs out, mornings start to suck. Same goes with snacks and candy bars.

Taxidermy
Most outfitters have a local taxidermist that can mount your trophy. There are advantages to this. Taxidermists that are used to doing that particular animal will do a better job. You don't bring a moose head to a guy that mainly works on deer heads back home. He might not know what a moose head is even supposed to look like. The key to good taxidermy is preparing the hide correctly. Capping the animal is critical and needs to be done quickly, allowing it to cool. Getting the flesh off and turning the eyes, lips and ears is all time sensitive. It needs to be done and salted as soon as possible. Many times, the guides do this if time permits, but in a pinch, getting it to a taxidermist is the best answer. If you do this, then a deposit as much as 50 percent of the taxidermy bill could be required.

Fines or trophy charges

Some outfitters will charge you fines if you do something outside their rules. Be sure you understand fully what those rules are. They might fine you for shooting a buck under a minimum score. You had better know how to score that buck. Some outfitters, especially those on black bear hunts, will charge you if you wound a bear, can't find it, and want to get back in the stand to hunt some more. Hunting Africa scares the shit out of me. You might get a few animals with your package but the rest are a la carte. I can see myself going ape shit seeing and shooting trophy after trophy and building up a huge credit card bill. Then there are places that charge more by how the animal scores. I am a little scared of that deal too. Honestly, who would want to pass up a gold-medal stag? Will power, baby! Hunts such as these require a huge amount of will and discipline that must be summoned and decided on in split seconds. I just am not sure I want to put myself in that position.

Conservation charges

In many cases, when you take an animal there is a fee that goes directly to the government or conservation department. I have seen $1000 fee for a grizzly bear, down to fees as low as $50. Your outfitter will communicate this to you, but be aware of the possibility.

Taxes

We are used to tax. It is on everything. Canada for example has two types of taxes that add a significant amount to your final hunt costs.

Cell phone usage

If you leave the United States, you run the risk of a huge cell phone bill if you make calls and texts. Be sure to research this ahead of time with your cell phone provider. Often you can add some sort of international plan to your phone just for one or two billing periods. Also remember that electric voltages are different in other countries, so your charger won't work. Luckily, they sold chargers at the hotel gift shop in Russia.

Emergency evacuation

You are going into dangerous, unforgiving countries where animals exist that push you down the food chain. You can get hurt and getting you out costs millions. There are insurances for this. I purchased the InReach satellite-communication device. They offered an insurance plan that was well worth the money.

Lesson – Carrying Money

If you add this all up, you can be carrying a lot of cash with you. If the outfitter asks for the last payment in cash when you arrive, you could find yourself needing to carry thousands of dollars. Credit cards work most places, until you get farther in the bush, or in a foreign country. I also found out the hard way that Russians think all traveler's checks are fake. They would not accept any of the traveler's checks that I brought on the trip. Luckily other hunters in camp brought extra cash and I could trade.

Lesson – Skimping on cost makes you bitchy

If you cannot afford it, you should not go! If you did not save enough money for the whole trip, the hidden costs and some insurance money on top of that, then you cannot afford to go. I have seen many people try to skimp on things during the trip. That pressure is a dark cloud that somehow follows them the entire trip. If it becomes dark enough, I believe it has a negative effect on your success. Even if you are lucky enough to bag your animal, it prevents you from having the fun you could have had.

If you cannot afford it, postpone the trip for one more year. Many outfitters will allow this if they have time to fill your spot. Continue saving at the pace you have been and you will have enough to cover your taxidermy, or better yet a deposit for the next hunt you will definitely want to go on.

Lesson – Remember it is hunting!

"Don't gamble what you cannot afford to lose." Not sure who said this first but a co-worker said this to me very early in my career. What you are about to embark on is a form of gambling. You are making the conscious decisions to spend a pile of money to have a *chance* at taking an animal. There are no guarantees in the hunting business. There are many factors that can work against you, most you can control, but others like weather and animals you cannot. Using the tips in this book will most definitely help swing the odds in your favor, but it is still hunting. Never, ever forget that!

Wolf Was on My Top-Five List

I had created the top-five list of animals I wanted to take. I tried for mountain lion in Arizona with some troubles. Wolf, moose, brown bear, and mountain goat were still animals of my dreams. When we were black bear hunting in Saskatchewan, we stopped at a taxidermist who had just completed a life-size mount of an arctic wolf. This giant, pure-white, gorgeous animal caught my eye and my dreams. It lit a fire inside of me, a burning urge to hunt wolf.

As soon as one hunt is over, you automatically start dreaming and plotting to go again. It is an addiction, I admit that and you should too. The white wolf haunting my dreams made me start to research the possibilities. For those of you reading this from the United States, wolves were at the time protected here and there is a ton of controversy surrounding them. In Canada, wolves are prevalent, so much so that you only need a small-game license to kill as many as you can. I will agree with the wolf lovers that these animals are beautiful, cunning, and majestic. For a hunter, they are a smart and elusive animal to hunt. We will leave the rest of the politics aside for now.

I found a couple of outfitters that advertised wolf-only hunts, but very few would take the responsibility because of the long odds of a hunter getting a wolf. This was also an off-season hunt, so taking just one hunter on a hunt would be costly to an outfitter.

I emailed Todd of *Rugged Outfitting* in Alberta, Canada, about hunting wolves. At that time, I don't think Todd had taken many if any hunters on a wolf-only hunt. His response to my email was that he was willing to take me, but he gave me slim odds at getting a shot at one. Most wolves are taken when a hunter happens across one while hunting another animal. The shots are long and fast and hardly ever planned. I loved Todd's honesty and that triggered me into saying yes, let's go hunt wolves.

The story you are about to read is exactly how it rolled off my lips when I told people about my hunt. Everyone I told said to me that I needed to write the story down. So, I did and that started this whole writing thing for me. The stories flow easy for me, because it comes from my heart and is simply my passion for the experience. The vision in my head is still as clear today as it was the day it happened.

So here is my story, one that was published in an online magazine called *Real Hunters Journal*.

The Plan

Every day of our lives we make plans. We plan our day; we plan for the future and for our next hunt. All plans have goals and our personal goals are often based on our dreams. Sometimes dreams are wishes with little chance of success. They are still our dreams, so we plan and we try and we work toward fulfilling them. Because of the low odds of success, plans are constantly changing, but when a plan comes to attrition, there is nothing more satisfying. There is nothing better than when a "plan comes together."

As with you, I love to hunt. I've become hooked on hunting trips for different species of animals, always in a new area of North America. For some reason I have been blessed with hunts that turn out just as I'd dreamed. I recently had a successful spring black bear hunt in Saskatchewan. I had taken my chocolate color-phase bear, just as had hoped and planned.

To avoid disappointment, I try to keep my dreams realistic. When I got the urge to hunt wolves, my dreams may have gone a bit over the top. I take that back — it was way over the top. I contacted Todd, owner of Rugged Outfitting in Alberta, Canada. My sole purpose was to go there and hunt wolf. In swapping e-mails, Todd gave me a 25-percent chance of success. Either Todd is the most honest outfitter known to man, or the percentage was much lower and exaggerated up to 25 percent. Either way, if I was in it for success only, this may be a bad investment.

No matter how hard you plan, things happen! One mistake in my plan forced me to change flights and we didn't get into to camp until two o'clock in the morning. Needless to say, we were a bit groggy at 4:30 AM and a morning of road hunting and bait checking was pretty nice. I didn't see any wolves that morning, but I saw what seemed like every possible North American game animal in existence. In a few short hours we saw countless elk, a few moose, a lynx, whitetail deer and bald eagles. Then to hear the stories of taking antelope in the morning and rams in the afternoon, while passing up mule deer in between, made me think I was in hunting heaven. Alberta has it all; the variety of land features makes this place ideal for all sorts of game animals.

The plan was to have some lunch and a giant cup of much-needed coffee, then do some calling that afternoon. Wolves and coyotes are hunted on a small-game license in Alberta and any number can be taken. Calling and baiting are the methods of bringing the wolves out in the open, but in reality, most wolves are taken by hunters pursuing other game and shot at long distances.

Another hunter, who has hunted all over the world, was with us at this time, as he had extended his stay to hunt a couple more days. We checked baits that showed no signs of action. Todd mentioned as we traveled the logging roads that there was a herd of wild horses roaming the area. This pack of horses was descendants of horses abandoned by a rancher many years ago. The locals had seen that one of these horses was lame with a broken leg.

We proceeded to a valley that was known as the stomping grounds of a pack of wolves. Here we would try our first calling sequence. I set up in a 100-acre clear cut as Todd disappeared into the spruce to do some predator calling. Moments after Todd disappeared into the trees, he reemerged, motioning me to come over. I had no idea what he wanted, but I was pretty sure we weren't stalking a pack of wolves.

I got to the edge of the tree line where Todd stood and he explained that on the other side of the trees, in an open area called a lick, something had caught up to and killed that lame horse. Wolves, cougars, or bear may have taken this animal down.

The plan was unveiling itself right before our very eyes. The kill, now my bait, was exactly 100 yards from a stand placed twenty feet high, just inside the edge of the woods. This was at the bottom of a long valley where the wolves were known to run. It was only a matter of time before they found their meal and I had all week to wait for them. The wolves were sure to visit this lick knowing the frequency the other animals, their potential prey, came here to drink the mineral-enriched spring water. Hence the name "lick"; animals loved the taste of the much-needed mineral water. A natural salt lick!

We sat in watch over the bait that afternoon and then again the next morning. We saw nothing but a few ravens flying about. The other hunter in camp had to pack up and leave the afternoon of the second day. As we ate lunch the topic of "beating the ravens" came up.

I had to ask what they were talking about. "Beat the ravens?" They explained that the ravens, being very leery creatures, would not feed on the bait when they knew there was danger near. If they knew we were near the bait, they would not feed. If I could only get into the stand without them knowing it, they would feel comfortable enough to feed. When they feed they make noise that sounds like the dinner bell to the wolves. First of all, if the ravens think it is safe and are eating, the wolves think it is safe. The wolves are also a little ticked off because the ravens are stealing their food. Either way if the wolves are near and hear these ravens on the bait, they will come right in to chase those thieving birds away and enjoy a free meal.

Problem is, I was walking to the stand in the daylight, and the ravens would spot me as I got closer. To fool them, Todd wanted me in that stand before sunrise. Get there before the ravens start to stir. We had to drive over an hour to get there and it was a mile walk in. We would have to get up pretty early in the morning to pull this off. Todd suggested we pack up camp and move to a hotel within ten minutes of the hunting area. It was obvious with bait like this that I would hunt this area all week. So, we moved.

The next morning we were at the drop-off point on top of the hill, before 5:00 in the morning. We agreed that Todd would check back with me by radio at 11:00. If the bait had been hit, I was staying all day, knowing whatever ate there would eventually be back. I piled out of the truck; Todd wished me luck and drove off. There I was alone in the dark, ready for my mile walk to the stand.

I'm from New York and the meanest thing we have is black bear, and very few of them. They live in other parts of the state. Luckily the grizzly bears were probably still sleeping. I had mountain lions on my mind, and I was walking to a place that I hoped had a pack of hungry wolves. Mind you, we saw wolf tracks the first day that were the size of my outstretched hand. I have pictures! Todd said those tracks were probably from a 175-pound wolf. My worst thought was the fact that you won't see just one wolf, because these animals come in packs. The four shells in my rifle versus a pack of wolves in the dark—I didn't figure this into my plan.

Alberta had a warm spell, melting most of the snow. It wasn't deep, but what was there was frozen and terribly crunchy. It was the kind of snow you could almost walk on, and then at the last second, you'd fall through. There was no way to keep quiet. This helped calm my nerves; I told myself there was no way that wolf would stick around with me making all this noise. In all reality, they would just slink to the cover, knowing exactly where I was at all times. Nonetheless, I made that mile walk rather quickly; if was going to make noise no matter what so I may as well get there and get settled in.

I entered the lick, an open area probably 300 by 500 yards long. Little vegetation grew there because of the high mineral content of the water. I had to cross the lick to get to the stand. The bait was on the way, so I would check and see if it had been chewed at during the night. From the edge, I glassed and could see the bait in the moonlight, and no other movement around it. If they were there, I chased them out of the lick. I was feeling relatively safe now. I felt more and more safe the farther into the open I walked. I got to the bait to find that it had been hit. "Good." I thought, "I'm going to stay all day."

Just then a fire siren went off. I was confused and a bit shocked. "Was there a fire tower nearby?" I said to myself as I looked into the hills for signs of a tower. Then another went off from a different direction. Then it hit me. "That's no siren, its wolves!" At that moment I felt I was surrounded by up to twenty wolves. Howls came from all directions, echoing through the valley. Worst of all, I'm standing by their food. I start toward the stand, wanting to run the 100 yards, but two things stopped me. First it would be real noisy running, and it might chase them away. After all, I am here to hunt them. The second and more truthful reason was that the stand was in the edge of the woods, it was dark over there and there were wolves howling in the trees. Believe me: the "chicken" reason was overriding the "big time hunter" reason, but I went anyway.

I made it to the stand and scaled the twenty-foot ladder in no time. I was sure glad to get off the ground. Sweat poured off my forehead. I thought I'd probably freeze solid before 11:00 came. Fear faded away quickly and reality started to hit me. "There are wolves here!" I was here to hunt and I had better get ready. I got my video camera and other gear out and set it down. I put on my head net, then my camo cap, and as my hand started back down from the brim of my hat, I heard the wing beats of a bird landing in the tree not fifteen feet from me.

I stopped and rolled my eyes toward the bird. It was the lead raven. He came to investigate whether I was part of the tree stand or danger. I froze, hand still in the air. I didn't even blink as the raven stared at me. He tilted his beady little head from side to side like a curious puppy would. The raven was trying to get me to move. It felt like I didn't blink for seven minutes, even though it was probably a lot less time than that. He finally became convinced that I was part of the tree stand, cawed and flew to the ground. Immediately ravens came from every direction, landing and circling the bait. I did it. I had beaten the lead raven. The plan was working.

There are things in nature that can only be seen to be believed, and the ritual of the ravens is one of them. You'd think that if it were safe, the ravens would immediately start eating. It is much more complicated than that. The birds first circle the bait standing a few feet away. They hop toward it as if their legs are handcuffed together. Then they hop back. This dance was done three times. All at once they jump on the bait, cackle and immediately fly off, as if they are practicing their escape plan. This ritual is practiced multiple times. As the others stand in a circle around the bait, two ravens take off like fighter jets circling the speedway moments before the start of the Daytona 500. Farther and farther out their circle goes, until they are buzzing the trees at the edge of the lick. When they are done, they land, give the all-clear squawk, and all the birds jump on and start to feed. When ravens feed, they fight, a ton of meat setting in front of them and they fight for one little piece. The racket they make is unbelievable. They are ringing the predator dinner bell.

Everything is going as planned. I beat the ravens. I stare across the lick to the farthest edge, in the direction I heard most of the howls. I'm convinced the wolves will come from that direction. But will they come all the way in? I sit for maybe fifteen minutes, barely cooling off from my panic attack. All at once I hear the ravens take off and fly away. "Did they see me?" I thought. Did I ruin the plan?

As I turn and look toward the bait, I see a gray dog-like creature running out of the woods toward the bait. Since the animal was gray, alone and still a long way away, I thought it was a coyote. Todd said coyotes were huge and often mistaken for wolves. I didn't care; a Western coyote would be a great trophy. As this creature gets closer to the bait, behind it a black figure comes out of the woods taking the same path, then another gray and another black. I'm in shock! These are wolves, this is a pack of wolves. I couldn't believe this was happening to me. I dreamt it, we planned for it, but I never expected it would really happen. Six wolves reached the bait, three of them black and the rest were different shades of gray.

The animals tear into this bait, ripping massive chunks of meat off the bone. Pieces of carcass are flying in the air. Their powerful jaws severe meat and bone in one powerful crunch. I first though I had to get this on video, so others could see and believe this vicious show of power and fury. I didn't dare pick up the camera. I couldn't blow this chance of a lifetime, so I got ready, bringing the gun to my shoulder.

Choices! Which one do I take? The wolf on the right was almost pure white with a gray bandana on the back of its neck. I wanted a white wolf ever since I saw an Arctic wolf at the taxidermist in Saskatchewan. This wolf was the smallest of the six. The wolf on the left was a black one and would be the choice of 99 percent of the hunters. A black wolf defines the mystic and horror of all wolves portrayed in movies. Either would make an awesome mount.

Out of the corner of my eye another black wolf comes into the field. He walked slowly, with confidence, I wondered if this could be the Alpha male. I could not judge his size and only hoped he would join the others so I could see if he was bigger. He circled toward me and disappeared behind the trees. I didn't know where he was heading and I feared he might scent me. I couldn't wait any longer; I had to take my shot at one of the wolves at the bait.

As I said earlier, my dream was a little farfetched. I dreamt of taking two wolves at the same bait. I didn't like thinking this way, being afraid I would blow the first shot while thinking of the second. Making a second shot would be tough. Try for two and come home with none, was not what I wanted to do. I tried not to think of this scenario, but I couldn't shake it. When I dreamt of the hunt, I dreamt of pulling this off.

The only possible way of taking two wolves was to take the black one on the left, and hope that the white one with the gray bandana ran to my right. I had about a fifteen-foot opening to shoot through on the right. I settled down on a firm rest and put the crosshairs on the black wolf's chest. I kept telling myself "finish this before you do anything else." I squeezed the trigger. As the muzzle came back down and the scope focused on the bait, there were no wolves to be seen. They were off and running in every direction.

The white one was running to my right and, quicker than Lee Harvey Oswald, I racked in another shell. The crosshairs came on to the wolf as he disappeared behind the trees. The wolf was totally stretched out; no way was I going to get a shot at it. Behind it came another wolf, a gray one. I threw the gun toward him, the cross hairs catching up to him as he hesitated and looked back for the others. The hesitation was a fatal mistake as I yanked the trigger and he spun. He changed direction, now running to my left. I could see the trail of blood in the snow. I had hit him hard. As he arced toward the woods, I shot again. As he reached the trees, he slowed to barely a crawl. He was hurting bad and I was sure he wouldn't go far.

I was confident I had a gray wolf. I sat back in the stand. My heart started to slow. What a morning, cold and brisk, the sun just rising, thinking of warming the day. The air was fresh and I was gleaming over the success of another hunt. The plan worked. My dream. It came true. Or did it? I couldn't see the black wolf. He could be behind the trees, but maybe I pulled the shot and missed. If that was what happened I still felt content in knowing that I would take the gray one home, no matter what.

I usually wait at least a half an hour before going after deer back home. I wasn't going anywhere because Todd wouldn't be back for four and a half more hours; it was only 6:30 in the morning. Besides, this wasn't a deer; this animal would bite. So, I decided to wait an hour and enjoy the morning from the safety of my stand. Just then the hair on the back of my neck stood up. The goose bumps rose on my arms. The same thing happens right now as I write these words. The pack started howling to each other. The Alpha male was calling in his division so he could assess the damages. You could hear their predicament in the tones of their howls, the loneliness, pain, and sadness. I taped the sound with my video camera. I couldn't tell until I got home if I actually recorded the sounds, but it worked. When the wolves are mounted, they will make a great trophy, but this tape is the real trophy to me. It brings back all the adrenaline, fear and emotion of that experience. Something very few people will experience. As Todd said, "They don't make a man big enough, not to be afraid of that sound, especially when you're alone and in the dark."

The hour had passed and I couldn't take it any longer. I got out of the tree and made my way toward the bait. I crossed a path of crimson red streaking through the snow. The gray wolf was hit hard. He couldn't have gone far.

I walked toward the bait, with no black wolf in sight. I hoped for a blood trail, but instead, there he was thirty yards away, lying behind a bush. What a beautiful yet frightening animal. Those black eyes staring out of the black fur, built to disappear in the dark. The pure white, inch-and-a-half-long fangs, polished from the bones of the victims they caught.

I'm not what you'd call a God-fearing person, but I thanked God: I always do. For making my dreams come true. For providing a guide like Todd who said and delivered exactly what he said. I was thankful for the creation of a creature like the wolf. I didn't hunt this wolf because I hate them. Some people do. They devastate rancher's stock. Wolves kill for fun, they kill for food, and they often eat before death comes to the animal. They are terrible, vicious animals, yet beautiful and deserving of our respect. These two animals will now live forever in my home and then my kids' homes one day. Most of all I thanked the horse for making the ultimate sacrifice for me. I'm glad the plan worked, making it worth the sacrifice. I love it when a plan comes together!

More to the wolf story

I shortened the story to be published in an online magazine, but there was still more. Remember the gray wolf and the huge blood trail it left in the snow? Well, I set off to track and recover that wolf. I easily followed the trail into the woods for a few hundred yards. I was getting to the point that I knew I would need help if I found it.

I decided to go back, then hike the mile back up the hill and see if I could get cell phone coverage enough to call Todd. Once at the top of the hill I got a faint couple of bars to call him as he waited back at the hotel. He was surprised hearing from me so early, shouting, "Did you get a wolf?"

"Um yeah," I said, "I shot two." I am not sure he believed me at first, and then what I said started to sink in. His reaction on the phone was priceless; he might have been more excited than I was. He excitedly said he would be right over.

We made the hike back to the bait and I showed him the black wolf. We took a few pictures and he heard the whole story. Then I showed him the blood trail of the gray wolf. He too said it couldn't go far. We followed the trail to the point I quit, and then followed it for a long way more. At times there was so much blood, it puddled getting on our boots we would leave bloody bootprints in the snow.

At one point, maybe a half mile in, Todd grabbed my shoulder and said, "I cannot believe it is losing that much blood." As he spoke those words, the wolf jumped up not ten feet away from us and started to run. I quickly finished it with a follow-up shot. If Todd had not grabbed my shoulder at that specific time, I likely would have stepped over that log and right on a very-much-still-alive wolf.

If you have not figured it out by now, I will make something very clear. I am a much happier person when I am looking to book or have booked a hunt. I do laugh at myself. When I am on that airplane flying home, the memories of the last few days hunting bouncing in my head, suddenly it always happens: "What am I going to hunt next?"

Even with a successful and memorable experience under my belt, there is this feeling of loss. Even after a long year or two of planning and anticipating, that moment when there is nothing left but the week of the hunt, I feel sad. I feel this way because I put so much time and energy into this and it is now over. I cannot stress enough how much joy and purpose you can get out of planning a hunting trip.

There is probably some psychologist reading this thinking, "Dude, you are messed up." Yeah, probably I am, but I know what brings me happiness. It is not the hunt itself, or the taking of a trophy animal, it is the pursuit of a dream that drives me and brings me joy. It gives me a purpose to live on, eat well, and stay fit and work hard.

Lesson – If you don't pursue dreams, whatever they are, you just exist.

If you don't pursue dreams, whatever they are, you just exist. If you don't pursue dreams, whatever they are, you just exist. I had to write that three times in a row, to make sure it sinks in. Pursuing dreams will fire up passion inside of you. The path you have to take may be difficult, but the journey will be worth it. You won't know until you get there. All I know is I don't want to look back on my life, from my old-age chair, and have regrets that I didn't get to do what I dreamed.

Pike County Illinois for Deer – The Story of Walmart and Kmart

At this stage in my life, things were not going very good. In 2003, a few months before I was to go hunt wolf, my wife handed me a list of people she had borrowed money from, money she then lost gambling. I am a problem solver. I knew nothing at all about addiction. It cost me a lot of money, but I made the problem go away. It was a tough decision financially to go on that wolf hunt. I had already paid most of the cost of the hunt, and paid for my airline ticket. Mathematically, I would lose more than I saved if I cancelled, so I decided to go. Mind you, this was a decision I made with my wife. I needed to know she was behind that decision.

I was done earlier than expected and the wolves were at the taxidermist. I decided I would fly home early and surprise my family. I was riding a high of adrenaline and I wanted to tell my story. I couldn't wait to get home. Once I knew I could change my flight, I called home to tell my wife the great news. My wife had some news for me. She had done it all again and had another list of gambling debts. The plane could have crashed and I would have cheered it all the way into the ground. I was not pursuing dreams anymore; I was living a nightmare that truthfully would never go away.

I tell you this to prove my point. Pursuing my dreams was never easy, but I kept pushing toward them. I am sharing these stories for you to learn that you can do it and to learn from my mistakes. I made many, but I learned from them all. They made me the person I am today, so for that reason, I refuse to have any regrets.

I sat at work one day with my frustration level at its highest peak and I had no hunting plans in the future. I knew money was an issue, but I also knew I was spending all mine on everyone else but me. I desperately needed something to look forward to. A giant whitetail would be nice and Pike county Illinois was a hot spot to hunt them. I made a couple of quick web searches later and boom, this is where I want to go.

Part of me just wanted to go on my own and get away from my life. I couldn't bring myself to do that without at least asking Dean to tag along. He quickly said yes. We would drive out, so there was room for more— little did I know, not much room for more. My brother-in-law Randy had always talked about archery hunting for a giant deer, so I decided to ask him. To my surprise, he was all in too. So, the hunt was set and the planning and anticipation had begun. It didn't solve any of my problems, but at least now I had something to look forward to and keep my mind occupied.

We would rent a van to carry the three of us and our gear. After all it would be a long ride and the extra space would allow someone to sleep while the others drove. A smart plan, at least until we started to pack the van. I had experienced taking too much gear with me before on the Arizona mountain lion hunt. I had a whole box I carried through airports that I never actually even opened, all gear that the hunting chain stores and commercials convinced me I needed.

We met to pack the van so we were ready to hit the road early the next morning. Dean and Randy laid their gear out, ready to be stuffed into the van. They had so much shit with them that I immediately nicknamed one Walmart and the other Kmart, because they brought everything in the store. We stuffed that van to the roof. Then we stuffed the back seat, the one we planned to sleep on, so full the third guy could barely fit in the van. We had to sleep sitting up. It was a hysterical sight. If we had been able to shoot any deer that week, we would have had to have a garage sale in Illinois or we couldn't bring any deer meat back home.

Packing for Your Hunt

Packing for your hunt will be a challenge and I advise you to work on it way ahead of time. Airlines have weight restrictions that need to be dealt with. Your gun or bow case will have its own issues. You need to spend at least as much time, if not more, thinking about what *not* to take. If you are new to all of this, the hunting clothes you have may or may not be the best choice. I will touch on these issues and give pointers on how I deal with them. I will also share my hunting list, a list that has evolved over all these years and gets manipulated many times before I finally pack.

Airplanes are the biggest detriment to taking the gear you want and need. They have rules on size and weight and they have baggage charges as well as significant charges for extra bags. If you are driving, great. You have a lot more leeway to pack what you want. I would still consider the things I am going to tell you so you don't carry all that stuff you really don't need.

Each outfitter will send you a recommended gear list. I have yet to see one that is correct. For the life of me I cannot understand why they refuse to tailor the list to the actual hunt you go on. I've carried hip waders hundreds of miles to find out there wasn't a swamp anywhere near camp. The last trip said to bring pipe insulation, cardboard, and duct tape. The idea was to protect your moose rack on the airline trip home. Airlines no longer allow racks, but the stuff was still on the list. All I can suggest here is to ask lots of questions.

Diary: August 5, 2015

Denny sent us the packing list
CHECK LIST OF ITEMS TO BRING FOR TRIP

AIRLINE TICKETS, VISA /PASSPORT
CASH, CREDIT CARDS
CAMERA, FILM, ADAPTER, EXTRA BATTERIES
SHAVING KIT, MEDICATION, WATCH, FLASHLIGHT
GLASSES, SUNGLASSES, CONTACT STUFF
HAT, GLOVES, SLEEPING BAG, SMALL PILLOW, BLOW UP AIR MATTERESS
WASH CLOTH, TOWEL, SMALL BAR OF SOAP
BACKPACK OR FANNY PACK TO PUT STUFF IN
HATS, GLOVES, GARBAGE BAGS
GUN, AMMO, CASE, CLEANING KIT
HUNTING BOOTS, SOCKS
MOSQUITO REPELLENT (FALL HUNTS), HEAD NET, RAIN GEAR (FALL HUNTS)
SMALL CUSHION OR BLOW-UP CUSHION FOR SPRING SNOWMOBILE HUNTERS
HEAVY DUTY PLASTIC BAGS FOR HIDES
GARDEN HOSE OR PIPE WRAP FOR HUNTERS TAKING ANIMALS WITH ANTLERS
THERMAL UNDERWEAR, UNDERWEAR, SWEATER, JACKET, ETC.
DUCT TAPE, HANKIES, CANDY BARS, SNACKS
HUNTING CLOTHING, (CAMO)
*SPRING HUNT TEMPS CAN GET INTO TEENS AND 20' AT NIGHT AND FROM 30 TO 60 DURING DAY

*HEAVY, WARM JACKETS, BIB OVERALLS, BOOTS, ETC FOR WINTER MOOSE HUNTS. CAN GET BELOW ZERO (ALTHOUGH UNCOMMON, DECEMBER HUNTS CAN GET TO 10 OR 20 BELOW!) ON THESE HUNTS! TAKE A WARM FACE MASK, SNOWMOBILE GOGLES OR MASK, ETC.

**NOTE: THIS IS A LIST THAT I USE TO PACK. IT IS ONLY A SUGGESTED LIST OF ITEMS TO HELP YOU PACK. THERE ARE SOME THINGS HERE YOU MAY NOT NEED AND OTHERS YOU MAY WANT TO TAKE ALONG. I TRY TO DRESS IN LAYERS AS NOBODY CAN PREDICT THE WEATHER. BY DRESSING IN LAYERS YOU CAN ADD ON AND PEEL OFF CLOTHES AS NEEDED. PLEASE DO NOT OVER-PACK AS YOU WILL BE CHARGED FOR OVERBAGGAE.

BAGGAGE LIMITS ARE MUCH MORE RESTRICTIVE THAN THEY USED TO BE. MOST FLIGHTS NOW LIMIT YOU TO A TOTAL 45 TO 50 POUNDS (AIRLINES TRY TO MAKE MONEY ON BAGGAE NOW). I KNOW IT'S HARD TO STICK TO THESE WEIGHT LIMITS, ESPECIALLY WHEN YOU CARRY RIFLES AND AMMO WITH HEAVY CASES. JUST TRY TO KEEP AS CLOSE TO POSSIBLE TO THE WEIGHT LIMITS.

IN THE PAST WE WOULD TAKE OUR HIDES AND HORNS BACK WITH US AND HAD TO PAY ENORMOUS BAGGAGE FEES FROM $400 TO $600 AS WE HAD BEAR AND MOOSE HIDES THAT WEIGHED OVER 200 POUNDS WET. NOW WE MUST LEAVE THE HIDES IN MOSCOW TO BE FLESHED AND DRYED. (SAME AS WITH ALL OTHER COUNTRIES LIKE AFRICA, ETC.) THE COST FOR THIS AND THE SHIPPING IS ABOUT THE SAME AS WE USED TO PAY FOR CARRYING THEM BACK WITH US. WE WILL KEEP YOU INFORMED ON WHEN THE HIDES ARE DONE AND WHEN THEY WILL BE SHIPPED BACK.

Lesson – Baggage Rules

Your first task is to go to the airline website and review the baggage rules for your flights. They are similar, but can be different enough to get you in trouble. If your flight is international, be sure to look at the rules of every flight because they are different. If you are flying smaller planes within a country, or float planes and helicopters you need to discuss the rules with your outfitter. Large bags stuffed with gear don't work well on many bush planes, and they might go through your bag and force you to leave gear at the dock before you can fly out to camp.

Diary: August 6, 2015 confirming baggage rules

United baggage rules
They have an online calculator based on the flights
SWISS Economy class is 1 bag 32 kg 158 CM equals 70 pounds 62 inches

Tariffs - Intercontinental

Additional baggage item	swiss.com	Check-in	Gate
Additional baggage item Standard (max. 23 kg, circumference less than 158 cm[1])	**swiss.com** CHF 140 EUR 115 USD 150 CAD 150 JPY 15000[3] JPY 20000[4]	**Check-in** CHF 180 EUR 150 USD 200 CAD 200 JPY 15000 JPY 20000	**Gate** CHF 200 EUR 160 USD 210 CAD 210 JPY 21000
Additional baggage item Oversize (circumference more than 158 cm[1])	swiss.com x	**Check-in** CHF 420 EUR 350 USD 500 CAD 500	Gate x
Additional baggage item Very heavy (24 - 32 kg)	swiss.com x	**Check-in** CHF 300 EUR 250 USD 350 CAD 350	Gate x
Additional baggage item Very heavy and oversize (24 - 32 kg, circumference more than 158 cm[1])	swiss.com x	**Check-in** CHF 540 EUR 450 USD 650 CAD 650	Gate x

Your Main Bag

There is a lot to be said about your main bag. That last diary entry shows the rules for my international flight to Russia. Sixty-two inches is typical and I have never seen anyone bring out a tape measure. If it isn't obviously oversized they might ignore it. That measurement means adding up the length, width, and height, and the total cannot exceed sixty-two inches. Of course, finding a bag that meets sixty-two inches exactly is near impossible, for reasons I do not understand.

The maximum weight for the international flight was seventy pounds, but for almost all U.S.-based domestic flights it's fifty pounds. I don't think I would take the chance; I would shoot for a fifty-pound bag. Take note of the extreme charges for oversize or overweight bags. Just one pound over can cost you a lot of money at the gate. Trust me; they will not have any sympathy for you. They will give you time to take something out, but where do you carry it then? The rules also show it is cheaper to pay for the oversized bag ahead of time. That might sound like an easy answer, but be careful. Baggage handler union rules say it takes two people to pick up an overweight, oversized bag. If two people aren't available, your bag may never get on the plane. Also, the fine print says the airlines don't guarantee taking overweight items if the plane is full. It is not worth the risk.

I carry a little electronic archery scale in my carry on. This allows me to check, recheck, and adjust the weight before I get to the counter. You will spend days getting this right at home before you leave. When it is time to come home, you have minutes to stuff your crap back in the bag. Not knowing the exact weight will cost you.

Wheels and extendable handles make carrying bags through the airport a breeze. I have been there and made this mistake. The $190 monogrammed duffle bag with wheels and handles weighs fifteen pounds before I put anything in it. It no longer leaves my storage closet. Get the lightest bag you can find that measures sixty-two inches.

If you are carrying a gun to hunt with, typically they require you to keep the ammunition in its original box, in a checked bag separate from your gun case. I will discuss this more in another section, but my point here is, your main duffle bag will have five or more pounds of ammo in it. That takes away from weight available for other gear.

They will search this bag. If you are flying with a gun, the rest of your luggage will go with the gun case. This is cool because it all gets very special handling. But it also guarantees that your bag gets manually searched. Do not pack your bag so tight that they cannot re-zip or re-latch the bag. They won't have your wife there to sit on it so it can be zipped back up. They will leave it open and underwear and hunting gear will be scattered throughout the airport.

Also remember that you are likely going to buy things on your trip. You should have room in your bag to bring things home. Souvenirs should not take you over the weight limit. That is why I carry that archery scale with me; it is even more valuable packing for the trip home. If your trip took you out of the country, then there will be customs rules that apply for anything you bring back. My Russian outfitter had a meat-packing business that made sausages and mustards. He was nice enough to give us one each and I carried it over fourteen time zones, just to have it confiscated at the U.S. Customs checkpoint. That sucked, because that sausage was awesome!

Before you pack your bag, remember all that space you took up when your gear was scattered all over your house? You won't have that kind of space to spread out at any camp, cabin or tent. My advice is to pack things you might not need to use first, then things you will use on top. I have seen so many people digging through and unloading an entire bag in a panic just to find one little thing. Unused gear is best left right where it is. You will thank yourself and your cabin mates will refrain from kicking your ass.

Packing the Gun or Bow Case

Your second bag is always going to be your gun or bow case. It is always going to be oversized. There is no way you aren't paying some extra fee every time you board a new airline. I make very sure it is full. I have a double bow case that I use for every trip. It could have a gun, a bow, or sometimes both inside. I take advantage of every possible spot to put extra gear. Binoculars or any electronics that can benefit from the extra padding and protection go inside. This is also a good place for knives and other tools that might be better protected in this case.

The main cause of damage, especially to a rifle scope, is because the gun moves inside the case when they drop it, and they will. The gun's momentum slides it hard against the inside of the case. For that reason, I also pack soft clothes and gear around the gun to prevent any of this motion. My case always has new gouges and scars, but knock on wood, I have not had a scope jarred off center yet.

At the ticket counter, they need to see the gun. They will put a card in the case to tell the inspector that you declared your firearm. Do not take that card out of the case. If they think you didn't declare a firearm, there will be big trouble brewing and for sure you will not get your gun at the end of your flight. So, keep this in mind when jamming clothes and gear around your gun. It needs to be declared and someone will always open it up and check it before putting get on a flight. Don't make it hard for them to see what is in there. You don't have to declare a bow, but because it looks like a weapons case, I always offer to open it up at the ticket counter.

TSA rules now say you must leave all baggage unlocked for inspection. This is very hard to do, letting your baby go off on its own without being protected. In rare cases, they will inspect it in your presence then ask you to lock it. My case has four locks. I never lock them all. They will break them open if they want to get in and I don't want all four locks broken. I also put Duct tape over each lock so no latch can be knocked open and broken off.

I want to make sure it is evident that the rifle can in no way be loaded or fired. There is no reason to lead anyone to believe that anything is unsafe. I remove the bolt and often pack that in my other bag. I am not leaving anyone with a working gun. I add a padlock through the chamber, where the bolt once was. I also add a trigger lock. I make it very evident that this gun is locked and unable to fire. It only takes one person behind you with a deadly fear of guns to yell, "Gun" and you will have police there with their guns drawn. Be respectful of others and always assume the worst and the trip will be much smoother.

I have never had an issue taking a gun on a plane, or through any customs check. In most cases I find people to suddenly take their job much more seriously and become very helpful. A lot of times I have had them leave their counter and personally escort me to insure my gear gets where it needs to go. All your bags will go to a secure area and be handled specially. This also means that it probably won't come out on the usual baggage claim like the rest of the common passengers. Check the baggage office, or sometimes there is a special room.

My case is all stickered up and has my name and address in big letters. Some will say this can be a home security risk, showing off your address to the world. All I know is this: I can see my case from a mile away and if it is on its way out of the airport in someone else's hands I will see it.

I take pictures of the contents of the case and carry it on my phone. I also snap a picture of the firearms declaration card lying in the case before I close the case up. This is your only proof of what was in there at the time they took it from you. Honestly, I am not sure it will help, but it is your only chance to prove that there were thousands of dollars of gear in there if it becomes lost or stolen.

Everything I have told you to do has worked well for many trips. Then I tried to fly across Russia. Tracking guns and ammo in Russia is a big deal, since most Russians cannot own firearms. Easily two and a half hours of paperwork per airport had to be completed before we could move on. But the bigger issue in Russia was they would only allow the gun and ammo in the case. All that other stuff had to be stuffed in another bag and that caused chaos. They aren't real keen on people carrying knives in the country either. The bottom line is, make sure you discuss these kinds of details with your outfitter before you pack and go.

You Usually Get Two Carry-on Items

Be sure to check the airline's regulations for carry-on bags. Most let you bring a carry on and a personal item. But, I had one flight to Russia that only allowed one item.

> **Each traveler can bring on board one carry-on bag plus one personal item free of charge. To ensure a smooth boarding experience, it's important to make sure that these items will fit into the overhead bin or under the seat in front of you.**
> **Carry-on bag**
> **The maximum dimensions for a carry-on bag are 9 inches x 14 inches x 22 inches (22 cm x 35 cm x 56 cm), including handles and wheels.**
> **Personal item**
> **The maximum dimensions for your personal item, such as a shoulder bag, backpack, laptop bag or other small item, are 9 inches x 10 inches x 17 inches (22 cm x 25 cm x 43 cm).**

The carry-on is where you can carry things that would have made your checked bags overweight. It is tough to carry heavy bags through airports, but weight does not usually matter, it is usually just size. I only saw one instance where they measured and rejected a carry-on. Of course, all the items in your carry-on must meet the rules or they will take it away from you at the security screening. Binoculars, rangefinders, phones, and tablets all will make it through. Of course, you can then fill every nook and cranny with clothes or other small items.

I like to carry on anything I may need up to the point I start hunting. My goal is to not to get anything out of my checked bag or my gun case until I reach my final destination. That way, those bags and cases stay packed neatly and the weight cannot change. I carry on my toiletries, following the rules of course, so if I lose a bag or it is delayed, I can at least wash up and be human again.

Lesson – There is no weight restriction for you.

There is no weight restriction for you. You can weigh as much as you want. No, I am not giving you permission to eat that donut. You can wear hunting boots versus travel shoes. You can wear a hunting coat instead of a casual coat. There might be other clothing items you could wear versus street clothes. Why pack a hat when you can carry it on your head? A camo belt holds your pants up just as good as a dress belt.

Lesson – Compare and Share

If you are lucky enough to travel with other hunters, or can get to know other hunters in camp, you can compare hunt lists and identify items that you all don't need to carry. Tools, gun-cleaning supplies, duct tape, knives and sharpeners are all things that can be shared. There are also things that you might need if your hunt lasted all ten days, but some of you will tag out early. Snacks and hand warmers are things you can cut back on since some of you may not need them all week. If you all shoot the same caliber gun, maybe you can share a box of ammo. Does everyone need to carry satellite communication? You can share charging devices. Toiletries and medicines can be shared. The only thing I wouldn't share is toilet paper. You need to be selfish with your toilet paper!

Bush Planes

Everything I have said in the previous paragraphs might be for naught, if your final leg into camp requires a float plane or helicopter. In these cases, the total weight of you, your body and all you wear, plus your gear is important to the pilot. Overall weight and balance needs to be calculated before they can fly. Be sure you have a conversation with your outfitter on this, long before you pack.

Large bags full of loose gear may be a problem. Packing in multiple small bags versus one giant bag could be important to them. Often, they want to break down your gear to literally stuff things in corners or little compartments. In this case having smaller bags inside your main bag may be important. You should also be conscious of items such as street clothes that don't really need to go all the way into camp. This is also a case to pack with some sort of strategy so you don't have to paw through a bag trying to figure out, under duress, what things you can live without and leave behind.

Riding in on horseback will also require you to think about how you pack. In that case, you likely can take only the gear you must have to hunt. Guides are good at sorting your gear, they have no qualms about throwing unneeded gear into a pile, if you cannot.

Large gun or bow cases sometimes need to be left behind at the point of the final leg into camp. If this happens, a gun sock or soft case is a nice thing to have, otherwise your gun is unprotected during the trip. Riding four-wheelers or other ATV's during the hunt is another reason a soft case can be worth its weight in gold. It needs to be safely stuffed in a spot, or tied to a rack.

Packing Summary

I have seen it happen repeatedly; the stress that can occur when a person does not take the time to pack properly and with a purpose is not worth it. Trust me when I say that taking your time to do this up front will make your trip more enjoyable. While others are frantically trying to deal with packing issues, weight restriction, or finding that one piece of gear they think they need, you can be talking with your guide about the hunt, or listening to the hunt stories of others. You will miss a lot with your head stuck in a duffle bag rutting around for gear.

Lesson – Steps to take when packing

1. Check the airline regulations before you book your flights.

2. Buy the appropriate-size bags. Do not get wheels and handles.

3. Check the airline regulations for transporting a firearm before you book your flight. I suggest printing this page out and taking it with you, in case the ticket agent has some other idea what the rules are.

4. Check with your outfitter to see if there are any packing guidelines when bush planes or horses are to be used.

5. Get a suggested hunting list from the outfitter. Be sure to review this with them to make sure it is accurate.

6. Make your own checklist ahead of time. This way you can identify what you may need to purchase and weed out what you can leave home.

7. Pack strategically. Things you need to access on top. Gear you may never use on the bottom.

8. Determine what you can wear on the plane, or carry in your carry-on bags to keep the weight of your main bag within the required poundage.

9. Buy an archery scale and weigh your gear.

10. Photograph your gear with your phone so you have a record of what you carry with you.

11. Remember, you will use some things up, freeing up space, but you will also buy souvenirs. Make sure you leave room for things you bring back.

12. Make sure guns, ammo, and knives are in the right bag. Stowaway knives left in pants pockets can get you in trouble. Check then double check that you have everything where it should be.

My Pack List for the Russian Moose Trip

Here is my hunting list as it evolved over many hunts up to what I carried on the Russian moose trip. Yellow Highlighted items were taken directly off the gear list sent to me by the outfitter.
- "Camp gear" refers to items that stay in camp.
- "Clothes-camp" are items I would wear at camp, leaving my hunting gear away unwanted odors such as cooking and fuel.
- "Clothes Travel" are clothes I would wear while travelling to and from the hunting spot, or the street clothes I would wear getting there and back home.
- "Hunt" refers to gadgets or tools that I carry on me when I hunt.
- "First Aid" and "Survival" are general lifesaving items that should always be in your backpack.
- "Toilet" and "Travel" are items I need while I am on the road, so they usually go in my carry-on.

I have different categories of hunting clothes depending on the weather.
- "Warm weather"
- "Cold Weather"
- "Rain Gear"
- "Extreme Cold"

Then there are categories for the equipment I take.
- Whether the "gun" or "archery" goes determines the list of gear that go with them.
- "Climbing" are items I take when I am climbing a tree or in an elevated stand.
- "Misc. Equip." are items that I may or may not need, such as tools. These things typically stay in camp.
- "Game care" are items I might take to help process and store the hide and meat.
- I also do my own "Taxidermy" preparation, so I carry the tools I need to do that right.
- "Shipping" These might be special items needed to pack for shipment.
- "Packing out" are special items I would take if there is a chance I will live out of a back pack.

As for the columns, you will notice two columns "carry" and "get there." I spend a lot of time on the columns "Get there" and "carry." "Get there" is how I pack to get there, during the travel process. This is usually driven by weight and other airline restrictions. The column "Carry" is where I move items so they are in the correct bag for hunting. Once things are moved over to the right bags, I am good to go. I know when I grab my gear that I have what I want with me all the time; I am sure I am carrying what I need in the field. There is nothing worse than carrying something thousands of miles and then leaving it in camp when you need it in the field. I know, I know, you are thinking this guy is over the top. I am! But, I have seen many hunters in a panic because they are disorganized and rushing to go out hunting.

The "Used" column is the results of a little debrief that I do after the hunt. I write down if I used it or not helping me decide next time if it is something I can leave home.

Russian Moose Packing List

Description	Category	Take	Used	Carry in field	To get there
blow up mattress	camp gear	Yes		Duffle Bag	Duffle Bag
pillow case	camp gear	Yes	Yes	Duffle Bag	Duffle Bag
towels	camp gear	Yes	Yes	Duffle Bag	Duffle Bag
washcloths	camp gear	Yes	Yes	Duffle Bag	Duffle Bag
sleeping bag / pillow	camp gear	Yes		Duffle Bag	Duffle Bag
shirts 3	clothes-camp	Yes	2	carry on	carry on
jeans 1	clothes-camp	Yes	Yes	carry on	carry on
long socks 3	clothes-camp	Yes	Yes	carry on	carry on
shorts	clothes-camp	Yes	Yes	carry on	carry on
sneakers	clothes-camp	Yes	Yes	carry on	carry on
sweatpants	clothes-camp	Yes	Yes	carry on	carry on
sweatshirts 1	clothes-camp	Yes	Yes	carry on	carry on
underwear 6	clothes-camp	Yes	Yes	carry on	carry on
shirts 1	clothes-travel Home	Yes	Yes	carry on	carry on
jeans 1	clothes-travel Home	Yes	Yes	Duffle Bag	Duffle Bag
regular socks 1	clothes-travel Home	Yes	Yes	Duffle Bag	Duffle Bag
underwear 1	clothes-travel Home	Yes	Yes	Duffle Bag	Duffle Bag
jeans 1	clothes-travel up	Yes	Yes	Duffle Bag	Wear it
regular socks 1	clothes-travel up	Yes	Yes	Duffle Bag	Wear it
shirts 1	clothes-travel up	Yes	Yes	Duffle Bag	Wear it
underwear 1	clothes-travel up	Yes	Yes	Duffle Bag	Wear it
ibuprofen	first aid	Yes	Yes	plastic bag	BP Carry on
Alka Seltzer	first aid	Yes		first Aid	Duffle Bag
aspirin	first aid	Yes		first Aid	Duffle Bag
First-aid kit	first aid	Yes		first Aid	Duffle Bag

Item	Category				
safety pins	first aid	Yes		first Aid	Duffle Bag
Tums	first aid	Yes		first Aid	Duffle Bag
Tylenol	first aid	Yes		first Aid	Duffle Bag
soap	first aid	Yes		out of camp	Duffle Bag
gun slinger	gun	Yes		batman belt	bow case
rifle	gun	Yes	Yes	Rifle	bow case
rifle sling	gun	Yes	Yes	Rifle	bow case
rifle ammo 1 box	gun	Yes	1/2 box	Rifle	Duffle Bag
video camera tripod	Hunt	Yes		batman belt	bow case
handy wipes	Hunt	Yes	Yes	batman belt	bow case
ibuprofen	Hunt	Yes	Yes	batman belt	bow case
wind indicator	Hunt	Yes	Yes	batman belt	bow case
florescent tape	Hunt	Yes		batman belt	bow case
predator call	Hunt	Yes		batman belt	bow case
camera	Hunt	Yes	Yes	batman belt	BP Carry on
almonds	Hunt	Yes	Yes	batman belt	BP Carry on
binoculars	Hunt	Yes	Yes	out of camp	BP Carry on
paper towels in plastic bag	Hunt	Yes	Yes	BP Hunt	Duffle Bag
scent killer - small	Hunt	Yes	Yes	BP Hunt	Duffle Bag
backpack	Hunt	Yes		BP Hunt	Duffle Bag
socks hunting (4 pair)	Hunt	Yes	Yes	Duffle Bag	Duffle Bag
newspaper, in plastic bag	Hunt	Yes	Yes	Duffle Bag	Duffle Bag
hand warmers (20)	Hunt	Yes		Duffle Bag	Duffle Bag
gloves - archery	hunting clothes	Yes	Yes	batman belt	bow case
light mask	hunting clothes	Yes	Yes	batman belt	bow case
camo ball cap	hunting clothes	Yes	Yes	BP Carry on	BP Carry on

colored handkerchiefs	hunting clothes	Yes	Yes	Duffle Bag	Duffle Bag
belt	hunting clothes	Yes	Yes	out of camp	Duffle Bag
base Layer shirt	hunting clothes	Yes	Yes	out of camp	Duffle Bag
flannel shirt	hunting clothes	Yes	Yes	out of camp	Duffle Bag
gloves-camo heavy	hunting clothes	Yes		out of camp	Duffle Bag
rocky boots	hunting clothes	Yes	Yes	out of camp	Wear it
Batman belt	hunting clothes	Yes	Yes	batman belt	bow case
camo winter Hat	hunting clothes cold	Yes	Yes	batman belt	bow case
Dicki - Camo	hunting clothes cold	Yes	Yes	batman belt	bow case
gloves - mitt and liner	hunting clothes cold	Yes		batman belt	bow case
sweater	hunting clothes cold	Yes	Yes	carry on	carry on
jacket heavy - camo	hunting clothes cold	Yes		BP Hunt	Duffle Bag
long johns - medium	hunting clothes cold	Yes		out of camp	Duffle Bag
long johns - heavy	hunting clothes cold	Yes		out of camp	Duffle Bag
Marion Wool shirt	hunting clothes cold	Yes		out of camp	Duffle Bag
pants heavy - camo	hunting clothes cold	Yes		out of camp	Duffle Bag
rain bibs	hunting clothes rain	Yes	Yes	BP Hunt	Duffle Bag
rain jacket	hunting clothes rain	Yes	Yes	BP Hunt	Duffle Bag
jacket archery scent lock	hunting clothes warm	Yes	Yes	BP Hunt	Duffle Bag
pants archery scent lock	hunting clothes warm	Yes	Yes	out of camp	Duffle Bag
windshear shirt large	hunting clothes warm	Yes		out of camp	Duffle Bag
lense pen	Misc. Equipment	Yes	Yes	bow case	bow case
duct tape	Misc. Equipment	Yes	Yes	BP Carry on	BP Carry on
goggles	Misc. Equipment	Yes		out of camp	Duffle Bag
flashlight	Survival	Yes	Yes	batman belt	bow case
flashlight	Survival	Yes	Yes	batman	bow case

batteries				belt	
GPS, compass & whistle	Survival	Yes	Yes	batman belt	bow case
hand warmers (4)	Survival	Yes	Yes	batman belt	bow case
knife - orange hunting	Survival	Yes	Yes	batman belt	bow case
space blanket	Survival	Yes	Yes	batman belt	bow case
cotton balls and *Vaseline*	Survival	Yes		batman belt	bow case
lighter	Survival	Yes		batman belt	bow case
matches	Survival	Yes		batman belt	bow case
stop bleed	Survival	Yes		batman belt	bow case
water bladder	Survival	Yes		batman belt	bow case
parachute cord	Survival	Yes		BP Hunt	Duffle Bag
garbage bags - heavy	Survival	Yes		BP Hunt	Duffle Bag
GPS batteries	Survival	Yes	Yes	Duffle Bag	Duffle Bag
collapsible water bottles	Survival	Yes		out of camp	Duffle Bag
sheets how to measure	taxidermy	Yes	Yes	batman belt	bow case
tape measure	taxidermy	Yes	Yes	batman belt	bow case
scalpels	taxidermy	Yes	Yes	bow case	bow case
brush	toilet	Yes	Yes	plastic bag	BP Carry on
eye drops	toilet	Yes	Yes	plastic bag	BP Carry on
razor	toilet	Yes	Yes	plastic bag	BP Carry on
shampoo	toilet	Yes	Yes	plastic bag	BP Carry on
toothpaste	toilet	Yes	Yes	plastic bag	BP Carry on
toothbrush	toilet	Yes	Yes	plastic bag	BP Carry on
vitamins	toilet	Yes	Yes	plastic bag	BP Carry on
Kleenex	toilet	Yes		plastic bag	BP Carry on

Scent-free liquid soap	toilet	Yes	Yes	Duffle Bag	Duffle Bag
sun glasses - hunting	travel	Yes	Yes	batman belt	BP Carry on
books or magazines	travel	Yes	Yes	BP Carry on	BP Carry on
cell phone and charger	travel	Yes	Yes	BP Carry on	BP Carry on
hunt paperwork	travel	Yes	Yes	BP Carry on	BP Carry on
passport	travel	Yes	Yes	BP Carry on	BP Carry on
spare glasses	travel	Yes	Yes	BP Carry on	BP Carry on
travel visa	travel	Yes		BP Carry on	BP Carry on
watch	travel	Yes	Yes	out of camp	Wear it
bow - release	archery	No			
bow sling	archery	No			
Lineman's belt	archery	No			
quiver attachment	archery	No			
range finder	archery	No			
blades	archery	No			
bow	archery	No			
bow - arrows	archery	No			
bow - broadheads	archery	No			
quiver	archery	No			
camera bow bracket	archery	No			
stabilizer mitt	archery	No			
blunts	archery	No			
bow - press, serving, strings	archery	No			
fletching waterproof	archery	No			
pull up rope	Climbing	No			
strap to hold pack on tree	Climbing	No			
tree steps	Climbing	No			
bow hanger (2)	Climbing	No			
tether	Climbing	No			
safety harness	Climbing	No			
5 Fingers	clothes-camp	No	Yes		
mag. starter	first aid	No			

bug itch relief stuff	first aid	No			
Septic Stick	first aid	No			
GPS instruction book	first aid	No			
cheesecloth bags	game care	No			
knives - meat cutting	game care	No			
cape salt	game care	No			
plastic wrap	game care	No			
pack frame	game care	No			
foodsaver	game care	No			
foodsaver bags	game care	No			
shipping box	game care	No			
Zip lock bags	game care	No			
silicon cloth	gun	No			
bipod	gun	No			
gun-cleaning equipment	gun	No			
rifle - bore sighter	gun	No			
hand saw	Hunt	No			
calls can	Hunt	No			
calls rattle	Hunt	No			
calls snort weeze	Hunt	No			
deer drag	Hunt	No			
deer scent	Hunt	No			
radio and headset	Hunt	No			
seat cushion	Hunt	No			
water bottles	Hunt	No			
calls grunt	Hunt	No			
calls Grunt call	Hunt	No			
calls mini doe bleat	Hunt	No			
calls small grunt	Hunt	No			
cover scent	Hunt	No			
piss bottle	Hunt	No			
trimmers	Hunt	No			
hip waders	Hunt	No			
mat to stand on	Hunt	No			
white cover	Hunt	No			

pants					
bug net	Hunt	No			
fanny pack, small camo	Hunt	No			
scent lock mask	hunting clothes	No			
gloves wool	hunting clothes	No			
knit hat	hunting clothes	No			
gloves - thin camo	hunting clothes	No			
flannel shirts (2)	hunting clothes	No			
lacrosse boot Hunting socks	hunting clothes	No			
scent lock old coat	hunting clothes	No			
boots camo alphas	hunting clothes	No			
camo pants - light	hunting clothes	No			
camo jacket and liner	hunting clothes	No			
boots old lacrosse	hunting clothes	No			
camo long sleave shirt	hunting clothes	No			
camo pants - fleece	hunting clothes	No			
camo sweatshirt	hunting clothes	No			
camo vest	hunting clothes	No			
gloves - camo mesh	hunting clothes	No			
Lacrosse boot *Gortex* socks	hunting clothes	No			
orange ball cap	hunting clothes	No			
orange vest	hunting clothes	No			
turtle neck	hunting clothes	No			
white cover suit	hunting clothes	No			
treestand umbrella	hunting clothes rain	No			
Windshear shirt	hunting clothes warm	No	Yes		
sun screen	Misc. Equipment	No			
bow - allen wrenches, screw driver	Misc. Equipment	No	Yes		

bow - release spare	Misc. Equipment	No			
food - snacks	Misc. Equipment	No			
boot dryer	Misc. Equipment	No			
knife sharpener	Misc. Equipment	No			
video camera cables	Misc. Equipment	No			
spot light	Misc. Equipment	No			
Thermacell	Misc. Equipment	No			
Thermacell refills	Misc. Equipment	No			
cushion for snow sled	Misc. Equipment	No			
camera - disposable	Misc. Equipment	No			
knives - folding (2)	Misc. Equipment	No			
9-volt battery	Misc. Equipment	No			
bourbon	Misc. Equipment	No			
jock strap	Misc. Equipment	No			
camp pots	Packing out	No			
food - dehydrated	Packing out	No			
gas bottle	Packing out	No			
pack hiking	Packing out	No			
stove	Packing out	No			
tent - two man	Packing out	No			
Musk-ol	Survival	No			
toilet paper	Survival	No			
stick lights	Survival	No			
tarp	Survival	No			
Stop Rot	taxidermy	No			
pipe wrap	taxidermy	No			
hair dryer	toilet	No			
shaving cream	toilet	No			
birth certificate	travel	No			

Lesson – Spending Money on Hunting Clothes

I have no regrets regarding any of the money I spent on hunting trips. I am disappointed in myself with the money spent on various generations of hunting clothing. Hunting clothing, good quality hunting clothes, are expensive, or it seems that way at first. I have spent countless hours staring and comparing items in catalogs like Cabela's. I would narrow it down to a specific jacket or pants, but bringing myself to spend that much money always stopped me. Then, I would settle on a cheaper brand or style in the guise of "saving money." In doing this, I "saved money" so many times, that I could have easily paid for that higher priced but higher quality gear.

The fact is that higher quality gear is worth every penny you spend when you are on a hunt of a lifetime. Cold and wet make miserable hunters and you cannot afford to let those conditions get into your head. Even back home in my own tree stand, these higher quality clothes kept me in stands longer, with more comfort and this translated to more success. I sure wish I had back all that money I spent on clothes that didn't quite cut it.

My advice is to hold off until you can purchase good quality hunting clothes. I would rather see you hunt in Carhart work clothes for a couple years than waste money on cheaper clothes that just don't cut it.

You might be thinking, "But Pete, don't we need good camouflage?" This will ruin my chance of getting a camouflage sponsor, but camo is bullshit. The animals do not care. High-definition camouflage is made for human eyes and marketed to our egos. Do I have it and wear it? Sure I do, I like to dress cool too. But I know it doesn't make or break my hunt. If you break up your pattern at all and be sure to limit your movement, you can still fool animals. A hunter goes out west and dresses in full camo and face paint and is meticulous with scent control, but stands next to the guide in jeans, Carhart jacket, and cowboy hat. They are still successful. The point is, you can wait an extra year and save money for good stuff. Good, high-performance gear can make you a better hunter.

Accommodations

It is a good idea to be conscious of the accommodations of the hunt before you considering booking. Accommodations can range from a five-star resort to being dependent on what you can carry on your back. Each of these experiences has their pluses and minuses and I suggest you make sure it is really what you want. Along with the fun of planning a hunt, accommodations can also add or subtract a lot from your story. I have been on hunts based out of giant log cabin, soft beds, showers and gourmet-style meals, and I have slept on a mountain with my legs stuffed in my backpack to stay warm. Each method can create positive memories, but that depends on your attitude.

Many times, your choice may depend on your health. Often plush accommodations mean an easier hunt, but that cannot be assumed. I like to push myself out of my comfort zone, but not too far out. I want to hunt for my animal and not have it be too easy. When I say easy, I don't mean that the animals are out in the yard waiting for me; it is still hunting and there are no guarantees. Staying at a nice cabin and driving out to a tree stand is an easier hunt than spiking out with a tent and sleeping bag on your back. As I have said before, you need to be honest with yourself and honest with your outfitter and guide because unrealistic expectations will surely sour your hunt.

Coming back to a cabin or resort is nice to clean up, rest up and go at it again tomorrow rested and refreshed, but remember you can only hunt a certain radius if you must come back each night. That is the same radius that the hunters there the week before hunted. Point being, there are only so many animals in that area and over hunting can occur. When you spike out to an area to hunt, you are spiking out into a new area and a whole new set of animals. Researching ahead of time the quality and the number of animals in the area will help you make this decision, but there are many factors like this that can help or hinder your success. I am not going to pretend to be an expert on this, but I will try to break each down with some tips to think about.

The Resort Style

Sometimes you just need to get away from the hustle and bustle of your world and be a little pampered. Yes, even guys need to bask in luxury one time or another. A nice rustic-style cabin, with soft beds, great food, a hot tub or a sauna to relax in and a little bourbon and cigars can be a nice break. Then to be able to go out during the day and chase your favorite game, well it cannot get much better than that. This is a great option if you are getting away with friends or family because you all come back to the same place each night. In many cases, such as Africa, these are awesome places to take the wife along, even if she is a non-hunter. She can spend a quiet day with a good book and the great outdoors while you are chasing your dream animal.

I think my favorite thing about the resort style is that they have clothes dryers. Spend the day hunting in the rain and you will appreciate being able to dry those clothes for the next day. If you are in the bush, you stay wet until the sun shines. Being wet, cold, and clammy is for sure my least favorite thing. Great cooking and a nice bed are an awesome benefit too!

If you come back every night, then you didn't get very far away from the resort. Depending on the game animal you hunt, that might not be a bad thing. Things like waterfowl and wing shooting are typically well suited for this type of environment. Whitetail deer operations often are run from central lodges; now we are leaning toward it becoming an issue. Are the stands fresh? If you are the third week into the season and your stand has been hunted hard for two weeks, then deer might avoid the stand because of human scents left behind, or perhaps the deer were spooked by previous hunters. What if the guy before you tagged a giant and that just happened to be the only giant in the area? These types of lodges often have many hunters at the same time. When they choose stands based on wind direction and other factors, some stands stand out as great, good, and really not so good. If you are last to be placed in the stand, what stand do you think you get that day?

Going after larger game out of a resort is even trickier. You often spend a lot of time getting there and back. I can think of many times where you might finally see an animal to pursue, but it is too far away or too late in the day to go after it. Will it still be there when you get back the next day? I highly doubt it. If you are using vehicles to get in the field, then you are typically road hunting. You won't get off the road until you see an animal worthy of stalking. Horses get you deeper in the bush, but they also take a lot of time getting there. If you are hiking from the resort, then you aren't getting very far away at all. Hunters will boast how many miles they walked in a day, but the truth is they didn't go that far at all. Strap a GPS on their ass and the bullshit stops. In all cases you are limiting yourself to how much ground you can cover and you are at the mercy of the animal population in that little area.

Cabin in the Bush

In this case you typically travel a long way into the bush by 4-wheel drive, ATV, or maybe horse. If the cabin is near a lake, we might be talking about a fly-in hunt using a bush or float plane. No matter how you get there, you are spending time getting into the wild first, and then you stay there in some sort of remote cabin. Because it is hard to get you back in that far, then it is safe to assume getting supplies in to build and furnish a cabin is even harder. It could be an actual log cabin, made on the spot with many man-hours of labor and sweat. It could be a shack, thrown together with any materials they manage to carry to that area. It could be a wall tent, or even smaller tents you carry in with you. Needless to say, things can get a lot less comfortable.

Non-hunters might be willing to tag along on this kind of trip, but I highly doubt it. Unless they are going right with you while hunting, they would be stuck at the camp with little to do. Venturing out on their own probably would be frowned upon unless there were good trails to follow. You should think that through for yourself because you might be the lucky one to bag your animal early in the week. What do you do to occupy your time for the remaining days? I have never had an issue with this because I just walk around smiling, relaxing and enjoying the tranquility of the wilderness. I also pitch in and help around camp, work on my trophy, and just maybe have a beer or two. It really comes down to what you want, a TV and a pool table in a resort, or free time just chilling in the wild.

Deer and bear hunts of this type are pretty good because you are now living in the middle of where the animals live. You will often hear stories of hunters bagging their game from camp. You might even get an unwelcome visitor at night. These types of hunts lend themselves well to bigger, more remote game. You might be at the base of a mountain range where you can climb after an animal if one of good caliber is spotted from the valley. You might venture out in all directions to spot and stalk game living in the adjacent areas.

You are still limited by this hunt based on what you have available to travel in or on. An ATV or snowmobile will help you increase your available range. A horse will too, but much slower. The horse's advantage is their ability to cross rough terrain. In most cases you are going to be travelling in just your boots. This is where you need to be real honest with your health and physical preparation. You will be limited by what you can do physically, and that can become very evident, very quick. The amount of time travelling becomes an issue and you might have to pass on a stalk because you need to get back to camp before dark.

Timing of your hunt is very important to consider. If the structure is permanent, then it will be more comfortable than a tent, but that also means many hunters have hunted out of it for years, and more importantly maybe the weeks before you arrived. I want the freshest area possible that has had no human scent left anywhere that might spook the animals. If your camp is a tent, then quite possibly they are moving that tent around to fresh areas each time. A fresh area does not guarantee animals. Outfitters and their guides are great at what they do, but they are only as good as the information they have. I think the lesson to consider is to do your homework and have realistic expectations.

Being in the bush means you have fewer creature comforts and you will have to pack in a different way. You typically live in your hunting clothes, often sleeping in them. Keeping dry and getting dry needs to be one of your top priorities. This means good gear that can take the weather and protect you at all costs.

Bush meals are awesome, but they won't be quite gourmet. Get in the mindset that you are eating to fuel your body and recover and you will be okay with what you get to eat. It will all be worth it when you bag your trophy and get to share the back strap with the rest in camp. Damn, my mouth waters just thinking about the taste of fresh tenderloin.

Spiking Out

You need to go where the game lives to be successful and spiking out is by far the best way to find those game-rich areas. Spiking out means putting whatever you need on your back and doing whatever it takes to get to where game likes to live. Packs filled with clothes, tents, sleeping bags, and food can be heavy to carry making your physical preparation for the hunt highly important. Trust me when I say, building up your core muscles so you can stabilize and support a heavy pack is a must. A weak core transfers the load to other muscles that are not designed to carry that weight. This will sap your energy quickly and I guarantee soreness and pain will quickly set in. If I could only work out one area of the body, the core would be my first choice. I know that I lost most of you by suggesting core training. I promise, once you have a solid core you will regret not doing it sooner. Yes, core training sucks!

The good thing about carrying everything you need on your back is that you don't have to pack much. You do however need to pack smart. Sadly, packing smart often comes with experience and only experience will tell you what gadgets you can leave behind. You need to be extremely conscious of every ounce you carry because they all add up to pounds. Light-weight gear can be costly, so you need to factor this into the cost of your hunt.

If it is worth carrying, it is worth carrying all the time. My guide and I were at a tent at the base of a mountain in British Columbia. I wanted a mountain goat. Legally, you must pack the entire goat off the mountain if you kill one. So, we emptied our packs of everything but the essentials and started to climb. Once we hit 5000 feet we had a decision to make. Unless we wanted to hike through grizzly country in the dark, we had to stay the night on the mountain. My choice was to stay on the mountain because I did not want to end the hunt. At 7000 feet we decided to make camp on a very, very steep slope in some spruce trees. Except for a wool sweater that I carried, I left everything else at the tent, even that space blanket I have carried for many years. As the sun set and the clear skies let all the heat from the earth escape, I could have really used that space blanket. My only choice was to put my feet and legs in my pack, cover my upper body with a garbage bag, and suck it up till morning. Luckily the rain and snow stayed away. Twenty-four hours later, when we looked back up the mountain from the tent, the spot on the mountain where we camped was covered in snow. Never, ever assume you will get lucky, like I did. If you carry it for your survival, then you should carry it each and every time you pack out.

The only way to hunt that area for goat was to spike out. We pushed ourselves to our limits and beyond making it a truly fulfilling trip. We never even saw a mountain goat, but it was one of the greatest experiences of my life. I did come home and purchase better and lighter equipment, which I will carry with me every time. I will not ever want to base my safety on luck ever again.

Montana Mountain Lion, Another Attempt for a Cat

Harrisburg Pennsylvania has a huge outdoor show that became a favorite mid-winter weekend trip for us. I was interested in mountain lion, and we first met Holly at the outdoor show. When we got home, Holly called and told me she liked talking to Dean and me, and wondered if we would hunt with her if she dropped her price. I jumped at the deal. I remember sending Dean an email saying just this: "You are going to Montana in December for mountain lion." He responded back, "Cool."

Lessons of a Lion Hunter

It never ceases to amaze me; No matter how many videos I watch, or stories I read, I never seem to fully understand what they are telling me until after I've been on my hunt and seen things for myself. After you return from a hunt, you watch videos differently. You don't see the steepness of the hills the hunters are on until you've walked those hills yourself. When they say, "You'd better get in shape for a lion hunt," this is advice that should not be taken lightly. For anyone planning on a mountain lion hunt, you should do yourself a favor and listen carefully to the lessons of a lion hunter.

Initiation Day

The first day of our five-day Montana mountain lion hunt, with Rebel Outfitting, started a little earlier than expected. Due to flight schedules, we flew in the day before and stayed in Missoula, Montana. Even though we slept late with respect to our usual work schedule, due to the time difference, we were still wide-awake at 4:30 in the morning. Little did we know it would be forty hours later before we would find our way back to bed. You see, you can't put your dogs on a lion track until one half hour before sunrise on opening day. But we hadn't truly considered the possibility of finding a lion track before anyone else. Holly, of Rebel Outfitters, picked us up at noon. Due to blizzard-like conditions we got to camp near dinnertime. The surprise came when we left to look for lion tracks at 9:00 that night. No time to sleep, the lion hunt was on.

Eight inches of new snow made the mountain trails look like a winter wonderland. These were perfect conditions for finding a lion track. Full of anticipation, we spent the entire night studying every dimple in the new snow. Elk, moose, bobcat, whitetail, and mule deer tracks were everywhere, all looking the same to me. As the night grew longer and eyelids grew heavy, the sight of wolf tracks brought me to the realization that this was the true wilderness. As the sun came up, and another "second wind" came upon me, I started to see that the trails and switchbacks were mere scars in the mountain side, dug out by some smoke jumpers, or a logger. The mountain walls went straight up on one side and straight down on the other. The thought of a mere slip of the truck sent shivers up my spine. Trees would catch the truck if it slid off most edges, but in spots, we'd tumble over and over for minutes. The vastness and the steepness of the country started to sink in. It was like an extension ladder leaning up against a house, but this ladder was not measured in feet—it was measured in fractions of a mile.

Rebel and I saw no lion tracks that first night. Early that morning we got a beep of a cell phone message from Chuck, who was guiding Dean. Let it be known that cellular coverage in the mountains is hit or mostly miss. It wasn't until after 11:00 AM that we could finally get service and hear the message. We learned that they had found a track at two o'clock that morning. As we drove toward where the tracks were found, we stumbled on a mountain lion track that also featured dog tracks. The cat and dogs had already made it over a very formidable-looking mountain that was littered with fallen trees. Listening very carefully, off in the bottom of the canyon, we could hear the faint barks of hounds at the tree. Somehow, we needed to determine if Chuck and Dean were going to make it over the mountain and into the canyon before darkness came. We drove on up the trail and found their truck. The GPS told me the distance from the parked truck to where we found the tracks crossing the road was six miles. That is as the raven flies, not how a lion runs. Problem was, it was straight up for thousands of feet, and we were pretty sure the cat did not run a straight line. Those guys were in for a long, grueling day. We thought this just might be a day they could not finish. This would prove to be Dean's initiation into lion hunting.

It is an unwritten rule not to start dogs on a lion track that someone else may be running. Besides, if the guys did make it over that mountain, they would have more than paid their dues and would truly deserve to get that cat. We decided we would circle the canyon and drop down the other side. With fresh dogs, we would hold the cat in the tree until dark, or Dean's arrival. If dark came before Dean, I would shoot the cat, and we would retrieve all the dogs. The only thing that stops the dogs is a cat in the tree. Treed cat or not, you follow the dogs' tracks until you catch them. If Chuck and Dean couldn't make it to the tree before dark, they would be extremely grateful that we saved them from having to chase dogs into the canyon in the dark.

We drove the 4 x 4 Dodge to the other side of the canyon. A gated road would allow us to walk to a spot somewhere above the dogs. This felt like a pretty easy trip, until we walked miles and miles without as much as a whimper of a hound. The lion had obviously jumped tree and the chase was back on. This took us even farther down the edge of the canyon. Finally, a faint bark led us to the spot where the only thing left was straight down. Over the edge we went, getting traction by digging the sides of our boots into the snow-covered bank. Loose rocks, weak twigs and slippery grass made it a tensioned filled descent. As I scaled down the bank, I wondered just how fast I would hit the bottom, if my feet slipped.

As I crossed the creek at the bottom of the canyon, I looked straight up to the next phase in my initiation. The cat and dogs went up, and so I had to as well. In a matter of minutes everything in my body started to burn. My thighs creaked as I pressed my weight, the weight of my pack and bow up the hill. Not being used to the thinner air overtook me. I felt as if I were going to exhale my lungs into the snow. I was physically spent in no time, yet the only way out of that canyon was up. I had no choice but to push on. Rebel, who I think is part mountain goat, was up the canyon wall in no time. Rebel yelled to me to keep following his tracks, as he disappeared out of sight. The only thing that kept me going was the thought that the road, where we first saw the tracks, was somewhere near the top of this hell that I had gotten myself into.

Near the top, Rebel passed me again, heading back down toward the bottom of the canyon. The cat had changed directions and was heading down the hill. Before I started back down the way I came, I stopped for a moment and took a picture. I figured when they found my camera they would know where I had been, and would understand why I was frozen in the snow with my lungs lying by my side. As it turned out, the cat had circled me while I was gasping for air. The lion walked on my footsteps and headed to the bottom of the canyon. In the confusion, the dogs started to run the cat trail backwards. Our day was over, and the only thing left to do was to climb out of the canyon and make the multi-mile walk back to the truck. Of course, the dogs were headed back toward Chuck's truck, probably ten or more miles away. It would be very late before we ever saw a dog again.

Even the walk on the gated road was painful. My hips and knees had not experienced this kind of prolonged stress before. At this point, I still was unsure of making it to the truck. The pain was growing extreme. As we rounded a corner, there stood Rodney with all our dogs. Somehow, he heard them in the canyon and was able to cut them off. This was a welcome sight. Now all we needed to do was get to the truck and go home. But, now that Rebel had his dogs, he turned to me and said, "I can get that cat, if you can make it back into the canyon." One of the most painful things I have ever had to say was "No, I just can't make it." Now, my pride hurt worse than my body. Little did I know that my personal failure would haunt me more and more each day.

Getting into dry clothes and a warm meal was a great way to end the day. My knees and hips could only muster one more climb up the stairs to bed. The forty-hour initiation day was over, and we could finally get some sleep. But, when they say lion hunting is not for the meek, they mean it. Rebel and the others, still with no sleep, went back in the mountains looking for the next day's cat track. For these guys it is a passion, not a job. It is what they live for.

Day 2: How we thought lion hunting might be.

The phone rang at 4:00 AM, but Dean and I were already awake and refreshed. Rebel had cut a "smoking fresh" lion track and Chuck was on his way to get us. Adrenaline spiked as we gathered our gear. Another fresh coating of snow met us at the door. Stars filled the sky. The smell of the wood burning stove mixed with the cold crisp fresh air. Not even a cup of coffee can start your day like the news of a fresh lion track.

We met at a mountain road intersection to discuss the game plan. Two trucks would circle the timber, making sure the cat had not left the area. This is where teamwork proved itself. When all the trucks convened at the cat track, we had verified the cat was still in the timber, and probably very close.

Rodney, Dean, and Cory would go with the dogs. This was Dean's turn, since I had turned down my chance at the first day's cat. A hard lesson for me to handle, but I was excited for Dean. Rebel, Chuck, and I would stay with the trucks until we could hear the lion treed. We would then take the opportunity to walk young dogs to the tree for their first experience at a treed lion. It wasn't long until we heard the sweet sound of dogs barking at the tree. Off we went up the mountain, young dogs pulling us up the hill. I'll tell you, it is so much easier climbing up those hills when you can hear the ever-louder bellows of hounds at the tree. As I approached, I could see the cat in the tree. What an awesome sight: such a beautiful, majestic, terrifying animal. Then I saw a campfire, which is the first thing Rodney always builds to ward off the cold. Dean was bouncing between taking pictures and getting his bow ready. It felt more like a campout than a hunt. You can take your time getting to the tree, and getting ready. If the cat does decide to jump tree, you just start the process over again.
To be able to witness my hunting partner get his cat was a great experience. I was able to watch him live out what I had dreamed of doing. His tomcat was a great cat with a large head and huge paws. Video tape and pictures were taken of the whole event. It was a bunch of men and dogs who love to hunt celebrating a textbook lion chase. If our hunt ended right there, it would still have been one of the greatest memories in my hunting career.

Day 3 – The roller coaster ride to the bottom.

Hunting is always a roller-coaster ride. Long, agonizing climbs to a point where you break over the top and experience a short but very intense thrill. Then you hit bottom again, where the days are long and doubts of when you might make it to the top fill your head. At the start of the day I was confident and still reeling from the excitement and success of Dean's cat. As the miles of mountain trails went by, and fatigue settled in, the day grew very long. As we headed home I had mixed emotions. On one hand, I had two days left and all the resources working for me. On the other hand, I couldn't help but think that I might have already passed up my chance.

Day 4 – Superman, 0 to 100 in 6 seconds.

The fourth day was every bit as long as day three. To make matters worse, this was the first day without a fresh coating of snow. Now the numbers of tracks were doubled; both fresh and old tracks drove us crazy. To top it all off, the quota for the area had been filled and no more cats could be taken after days end. Now, all the competition on these mountains would move to the next nearest area, doubling the number of lion rigs looking for that now allusive cat print. As two o'clock that afternoon grew near, I had started to come to grips that I would be going home without a mountain lion. We had to hit the new area hard and early, so we decided to quit for the day, get some sleep and start out early that evening. I was at the bottom of the Superman coaster and the chain was broken. There was no way to the top. Worst of all, I might be going home empty handed and the only person I could blame was myself.

Dean and I were riding with Chuck as we followed Rebel and Rodney down the road, a long and quiet trip home. All the sudden, Rebel slammed on the brakes and Rodney jumped from the truck. He ran to the back of the truck and swung his hand over the trail in a crossing motion. A fresh lion track! The Superman coaster was fixed and the adrenaline coursed through me. The game was on, but we had less than three hours of daylight left to get this cat in a tree.

The dogs were dumped on the track. Rebel yelled to Rodney to grab his pack and follow the dogs. The rest of us would split up with the trucks and see if we could guess where the cat might tree. Rebel and I went up one path and down another, reminiscent of a scene from Dukes of Hazzard. We stopped and listened along the way. Sometimes we could hear a faint bark, but we weren't sure if it was real or just our minds hoping to hear a dog. Rebel described the cat as a long, lanky female, one that was sure to be a runner. He feared this cat was not big.

We met up with Chuck and Dean. They had found the track. Gambling, we split up again and cut the track four more times. This cat was on the move. Cat tracks, dog tracks, and Rodney tracks streaked across the trails. We entered a canyon on a dead-end road. Luckily, we could faintly hear the dogs in the distance. The cat was treed. The sun was rapidly falling and the end of the day was near, so we geared up and started the climb toward the sound. Part way up the hill we cut the track, and saw Rodney running toward us. He had run all the way up and down the steep hills for miles. Probably the single most impressive super human effort I have ever seen. We had to hurry though—less than one hour until the day was officially over.

The dog barks grew louder as we approached the tree, a sound that brings incredible joy to a lion hunter. As we looked up into the tree, my heart sank. There was no cat in the tree! Disbelief overtook me, as I stood clinging to the bank struggling to catch my breath. Then Rebel yelled that the lion was in the next tree over. Somehow the dogs were barking at the wrong tree. To everyone's surprise, the cat was bigger than expected, but still difficult to tell as the cat crouched in the tree. The decision was quick: considering the effort put into this run and that my chances were growing thin, there was no way I could pass a second time.

I climbed the hill above the tree. It was so steep it was difficult to stand. Dampness in the snow made every footprint slippery as ice. I prepared my bow. Ice had encrusted the cams and string and covered my arrow shafts. All the ice had to come off before I could even think of drawing the bow. I chipped at the ice and warmed the string. I slowly drew the bow, cringing in fear the string might pop from the icy cams.

The cat was positioned such that branches and pine needles covered its vitals. She was probably thirty-plus feet up in the tree. She shifted only to better her position on the branches. For the most part she seemed only disgusted by the intrusion. Her eyes squinted as if she wished the dogs would just stop making noise. Every now and then she would growl like only a mountain lion can, her pure white fangs glowing in the shadows of the tree. We discussed the best arrow placement, but we didn't seem to be agreeing. Thank God for video cameras. I zoomed in close and froze the picture. Now we could point at the screen instead of thirty feet in the air. It was only then that we agreed on the best place to put the arrow. This would have to be the best shot I've ever made. There was no room for error.

Darkness came fast and I was worried about not being able to see my sight pins. The cat, already hidden in the shadows, blended in more and more as the light faded away. We knew Chuck and Dean would make it sooner or later, and we really wanted to wait for them to share this experience. But with rapidly fading light, I had to make the decision to shoot. At less than ten yards from the base of the tree, I tried to get my feet in position. My back leg had to be bent way up, almost like leaning against a barstool. The cat had moved a bit, but the shot would still be tight. Rebel and Rodney readied their handguns — safety of people and dogs is always the priority. Rodney asked me if they needed them. Unsure yet confident, I said "No." Then I explained, "I should be able to tell you if you need to shoot."

Archers call it the mystical flight of the arrow. Until you've shot an arrow the proper way, you don't know what this means. The best way I can describe it is "wishing the arrow into the spot." As I bent backward and raised my bow, everything felt perfect. The next thing I knew the arrow flew into the only spot it could for a clean kill. I yelled, "That cat is dead, don't shoot," as the cat fell from the tree. Two bounds and eight seconds later the cat tumbled down the hill. On the ground, we could see that the cat was far larger than we'd thought, turning out to be a great trophy. For six years I had dreamt of this moment.

Dean and I booked with Rebel Outfitting of Lone Pine, Montana, for two specific reasons. When we met them at an outdoor show their personalities and kindness outshined all others there. They also had the resources and dogs to run two hunters a week, in separate directions. Little did I know that the best part of the hunt was the teamwork involved in the chase, the ability to be at the tree when a good friend took his cat, and the celebration and jubilation of all involved when the team was successful. In most cases, a hunter-outfitter relationship is a business relationship. When I said goodbye the last morning, I felt like I was saying goodbye to a brother, and his family and friends. The type of people that would do anything for you, just because it's the right thing to do.

Being in Hunt Shape

The Montana mountain lion hunt was a humbling experience for me. I thought I was in shape, and I was wrong. There is no doubt in my mind that it cost me a chance at a giant lion the first day. Not only did my knee completely lock up, which was an unexpected experience for me, but I also did not have the lungs I needed to hike the mountains, especially at the pace needed to keep up with an aggressive set of mountain lion dogs.

I learned a lot from that lion hunt; being humbled is always a brutal teacher. The fear of a failed hunt focused me on what it really meant to be ready for a hunt. Failing to get an animal on a hunt is part of the hunting game. I can live with that. But being the cause of my own failure was the issue I needed to deal with and prevent from ever happening again.

Now there are a lot of hunts that might not require you to be in "mountain-climbing shape." But here is where I caution you. You might think a guided tree-stand hunt for whitetail in another state is easy. Hell, I hunt whitetail in tree stands back home with little to no issue. It isn't necessarily the same thing, so beware of what you are getting into. I have had to climb big hills to hunt a saddle on the hilltop. I have had to climb gully banks to hunt bean fields carved out of the top of hills. Granted they were short hikes, but I sucked wind nevertheless. My point is, do not underestimate the differences in terrain from your usual hunting back home. Also, don't forget, you still have to get that giant buck out of wherever he decided to expire.

Mountain climbing is a whole different ball game. There is an interesting phenomenon that nobody picks up on until they return from a brutal hike up a mountain. When you watch that stuff on TV, the slope never looks as bad as it is. The reason is that we all tend to lean out just a little when we take a camera shot or video. Leaning away from the slope makes it look less steep in the picture. If the camera were level, you would shit your pants about how steep it really is.

You cannot underestimate any hike that may or may not be on level ground or rolling hills. Add a heavy pack, heavy boots, constricting hunting clothes, and a bow or rifle and all the sudden you are trudging along with a ton of weight you are not used to. Then add the fact that most places where game live are in the Godforsaken, brush-filled, rock-covered areas that make it nearly impossible to walk.

The bottom line is, you will quickly find muscles that you did not know you had. If you did not know you had them, then obviously you forgot to train them. You might say, "Well I walked with a weighted pack on to get prepared." What you fail to realize is that every degree difference in your step requires a different muscle or the same muscle to react a different way. Training one-dimensionally, like running for example, only trains your muscles in one specific way. That way is always the wrong way, because the conditions are always different.

Doing the same routine over and over is only good for so long. Yes, you still might be burning off calories, but you are only training certain muscles in the same direction every time. As a matter of fact you can, and people often do, train their muscles in the wrong direction or use a muscle that is not suited for that task. For example, if you have a poorly developed core because you hate core work like everyone else on the planet, you will lift with your back. Next comes back strain, then back pain, and you sitting on your ass not doing the hunting you want to do because you are now laid up.

Lungs rank right up there with the much-needed things for a successful hunt. I don't care how well you shoot, if you are gasping for air at the moment of truth, you will fail to make that shot. Or worse, you will fail to even get to the spot where you might see an animal.

Reminds me of the smoking farmer in his work coveralls that claims profoundly, "I always get a deer," Yeah, you shoot the dumb ones. The big ones never show themselves because they know exactly where you are and avoided you long ago.

Cardio is a wicked bitch too. You can train your ass off for a year, then get twenty yards into the hike on a hunt and be gasping for air like you are trying to breathe through a clear plastic bag. That really isn't a cardio problem, it's an anxiety issue. Hiking and climbing is really a simple task. Just breathe normally and take a step. I consciously had to tell myself just to breathe and walk. When climbing the mountain, every now and then I would look up at a steep part and a little panic would set in and I would start gasping for air. Gasping is fruitless because you don't really get the oxygen your body needs, then your muscles want to quit. Telling myself to simply breathe would immediately bring more oxygen in and the body would respond. Next thing you know you conquered that steep part that had just scared you. Always take time to calm down, breathe, and talk to yourself if you need to.

This all sounds great Pete, but I have only worked out on January 2nd of each year, after I got drunk and made a stupid New Year's Resolution. I get that. Now I will explain how scheduling hunting trip one or two years in advance serves as my motivation to get in better shape.

None of us want to do anything we don't have to. Half of us would never get out of bed unless you had to pee, eat, or work. I want to live longer and healthier, but have trouble motivating myself to work out. But when I have a hunt booked, I Immediately put this pressure on myself to be better. One, I don't want to fail because I was not in good enough shape to get the job done. The mountain lion hunt taught me that. Then, when dangerous game is concerned, I owe it to myself, my loved ones who want me to come back home, and the guide whose life is also on the line at the moment of truth to be the best I can possibly be. I need to be a great shot, so I practice shooting diligently. I need to be calm and not gasping for air, so I get myself in the best shape possible.

Booking a hunting trip is the excuse I use to make myself a better person, becoming stronger and fitter each day. This is an unknown benefit to booking a hunt ahead of time. The days I don't want to do it, I think about the hunt. I think about the money I will be spending. I think about the danger I could be in. I think about the success I will have because I am in shape and tough as nails.

Lesson – Living your life

I just made a comment that I wanted to stay healthy and in shape to live longer. Most of us would make that comment. That is not what I really think; I could give a shit if I live longer. What I really care about is that I "actually live" during the years that I have. Getting old and sitting on my ass is not my goal. My goal is to do things while I can that have meaning to my life. I will bank those memories for the time I finally have to slow down and start to take it easy.

Lesson – It starts in your head

The first few minutes of anything, an exercise routine, a hike with extra weight, or a mountain climb can make you or break you. First, getting moving is harder than staying moving, especially when you are getting older. It takes time to get the body warmed up and moving fluidly. Second, for most of us these demons creep into your head and you immediately doubt you can do this. When that happens, a little anxiety kicks in, a little panic feeling takes over and you start to breathe harder. Gasping for air does nothing but rob your muscles of oxygen. In a few short steps, your body feels like it cannot continue.

BREATHE!!!

Just breathe and put one foot in front of the other. If you simply concentrate on that, you will make it up that hill or through that exercise routine. We tend to look far ahead to the end and that end looks unreachable, but if you just keep chugging, next thing you know you will be there.

This isn't easy and it takes some willpower. Sometimes you need to talk to yourself. Part way up the mountain in British Columbia, I was holding my own. It was hard work, but I just kept stepping up. I was feeling quite good about myself. We paused to take a drink. When we decided to start again, I looked up to the top of the mountain. It immediately got into my head. I cannot make it up there, I thought. Each step after that was agonizing. My heart raced, and I gasped for air. Doubt filled my head and I thought we should turn back. I literally said to myself, "You dumb fuck, two minutes ago you were kicking ass." I paused to take a few deep breaths to slow my breathing and my heart, and then said to myself, "One step at a time." Next thing I know I am busting up the mountain again with no issue. Don't let shit get into your head! More importantly, be aware when it does and fight it.

Wisconsin and Minnesota Deer – Combining Your Trips

I have been to multiple states hunting big whitetails and failed each time. Each trip had its memories and experiences and I wouldn't trade them for the world. As you can figure out by now, the planning and the trip is most of the fun.

I do believe that in order to kill a giant whitetail, you need to be either really lucky or really good. They don't get big and old without being smart. These hunts have humbled me, thinking maybe I am not in the league yet to kill a giant. But I will put my time in and bet on a little luck coming my way one day.

The lesson to be pointed out on this particular trip was the fact that we combined hunts and visited friends. We had booked a hunt in the famous Buffalo County, Wisconsin. On the way, my brother was in Minnesota and had some friends that would allow us to hunt their land, so we grabbed some Minnesota tags and climbed some trees. For a few extra bucks we got in a few more days hunting and got to spend time with family and new friends.

Hunt trips don't all have to be big and expensive to be good. There is a ton of great hunting out there and the beautiful thing about hunters is they love to share stories and land with hunters that are willing to put in the time. Never underestimate how much fun you can have, and know that any tree stand might just be where your luck is waiting for you.

British Columbia Grizzly

The North East Outdoor show is deemed the largest outdoor show in the East. Held in a gigantic complex in Harrisburg, Pennsylvania, called the Farm Show complex, it proves to be an awesome sight for a hunter. In February, when the New York winter is getting very old and tiresome, a weekend trip to this outdoor show is a great getaway. I have gone there many years and made some outfitter friends. A few of my hunts were with outfitters who had booths there and it was always fun to stop and catch up. Some outfitter displays were hard to pass by, and Denny Geurink's eleven-foot standing brown bear mount was always one of them.

As you might recall from earlier in the book, I have always dreamed of hunting a brown bear with a bow. So, trying to walk by this beautiful bear mount without stopping and talking was hard to do. Denny has a great sales pitch: you can see many bears, it is in Russia, and the cost beats any bear hunt in Alaska. The difference this year was that I had just wound down the payments of my divorce. I had learned to live on nothing for years and now I had extra money in my pocket. Quickly doing some math in my head, I imagined I could do this hunt if I booked out two years.

I have never made a split-second decision at the show. I think it is prudent to think it over for a while at home. This one was really tugging on my shirttail, because I wanted to book it so bad. Being a thinker and a planner, I had to make sure I had all my bases covered. Everything was possible, except I had one nagging little thought in the back of my mind. I wanted to shoot a bear with my bow. Sadly, you cannot hunt brown bear with a bow in Russia.

That didn't really stop me from wanting to go. I had talked myself into every other aspect of it. Going to Russia was also a bucket list item and hunting there, especially that deep in the wild was an awesome thought. I thought however that if I could afford Russia, maybe I could afford to hunt in North America with the bow. So, the research started.

Brown bear in North America is expensive, but grizzly bear in British Columbia proved more in my budget range. There is a river that runs inland called the Fraser River. The salmon run up that river to spawn and end up feeding one of the densest populations of interior grizzlies on the planet. These grizzlies eat well and can get bigger than their brothers that forage the mountains for food. Brown bear and grizzly are of the same genus, but the brown bears live on the coast where the salmon run. They have better, fatter food to gorge themselves on, so they get bigger. This spot in British Columbia, nicknamed Grizzly Bear Mountain, is just a rare anomaly, where interior grizzlies have the same advantages as their coastal brown bear brothers.

A good population of grizzly bears, a spot on a salmon run river in the fall, and I could hunt them with the bow if I chose. I made up my mind, I had to pursue that dream I started thirty years earlier.

I found an outfitter, Kiff Covert, who had a camp right along the Fraser River. I told him my desire to hunt with a bow and that excited him. He had a tree stand along the river and he would guarantee it was mine, if I promised to try my best with the bow. It was a deal I could not pass up, so the planning and the saving started. I was now booked to hunt grizzly bear with a bow. A lifelong dream was coming to fruition.

Flying into Prince George, British Columbia, I overnighted in a hotel there. The next morning, I was to be picked up and driven to bear camp. I was warned by Kiff that my guide did not speak very good English, so I really had no idea what to expect. A dirty black suburban pulled up, and out climbed two Germans to greet me. The back seat of the suburban was already piled high with gear, and a large dog was in the very back. By the time we stuffed my gear on top of the existing pile, there was hardly any room left, and especially no place to sit. Thomas, my guide and the driver and owner of the suburban, had brought his brother Markus who was vacationing from Germany. One front seat for two guys; I was really starting to doubt my choices. Markus climbed through the back window on top of all the gear and lay there for the entire ride to camp.

I find the greatest thing about the hunting community is that we can still talk hunting, even when we don't speak the same language. It was awkward at first, but we could tell stories. I, being the foreigner in this situation, chose to speak loud and slow as if that was going to really help. They were learning English and would stumble to say things, often stopping and asking if they had said it correctly.

We took the long drive to a base camp, a cabin they used for some hunts like black bear and elk. There we waited for Kiff to arrive, and took the opportunity to sight my rifle in. I brought both the rifle and the bow. I would hunt hard with the bow, but I wanted the insurance that I could take home a bear with the rifle if time was running out.

Kiff arrived and we had our introductions. Grizzly camp on the river was still a long drive away. Thomas and I took an old beat up Bronco which was a truck they used to travel the mountain roads. Markus brought Thomas' suburban, because he would use it to camp in since he was not technically part of the hunt. Kiff would meet us at camp the next day, as he was going shopping for supplies.

There was a major highway that we had to travel for some time before turning off and taking logging roads to camp. The old Bronco whined and rattled as we sped down the road. We were talking about the chance of seeing a grizzly and getting a shot at one, when all the sudden a grizzly ran out in front of us. Slamming on the brakes, the grizzly passed mere feet in front of the beat-up four-wheel drive. We just looked at each other and smiled. It was going to be a good hunt!

Camp was nestled on a small lake in the bottom of a wooded valley. Near the lake was an old log cabin where the kitchen and dining took place. A very nice woman and her husband had been hired to care for camp and us. They would sleep in the back of this cabin. Another old cabin and shed off to the left were for the guides and the generator and wood. A nice new cabin was set back from the rest, this would be my home. I was the only hunter in camp for the first three days. This was a rare treat, as hunting camps go. The dining cabin walls were loaded with history. This cabin was over 100 years old, and one of the original proprietors was buried out front by the lake with a simple wooden cross marking his plot. A book by Jack Boudreau called *Grizzly Bear Mountain* describes in detail the history of the largest population of interior grizzlies on the planet.

We would hunt the next morning, so I was able to shoot some arrows at an old target setting near the outhouse. We had very few supplies, since Kiff was not due in until tomorrow, but our camp cook was amazing and she could cook anything out of nothing, keeping us very well fed. The day was bright and sunny and sitting on the cabin porch overlooking the lake was beautiful and peaceful.

We all sat around getting to know each other, them being as interested in my life as I was theirs. We in the lower U.S. think our Canadian neighbors are like us, but this is tough country. These people are hard workers, living as much off the land as they count on their jobs for income. Thomas told of his first winter in Canada, renting a trailer to live in. The first cold day his water supply froze. Walking a few miles to the neighbors to have someone to complain to, he expressed why he thought the owner was stupid not to have heat tape on the pipe. Thomas told us that his neighbor just looked at him and said, "It will thaw out in the spring."

We would head out the next morning as the sun came up. There was no need to go in when it was pitch black since the bears would feed on the salmon (if they were running) anytime during the day. Plus, it would be dangerous to walk through the trees in the dark since bears could be there sleeping off their last belly full of fish. We climbed the narrow trail out of the valley and onto the logging road. The spot was only a few miles down the dirt-logging road. Pulling to the side of the road, we gathered our gear and headed into the woods toward the river. Thomas asked me to knock an arrow because the possibilities were good that we could walk in on a bedded bear.

Nearing the river, I looked up into a giant tree and saw a wooden platform stand. I could hear the water rushing, but could barely see it through the thick brush. As we got to the tree, Thomas immediately started to climb the wooden ladder. As I looked up, watching him climb, he abruptly turned to me and motioned toward me with his open palm. I wrinkled my face to show that I did not understand and he put his finger to his lips to shush me, then point down toward the water. I turned toward the river and just on the other side of the brush, I could make out the form of a grizzly bear, less than ten yards away. Thomas was stopped half way up the tree, I had nowhere to go, and a bear was fishing a few feet from me. I stared at him waiting for our eyes to meet, knowing if they did I would be in big trouble. Luckily, the rushing water drowned out our sound and that bear never knew I was there. He fished on down the river. We finished climbing into the stand and stared, smiled, and high-fived each other. Two days and we were within arm's reach of two grizzlies. I must say, I was way more comfortable seeing the first one from a truck.

The platform was large. Thomas sat in a chair and I stood by the tree with the bow in hand. Blood was still pumping fast through my veins as I settled in for the morning. The sun was showing itself over the horizon and the morning fog gently lifted off the river. A slight chill ran up my back as the morning sunrise always drops the temperature a few degrees. The sunlight danced off the river waves like diamonds floating by. The river was about fifty yards wide where we were, so any bear walking by was in reasonable bow range. I was in heaven. I get emotional just thinking of that moment in time.

There were a few salmon swimming by. You could see their dorsal fins break the water as they pushed up river. In spots they had to wiggle across the shallow rocks. They proved to be very entertaining as the morning hours passed.

To my left and downstream, a tree had fallen into the river, about fifty yards away. For a bow hunter, this was such a perfect setup. If I saw a bear, there was a reasonable chance it was going to end up in bow range. We had a week to hunt and everything was feeling positive, like this was my time.

Later in the morning, out of the corner of my left eye, I saw movement across the river. It was a grizzly bear stepping out into the river by that fallen tree. My heart jumped into my throat and my blood pressure spiked so high I could see stars. We were only a few hours into the hunt and I was within bow range of a third bear.

Bear are hard to judge, especially when you have not seen one before. All I knew for sure was the bear was within range and getting closer. Being in the water made it even more difficult to judge. I slowly turned to look at Thomas behind me, hoping he would confirm it was big and give me the green light to shoot. He whispered, "Too small, look at the head." I relaxed and the adrenaline started to slow. I reached into my chest pocket and took out my camera to video the bear as it caught a fish. It took the fish up onto that fallen tree to eat it, offering me what would have been the perfect broadside shot. What a morning—it was obvious I would soon get a crack at a bear with my bow.

The rest of that day was without bear sightings. Back at camp, everyone was excited to hear about what we saw. Our cook had lived there her whole life and had never seen a grizzly up close. She was as proud as if I were her own son. Kiff arrived and was pumped to hear the news. He expected the salmon run to even get stronger, so when the salmon came, the bears would soon be there.

Hunting is hunting and this proved to be no different. You can have moments of extreme excitement and joy — and hours of nothing. We spent the next two full days in that stand and never saw another bear. Back in camp, I started to read between the lines. The population of bears here was great, but that did not make them easy to see. I had seen three bears, which was a lot; maybe I had seen all I was going to see. Another European hunter had come into camp with his wife, and he was on his second try. Last year he had hunted ten days and did not see a bear. He badly wanted my stand by the river and was willing to pay extra for Kiff to give it to him. Otherwise, he was going to have to spot and stalk from the many logging roads and trails. I give Kiff credit, he promised me the stand two years earlier and he would not budge from his word.

Those two dry days in the stand were not boring. There was a salmon with a black spot behind its dorsal fin that struggled to swim up the river past me. To the right of me it chose to spawn. For hours it thrashed around in the water laying eggs in different spots. It would tire and wash down past me only to regain strength and its will to spawn, and fight the current back upstream. Watching this battle of the cycle of life was amazing. The end of the second day, the salmon finally had expelled all of its eggs and all of its energy and passed away. It slowly floated down toward me and became lodged under a branch, all worn, tattered, and discolored. They almost rot away during their final hours. It was a humbling experience to watch this animal struggle so hard to continue the legacy of its life. The next morning it was gone; now it had given energy and life to a grizzly bear to survive the winter.

I was no longer as confident as we climbed into the stand on day four. The morning scene was just as beautiful and peaceful as the other days. The number of salmon swimming by had dwindled down to one here and one there. Not a good sign for bear-hunting success. Frustration is always a possibility; you never know what nature is willing to provide. I would hunt to the end and not give up.

The sun was hot as mid-morning came upon us. I had now stood motionless in that tree for more hours than I could count. We planned on leaving at lunch and try some spot and stalk hunting, so my time at the river was coming to an end. You try hard to remain confident, but the reality of the hunt can start to set in. There is no guarantee and going home with nothing is always a possibility. Then suddenly to the right of me, a bear appeared in the water.

I whispered to Thomas who I think had all but dozed off, and I pointed upstream. The bear was eighty yards away now, fishing into the river. My brain kicked into gear, sizing up my opportunity. If it turned left, toward us it would pass within bow range for sure. Turning right or straight would prove too long an archery shot that I would not dare take.

Now looking through his binoculars, I hear Thomas whisper in my ear, "That is a nice bear, do you want your rifle?" Just then it turned slightly right and I said, "Yes," as I slowly put down my bow and picked up my gun. I had done everything I could at this point to hunt a grizzly with my bow. I had seen more grizzlies than some who live with them. The odds were not in my favor to wait any longer.

He was fishing in a perfect quartering away angle as I squeezed the trigger. A loud roar filled the creek bed as the bear spun around once, tipped on his side and sank into the river. It was over just like that, I had just harvested a British Columbia Grizzly bear!

Thomas was as excited as me. We were brothers now; you tend to get that close spending that much time together in nature. Down the tree we scurried, as I wondered how we would get the bear from the middle of the river. That turned out to be an easy answer as Thomas just jumped right in. Dropping my gun and my pack, in the river I went too. The shallow spots where the salmon struggled were not as shallow as I thought; those fish are much bigger than they look. Of course, my bear was floating in waist-deep water, but we did not care.

I took all the strength we had to roll the wet, slippery bear up on the bank. That was as far as he was going to go. I stood in the water to take my trophy pictures. Balancing the camera on a stick pushed in the mud to get shot of both Thomas and I in a team photo. We were as happy as could be. This was the most beautiful bear I could ever imagine. It had black legs, a brown face, and the most gorgeous silver-tipped back that shined bright in the sun. I could not believe I was so lucky.

Camp that evening was a blast. Everyone was excited that I got a bear. We all played a part in the success of that hunt and everyone was ecstatic about it. Drying my clothes and boots in the sun, I finally got to take a nice, hot shower in a makeshift stall and had a cold beer as we enjoyed the success of the hunt.

A while later back home, I had recorded a hunting show on my DVR. I decided to watch it one night. It was called *Western Extreme* with Jim Burnworth. As I watched, he was practicing with his bow. Wait, I thought, I have shot that target before. He was hunting grizzly bear in the same camp I'd just been in, two years earlier. The scene eventually changed to that same stand I was in. Then a bear walked out on that same tree lying in the river. Damn if it was not the same bear I shot two years later. He passed it up for being too small. So, I not only have the life-size mount in my living room, but it is of a grizzly bear that is a television star.

Dome Creek Outfitters
British Columbia, 2011

Lesson – Being too hard on yourself

Maybe you are wondering if I was disappointed having to resort to the rifle to take my grizzly bear. I am not at all. Up until the very second that I put my bow down and grabbed the rifle, I was hunting for a grizzly bear with a bow. Up to that point I had done everything possible to make my goal happen. People tend to get so hung up on the final results; they don't give themselves credit for what they did to get there. There is a ton to be proud of throughout the entire process. Be thankful for every step you get to take.

Lesson – Just keep working toward your dream

It took many years for that burning desire to hunt a grizzly bear
with a bow to come true. The urge never left me even though I
never believed it could be in my cards. I am glad the dream stayed
alive and happy that I could push myself to make it a reality one
day. Every one of you reading this has some dream. That dream is
just always there, no matter how hard logic says it will never
happen. I am proof that one day it can happen. If it nags you that
much, pay attention and summon the will and discipline to pursue
it. Trust me, it will be the best thing you ever did.

Lesson – Buying extra tags

Canada is to hunters as Disneyland is to kids. When I booked my
British Columbia grizzly hunt, I could also buy tags for mountain
goat, moose, and black bear. Up front, I made an agreement with
my outfitter that I would pay a trophy fee only for the animals I
was able to take. When I saved my money, I saved enough for
three of the four, knowing time and luck would never allow me all
four. Luckily, Thomas my guide was a hunter and was always
ready to go hunt. After taking the grizzly, he asked me what I
wanted to hunt next. It was an easy answer for me because
mountain goat was on my top-five list. That story follows, but
even after we went after goat, we could look for moose in the
swamps and black bear in the area around the first cabin we went
to. In this case, these animals lived in different areas with different
habitats. Even black bears will stay out of grizzly country, but
nevertheless it kept me hunting and was worth the gamble.

British Columbia Mountain Goat

With my British Columbia grizzly bear hide salted and drying in the camp meat shack, and my boots drying in the sun from our recovery swim into the Fraser River, Thomas and I discussed what tag we wanted to fill next. This was a no brainer for me. I still had a few days to hunt and a mountain goat was still one of the animals on my top-five list. I wanted to go after a goat.

Thomas' face wrinkled up and he threw his head back like he was disgusted. Mumbling almost to himself, he said, "I was hoping I didn't have to go back there again this year." Then the hunter in him kicked in and he turned to me and said, "Pack up, we will head to main camp today and spend the night, then we can leave for the mountain early tomorrow morning."

I guess I was naive enough to miss all those signs. As I would find out later the hard way, this trip was not for the meek. There was a horse trail for part of the way; Thomas had spent weeks up there during the summer cutting trail further up the valley called Ptarmigan Creek. He had also guided others up this mountain, stories I will expand upon later. I knew mountain goat hunting was going to be tough; what I did not know is how tough getting to the base of the mountain would be.

I borrowed a large backpack to carry my gear. We would hike to a tent he left there and spend the night, then hike to the mountain and look for goats the next day. It was another beautiful, sunny morning as we ran the highway in that beat-up Bronco to a dirt road at the mouth of Ptarmigan Creek Canyon. The dirt road went from wide and accessible to narrow and rough. Brush scraped the sides of the Bronco as the hunk of junk pushed on. We drove through a few shallow creeks, bouncing off the rocks left behind by the rushing water. A few miles in, we stopped. We could not drive any further and boot leather would be the transportation of choice.

All I knew was that we would get to the tent by the evening sometime. It really depended on the pace I could keep. To me, I was just excited for a nice hike in the woods. A hundred yards into our trek and the first obstacle appeared: a river! I am not scared of too many things, but rushing water spikes my anxiety, especially when I must think about going in it. Waist deep and running fast we stripped down to carry our clothes across. The force of the water wanted to push us over, so keeping upright was difficult. The worst part was that the bottom was covered with rocks that were round and all different sizes. Trying to walk on them or trying to get your foot between them was tremendously painful. If it wasn't for the ice-cold water, I am not sure my feet would have survived. Making it to the other side, we dried and dressed and I wondered what I was getting myself into.

There was still a resemblance of a maintained trail, but it was quickly being overtaken by brush. After a long and reasonable walk the trail faded to a horse trail, about a foot wide and beaten deep into the mud. The problem was that all the brush covered it, so to even see it you had to continue to push brush away.

They had given me stiff leather gloves at camp. I was now understanding why. I cannot recall the name of it, but there was this thick and stiff briar stalk with briars like lion claws. Any exposed skin was immediately torn and infection and pain set in. Without leather gloves my hands would have been shredded. My nice hike in the woods was turning into a nightmare.

And let's not forget the horse bell. Thomas tied a large horse bell to the back of his pack. Every step he took — dong, dong, dong! This was to tell the grizzly bears we were coming. The theory is, if you don't sneak up on them and surprise them, they won't attack you. I was thinking, we were just ringing the dinner bell for them.

Thomas did not carry a gun, but he made it very clear that I was to never shoulder my rifle and always have a round in the chamber. This is not typical for hiking with a gun. We usually put the rounds under the bolt rendering the gun safe. That way, if you fall or make a mistake, your guide does not get shot in the back. When an animal shows itself, all the hunter needs to do is rack the bolt, loading a round in the chamber getting it ready to fire.

Yeah, we were headed right into grizzly bear country. As I pushed these Freddy Kruger-like briars away from the trail, I would look down and see grizzly tracks in the mud. It turned out the bears loved to use the horse trail. I could not see the trail well enough to place my feet, but I was supposed to feel confident with a loaded gun and a ringing bell. I thought back to my email to Kiff asking about bear spray. I did not want to be a pussy, but I wanted to have the spray if they thought I should. His response was, "You won't have time to use it. If a bear wants you, he will be on you before you can react." I was able to make myself stay pretty calm, until I pushed the briars away and saw baby bear tracks. Oh fuck! Would a baby bear know enough to run from a bell?

There are moments on a hunt where you get scared and really question what the hell you're doing. I was quickly slipping into one of those moments. All I knew was that I wanted a mountain goat; I asked for this and I needed to do whatever it took to accomplish it. So, I sucked it up and pushed on.

One would think hiking up a creek would be easy, except the old creek had a mind of its own. Zig-zagging from side to side it often choked off the path. The answer was to climb up the hill to find what might be called easier and safer hiking. Easier was a very relative term. Climbing hills and side hilling through brush-choked banks was easier than raging water over huge boulders, but it sure did not feel like it. Horses can go amazing places, but we were starting to go places that horses could not go.

I could only imagine how hard it was for Thomas to pick this trail. Hell, I was not sure how he even found it again. We were on the steep side hill pushing hard through the brush. You could see nothing, except the spot to put your feet. Through the forty-five minutes or so, I thought I noticed the river changing sides, but I did not think much of it. Later when we made it to camp, I looked at my GPS and it proved that we literally had walked back and forth in the same area six times, not knowing we weren't going in the right direction.

We were stopping to catch our breath more and more and grabbing a drink from the river when we could. Because the river swayed from valley bank to valley bank, we had to do the same. If it was too steep to hike the bank we were on, we had to get to the other side. In some case, we could go to the valley floor and walk the riverbed. In others, a new and more dangerous obstacle appeared.

The steepness of the bank forced us toward the river, but the river was fast, deep, and full of giant boulders. A giant tree had fallen across the water, spanning around eighty feet. Thomas asked, "How do you feel about tight-rope walking?" The first one was probable only twelve to fifteen feet above the water, but falling on those rocks would have been bone breaking and skull crushing. The old, wet, moss-covered log looked slippery. Luckily a large branch stuck up half way, giving us a place to grab on—that is, if it was solid. With a large fifty-pound pack on my back, an eight-pound rifle in one hand, and legs that felt like rubber, I thought, "Sure this is a good idea." Thomas went first, with ease. Then it was my turn to summon the courage. Maybe I summoned stupidity, but across I went, stopping first at the branch and then kind of lunging to the other side.

Well, I would love to tell you that was behind us, but we did it three more times. The logs got more slippery, higher, and longer, while the rocks below got more and more dangerous. I got more confident each time, but damn it could have gone bad quick. A fall from either of us would have changed both our lives.

We had hiked for hours now and I was completely soaked with sweat. Thomas never updated me on how far to go, I think for strategic reasons. Not knowing meant I could not let it get into my head. I would envision color up ahead and hope it was a tent. It never was. There was a time where we seemed to have walked out of the steep stuff and into a flatter valley floor. We spent a lot of time hiking the creek, hopping from gravel bar to gravel bar and rock to rock. The mountains on each side went straight up for thousands of feet. We would stop and rest and look for white Billy goats on the cliffs. At one point I could hear a waterfall and as we got closer I could see it was falling down the entire side of the mountain. It was an awesome sight to see.

Our little break did not last long enough and the steepness crept in again. Pushing on and on until I looked up, the color I thought I saw this time materialized into a tent. We had hiked all day, but we made it. This is where Thomas spent the summer. He had made a fire pit and benches out of log. There still were canned goods stored in a cooler and he had left a chainsaw there. We quickly peeled off the wet clothes and started a nice fire. The creek was a few yards away and I drank and drank as much of that cool, clean water as I could. All around us the mountains reached for the sky. The spruce trees could only grow so far up, then after the tree line it was just rock. Further up the valley the mountains stuck up like towers of rock. There we hoped to see mountain goats, but that was for another day. Now we would cook some food and rest by the fire. All the suffering, bitching, moaning, and whining from a few minutes ago turned in to the pride and joy of accomplishing something hard and ending up in a magical place.

The canned goods turned into peaches and potato soup for dinner. Thomas surprised me, bringing out grizzly bear steaks that he had carried in his pack. In any other situation I could find fault in this meal; after all, I hate peaches. But being here and doing what we just did, this meal was one of the best I ever had. It is amazing how quick our minds and bodies can recover. A lot of water, a little food, and some rest and I was looking forward to continuing the trip in the morning. Our only concern for the night was hoping a grizzly bear did not visit us in camp.

I slept pretty light, with my loaded rifle by my side. At the first hint of daylight and we were up and ready to go. A quick cup of instant coffee and a candy bar was our breakfast. We planned to hike to the mountains, stalk and kill a mountain goat, and come back to this spot to camp. It is law that you must bring the entire goat off the mountain, so we stripped out all the gear we did not think we needed from our packs.

The sun was just lighting up the mountain peaks as we started up the valley. It was still cold, damp, and quiet at the valley floor. I was excited and confident that we would get a crack at my mountain goat. About an hour and half in and we came to the base of what I will call a forest-covered hill. It did not look as steep as it turned out to be. But up we went, pushing those demon briars away and taking a full climbing step up. The dampness and my spiking body heat got the best of my glasses and I could not keep them from steaming up. I'll remind you that the rifle was still loaded and ready because this too was grizzly country. It got so bad I had to take my glasses off. Now, I could not see well to shoot. I was just putting one foot in front of the other, pushing through the brush. It never got less scary, because often I would push through the brush and step into an area the size of a Volkswagen with the vegetation all matted down. It was a grizzly bed, even more proof that we were in their backyard. My mind and body might have felt recovered, but I was fading fast. Thomas had to stop and wait for me many times. I was tired and getting very frustrated with myself. Climbing was one challenge, but this fucking brush and briars were a real pain in the ass.

This battle lasted a couple hours, but we finally pushed over the top into a lake that was blue and beautiful against the mountain backdrop. We rinsed off and drank, all the while being very cautious of being at a grizzly watering hole. Candy bars were our mid-morning snack on the shore. This was the point where our adventure would start.

To our right, the mountains rose up for a few thousand feet. They looked like rolling hills tipped on their side. Our hope was that goats would be up there. The plan was to climb up, then sneak over those "rolling hills" hopefully onto a giant Billy goat. We had not seen any white animals on the slopes as we made our way up the valley, but Thomas knew they had been there before. From the lake, we could no longer see the whole mountain; tapering away you could only see a few hundred feet straight up. We would now start to climb. The good news was that we were out of the brush and briars, but this was straight up and all rock.

Time was getting away from us and we had to get up that hill, so off we went, one giant step after another. I won't lie, this was brutal from the first step. My head knew I had a long way to go and anxiety quickly overtook me and my breathing got short and fast. You can do a lot without food and much water, but you kind of need oxygen, and hyperventilation does not get you the oxygen you need. I had to stop and chat with myself. "Alright you pussy, you can do this. This is what you wanted and you cannot quit now. You need to breathe and you need to step, one after another after another. See that rock up there? Go there." With calm, deep breaths, I could climb like a maniac, but only for a few feet. I had to get into a pattern of rest, pick a goal, breathe, and go to that goal. Repeating this time and time again, I could go up the mountain.

The interesting thing about this mountain was that it always looked like the top was near, since the slope tapered out of view. But when you got there, it was not the end, just a few hundred more feet to climb. Each time, anxiety would creep in and breathing would go bad. Each time I had to literally talk myself off the ledge and get my shit back together to continue. This was a mental battle with my own brain and I could win it, but I had to be relentless. Thomas was good at it because he had been there before and knew what his body could do. He no longer had to deal with any anxiety. His mental game was strong.

We stopped for a candy bar break a few thousand feet up. Thomas told me he had come up here three times with hunters and they all gave up before this. I had done well. One was an Olympic athlete, but that does not guarantee mountain legs or the proper mental attitude. I guess his calves completely gave out and were black and blue. Thomas proceeded to tell me he would never bring anyone up here over thirty-five years old, because they wouldn't make it. I chuckled and asked him how old he thought I was? He thought I was in my early thirties, but this stubborn old forty-six-year-old was kicking some ass. That conversation put a spark in me that carried me the rest of the way up the hill. I now had something to prove to the world and there was no longer a moment of doubt or quit in me.

Off we climbed, out of the tree zone and into the rock. I marveled at how this mountain got formed. Sedimentary rock layers were no longer horizontal, but straight up and down. The pure violence that created this mountain must have been staggering. It humbles me when things like this put my puny little human existence in its place.

Another thousand feet clicked off and we stopped again. We were getting close to the top, maybe an hour or more to go. We drank water from a trickle running down the mountain. It was very dry and this could be the last water available from here to the top. Then Thomas said, "We have an issue." Concerned, I looked at him and wondered what it could be. He said," If we leave right now, we might make it to the tent before dark. We cannot go through that grizzly territory in the dark." He gave me a choice: we could leave now, or continue up the mountain and plan to stay the night on top.

My answer was quick because it was not even a choice. I said, "We aren't going to quit now, so I don't really see this as a choice." I hadn't come this far to not at least try to see a mountain goat. Thomas simply nodded and turned and started to climb.

It was getting very hot in the sun. We had left our source of water behind. The candy bars we had to eat today were only a tiny fraction of the calories I was burning on that mountain. Every time I looked up, it looked like the top, but when I got there, there was just more up. There were times climbing that I could only get about a quarter of an inch of my boot to bite into the rock, behind me was straight down. There was no stopping a slip from being a deadly slide to my death. They talk about your life flashing in front of your eyes. That happened two times on that mountain. As I placed my foot on a precarious foothold, I saw my kids flash in front of my eyes. I guess my subconscious was questioning what the rest of my brain was telling me to do.

A small finger of spruce trees made their way up the mountain, paralleling our path. That is where we decide we would sleep for the night. My GPS said we were at 7000 feet, I think we started at the lake at about 3000. We climbed higher than our camping spot to look for goats. The view from up there was amazing. We each found a shelf to sit on and enjoy the view. An airplane flew by, probably the same flight I took into Prince George. The funny thing was, I was looking down on it.

Thomas had carried a satellite phone for emergencies. It would not connect to a satellite. Jesus Christ, I can hit a satellite with a rock from here, I thought. My GPS tracking device was sporadic as we hiked the creek. There were times when the track was blank. So, don't bet your life on these things because they might not work for you when you really need them.

It was a bright blue and clear sky as the sun started to set. A beautiful evening on the mountain, but this meant trouble for us spending the night. Remember when I said we emptied all the unnecessary gear out of our packs at the tent? Well that included extra clothes, sleeping bags, and even the damn emergency blanket I have carried on every hunt, except now when I needed it. In an emergency! I had a wool sweater, extra shirt, and a hat in my pack. Thomas had brought some freeze-dried food and garbage bags in his. We had nothing else to prepare for the soon-to-be-frosty night. We needed to get a fire started and a stash of firewood to hold us through the night.

Down the mountain we went to those trees. There was no flat spot on this slope. We needed the trees to keep us on the mountain. We broke off dead spruce branches and picked wood from the ground to build a fire. Thomas had a little saw blade on a survival knife so we cut spruce branches to make beds. Now the ground was so steep, I had to dig my heels into the earth to keep my butt from sliding away from the fire. When I piled my spruce branches by two trees, to make a bed, they lay more on the tree to be level than the ground. Basically, I jammed myself into the sharp angle between the ground rising near straight up and the tree trying to grow straight up.

Dinner would be the dehydrated meal, except we had no water. Thomas took off in search for water while I tended the fire. He found some, bringing it back in ZIPLOC bags. Always carry good ZIPLOC bags. We boiled the water and made the meal. I had a hard time eating my share; I guess my body had given up on my stomach for food. There was no doubt I was eating my own muscle away for energy because my pants would no longer stay up. This adventure was a crash diet of an extreme magnitude.

As the light faded, the next challenge was to get into a position to sleep. Putting my sweater and hat on was all I had for the top half of me. Thomas gave me a garbage bag to use for a sleeping bag. My pack started as a pillow but as the bitter cold crept in, I ended up putting my feet and legs in it for warmth. I could reach the woodpile and feed the fire from my bed, but that was not going to last the night. Luck was on our side because around midnight clouds rolled in. That would help keep the radiant heat from the mountain from escaping, but then snow started to hit my face. The snow spared us for the night, but I often wonder how screwed we would be if the mountain ended up snow-covered and slippery.

Amazingly, I had to pee in the night. I did not dare move around in the dark, so I rolled on my side, up against the tree and peed down the hill. It kind of made me laugh because it was probably yards before my pee actually hit the ground. I did doze, but I cannot say I got much sleep. I was glad to see the twilight because that ended this charade.

So, maybe you thought this was a mountain goat hunting story. Well, it did not turn out to be. From our camp, there was this grassy little shelf on the mountain onto which we hoped a goat would come out and feed. However, I later ranged it with my rangefinder and it was 700 yards away. We talked about what to do, as I was not seeing this to be a productive spot to goat hunt. We did see goat sign, tracks and scat, but our guess was the lack of water sent them over the mountaintop. We could go over the top, or we could try to wander over those supposed rolling hills like we planned from the bottom. Thomas decided to check out the rolling hills. It quickly became evident that they were very dangerous and steep rock slides. If a goat had come out on that grassy spot and I had made a risky 700-yard shot, there was no way we could have recovered a mountain goat from that spot.

It was time to call it a hunt and head back. I had absolutely no regrets doing this. I had officially hunted mountain goat. This was not the first and wouldn't be the last time I would hunt game and not get one. That does not take away anything from the hunting experience. To make it this far up the mountain and to enjoy the view I got to see was well worth every calorie, infected scratch, and muscle ache I had. As I write this, I want to go back so bad it hurts.

There is something comforting when you climb up a mountain because the mountain is close to your face and hands. Falling up the mountain feels okay. Turn around to head down and it is scary as fuck. Immediately your knees start screaming from the shock of catching yourself every step. Different muscles are used coming down, so the pain and anxiety is all new and fresh. Nevertheless we decided to hike all the way out, non-stop. We were starving, tired, and ready to go home. Each creek-log crossing got scarier the weaker I got, until the last one, where I could not summon any more courage. I decide to strip down and wade that one. I felt like my luck and skill were both running out and I could no longer take the chance.

A crazy little story about how your brain works. I have had left knee issues. It hit me hard in Montana, mountain lion hunting, where I missed an opportunity on a giant cat because I could not go back into the canyon. I could not even walk up the stairs to bed that night. I had no issues on this hike until I hit a spot about 200 yards from the truck. As soon as I knew I was almost done, my brain gave up and that knee locked up tighter than shit. The interesting thing was I was able to regroup and talk to myself, calling myself a wimp, and the knee loosened up and I made my way to the truck. Don't ever underestimate the power of your mind and don't let it fuck with you either.

Dome
Creek
Outfitters

British
Columbia

2011

Ptarmigan
Creek

Mountain
Goat
Adventure

Lesson – Anxiety and Breathing

Ah yes, you would think breathing would be one of the easiest things we do, but it isn't. I proved it time and time again while climbing that mountain. I would get frustrated, scared, or anxious and my breathing would speed up, gasping for air, and my climbing progress would come to a screeching halt. I could talk myself out of it, but I had to recognize it was happening and take the conscious effort to deal with it in my mind.

Any good athlete knows how to breathe while doing their thing. Breathing is as important to shooting as aiming and pulling the trigger. None of this works if you have poor breath control. Learn to breathe!

Lesson – Value of a Range Finder

I carry the Bushnell Fusion range-finding binoculars on my hunts. These will range up to a thousand yards. These are not just valuable in ranging game, but I have also used them to range spots, like that grassy spot waiting for a goat. With my bare eye, I would have thought that spot was a long but very makeable shot. I would have been wrong. The size of the mountains distorted any guess I could have made in how far away it was. When I shot my moose, I had left the rangefinder at camp. The size of the animal distorted my range estimate and I could not tell it was a long, long way away. You may be good at ranging deer in your back yard, but different landscapes and different size animals can throw you off. Using a range finder is good insurance and you owe it to the animal to take the best possible shot.

Lesson – Crash Dieting

The mountain goat hike and climb was a calorie burner. We were burning thousands of more calories than we were taking in. It was very evident that my body was getting smaller. When we got back to the cabin, we ate everything in sight. I could not shove enough food in my mouth. By the time I got home, I was feeling and looking fatter than before I traveled to British Columbia.

What happened? I put my body into starvation mode. It had to burn my fat and probably chose to start burning muscle to meet my energy demands. When the body switches into this mode, called starvation mode, it does not come out of it immediately when food is eaten. Your body still remembers you just tried to starve it and it will first try to store that food as fat for next time you are starving. So, you might lose weight quickly by fasting and intensive exercise, but if you go into starvation mode, your body will put fat back on to prepare for the next time.

Consuming your own muscle for energy also creates chemicals that can hurt your organs, especially your kidneys. Intense exercise without proper carb intake can start this. A key symptom that you have gone too far is high anxiety, like you are scared and need to run away. Your body does not know what is hurting it, so the fight-or-flight chemicals start flowing and it feels like an anxiety attack. I learned this in the Emergency Room after I worked out too hard attempting double workouts a day all the while attempting to cut carbs. Work requires fuel and your body will get it from one source or another.

Lesson – Don't climb unless you see a goat

Getting back to the cabin after the long-ass goat adventure, the first thing we did was eat. A lot. We burned thousands of calories and I was having a hard time keeping my pants up. So, our bodies were craving carbs and calories and we could not stop pushing food in our faces. But, lying on the table was a book about how to hunt mountain goat. The first page said, "Don't ever climb after a goat unless you see one there first." I laughed. I guess we should have read that book before we left. Do your research ahead of time; it can save you a lot of work.

Lesson – Your head is the only thing stopping you

Whether it is pursuing a dream, or pushing yourself up a mountain, the only thing stopping you is the shit you allow in your head. Dreams are obtainable if you are willing to work at them and make the required sacrifices to achieve them. Mountains are climbable if you stay positive and trust that your body is much more capable than you might think. There are great rewards for pushing yourself out of your comfort zone, or for making the sacrifices to achieve something. Don't let your own head get in the way!

Be Prepared for Bad Weather – Ohio Deer in a Hurricane

Driving to Ohio from New York, I was pumped up. A weather front was passing over the hunting area and it should have cleared just as daylight hit. Because of this transition in weather pressure, the first day on the stand was going to be awesome.

My deal is a different animal or a different place each time. I don't want to do the same thing twice. I use hunting as an excuse to see the world and to see different species of animals and so far, it has proven to be a fun strategy. This Ohio trip was a deer hunt, the same critter I can chase at home, but this was a state I have yet to hunt and that excited me.

Friends booked this hunt with a new, up-and-coming outfitter. It was inexpensive, it was within driving distance, Ohio has some nice deer, and I got to hunt with friends; so how could I turn this down? Besides, a week in a tree stand with my bow in hand is always a good time.

As timing goes, weather was predicted to wash out any fun in New York anyway. A storm reminiscent of a hurricane was coming up the east coast and was sure to drown out the week in New York. The weather front I was driving into was going to create perfect deer-movement conditions, so life was good.

I got to the camp and met the guys. We dusted off our bows and shot some arrows, having a beer to start off the week. Viewing trail camera pictures got us all fired up. We were excited for each other because someone was going to put a deer down in the morning.

The hurricane was going to swing to the east of us, then curl into New York. The weather front would rain on us at night, but be gone by daybreak. So, we tried to sleep. But you know the drill: anticipation keeps you up all night.

The alarm went off to start our day, but most of us were wide-awake listening to the pouring rain thrash the house. The front did not pass as we expected, so we readied ourselves for a wet start, but still hoped for it to break and the animals to stir.

I was confident. I have some pretty good rain gear and I have sat in rain before. It was a challenge to dress in the pouring rain at the roadside, so we all started out wet. Getting to the stands in the dark was difficult, the ground was slippery, and there was water everywhere. Settling in the tree stand, I figured, *well now I can handle this*. I was wrong. It rained so hard, you could hardly see past twenty yards. There was so much water running over me that it easily found the weak spots in my rain gear. When it started trickling down the crack off my ass, I began to be miserable. Oh, and this was all before daybreak.

I was confident it would pass, but it never did. I sat there until nightfall and the downpour never stopped. Back at camp, we spread out everything to dry and went straight to the weather channel for an update. Turns out the hurricane decided to stall between Ohio and New York. It was now officially over us, but that weather front I expected to pass by had nowhere to go and the dark green line was stopped, right over my tree stand.

The next morning, we awoke to the same thing. A torrential downpour. We were here to hunt, and out we went. The day was much the same, just miserable. Back that night, the weather channel did not have any good news. I can tell you this over and over, but it was not going to change. I decided to drive home early and cut my losses; I could go back to work and save my vacation. The others could not, so they stayed and tried to be confident, but the weather did not change until their last day.

They say that you can control a lot of things, but you cannot control the weather. Mother Nature can help you in your hunt and she can destroy your chances. When you save all that money and put in all that planning you are still taking a huge risk. Weather is one of those risks. I cannot stress enough for you to enjoy the process, the research, the planning, the practice, the urge to get in shape, and the journey, because animals on the ground are far from guaranteed.

I could have easily left this story out, since as hunting stories go, there was no kill. For me this was a memorable experience. I loved the excitement of the preparation and the trip to Ohio. I enjoyed the company of my friends and to share their excitement. I loved the fact that we hunted our asses off in terrible conditions; those guys were studs for never giving up. I learned things that I needed to improve on to be a better hunter, like how to improve my rain setup. I got to hunt in another state. I got to hunt. It was a memorable hunting trip.

Manitoba Bear – My Son Devon's First Outfitted Hunt

I was sitting in a Manitoba bear stand, overlooking a bear bait about one hundred yards away, and all I could really concentrate on was the intense ninety-degree heat and the swarm of mosquitoes that my Thermocell was barely fighting off. We had travelled nearly all day on four-wheelers through rutted trails and mud-bogged beaver dam crossings to get here. I was the last hunter dropped off and the closest to camp, yet camp was still a couple hours away. We were hunting our way into camp. This was the first evening sit for a week of hunting deep in the Manitoba wild.

The sun finally set, bringing a few degrees of relief from the heat, but none from the bugs. A single rifle shot went off in the distance. I listened intently for more shots; I had a vested interest in what was happening a few miles back. You see, about an hour and a half before I got to my stand, I had dropped off my sixteen-year-old son at his bear bait. I was confident the shot was his and my excitement spiked, but there wasn't a damn thing I could do about it. I was alone and stuck in a tree until a four-wheeler came to my rescue. I had plenty of time to think and worry.

I had lots to worry about because anything in a hunt can go wrong. Devon was high in a tree, but we were still hunting wild bears and a wounded bear is nothing to screw with. I was confident that the single shot was Devon because the other hunters were still hours farther away and more importantly, no one shoots a rifle better than my son – no one! I was 100-percent confident he had a bear down. What I was not confident in was him being patient enough to stay in the tree until help arrived. I could visualize him snapping pictures with his phone as other bears snuck in on him.

About an hour after dark the guide came back from camp and got me. I told him about the shot and that I was confident Devon had a bear on the ground. We both now were excited and we couldn't get there fast enough, but it was still an hour and a half away. All the while poor Devon waited in the darkened woods, high in a hot tree stand with his trophy bear lying a few yards away. Devon was not built for that kind of patience.

Three happy guys gathered around Devon's first black bear from his first real outfitted trip. I am not sure which of the three were happier. When Jason, the owner of *Hunts from the Heart,* met us at camp, it was obvious he was the happiest of all. As the hunt ended at the end of the week, Devon's bear was by far the biggest of the ones taken. Three out of the four of us took bears in some of the hottest and worst bear-hunting weather conditions you can imagine.

Devon got to spend the rest of the week hanging out with Jason, doing outfitter-type stuff. Checking baits and preparing trap lines for the winter kept them busy while the rest of us were in the tree. Old Dad got to spend every night in a hot tree, and we even tried to capitalize on the slightly cooler mornings. I didn't mind it at all.

Bear stands have this smell that is unmistakable and I love it. There is a musty, crusty, spruce odor that always snaps my brain to bear camp, in a deja vu kind of way. Most people would probably be grossed out by it, but it tells me I have found the correct deep, dark, and damp spot in which bears love to hang out. You know how the smell of fresh-cut grass makes you feel? Well, stinky old bear baits do that to me too!

We hunted hard, but animals with thick fur coats do not want to come out in ninety-plus-degree temperatures. Jason decided we would hunt our way out of camp much like we hunted our way in. Then we would try another area for the last night just to see if we could get lucky. A few hours of riding through the mud of the wild and I was perched in yet another tree. This spot did seem promising. The game cameras showed action, and it was near a small lake. Maybe a spot that was a little cooler than the others.

It was still hot as hell. Wearing dark camouflage in the hot sun made it even worse. So, yes, I did it. To keep from sweating so bad the water ran off me, I did strip down and hunt in my underwear. To pass the time I thought about Devon's success and his hunting skills. He really is quite good at it.

Excitement, also known as "Buck Fever," takes over for him as bad as it does for as the rest of us, but his other skills are top notch. The kid can shoot a chipmunk between the eyes with his bow. Ask him, he will show you the picture on his phone.

I really wanted a bear. There would be nothing cooler than the two of us taking bears home, together! There were big bears here. We could see their big asses on the game cameras, so it was possible to shoot one bigger than Devon did. I didn't really want to beat him. I was hoping for a tie. As time went on and darkness started to fall the pressure grew in my head by the minute.

And then a bear appeared! Tunnel vision crept in as the blood raced to my head. The bear walked in right passed the bait and up the trail. Shit! A few minutes passed and back down the trail it came. My adrenaline was pumping twice as bad as the first time he passed—I had to take advantage of the second chance. As the bear walked past the barrel it sized up to be pretty fair. This bear would not beat Devon's. Check! This bear looked decent against the barrel. Check! Daylight was fading and the day was almost over. Check! I wanted a bear really bad. Check! I might not get another chance. Check! The bear is now broadside with its head in the barrel. Check! BOOM! The bear dropped right there. It never even twitched.

I did it! We did it! Devon and I both got our bears on our first big game trip together. I was pumped.

I had no idea when I would get picked up. Now my bear was just lying there like more food on the bait pile. In the dark, if a bigger bear came in, I could do nothing if he wanted to eat my bear. So, I decided to get down and drag it over near my tree. I could even start to skin it, I thought. I climbed down and walked over to the bait sight to look over my bear. I almost puked.

The bear lying by the barrel was not the bear I saw and shot. It was tiny. *What the fuck did I just do*, I asked myself. Bile rose into the back of my throat and I choked it back down. Tears formed in my eyes, because I killed a small bear and my pride was shattered badly for the very first time. I was embarrassed to face my kid, the guide, and Jason the outfitter. How could I go home with this bear and have any pride in what I just did? I have a pretty decent hunting resume and have done some pretty cool things, but this could erase all of that. I climbed back up the tree to pout and wait. I hoped they would never pick me up.

Everything I told my son to do or not to do he absorbed and did right. I completely and utterly forgot everything I told him and did the opposite. I could not have made that many mistakes in that short of time in anything else in my life. I had sat there so long putting pressure on myself to succeed that I forgot everything I knew about hunting. Now, somehow, I would have to live with the embarrassment.

There was no way out of this. Trust me, I sat a long time looking for a way. I remembered stories from Saskatchewan about a hunter who tried to cover a dead deer up in the snow, so no one would find out he misjudged the rack. That coward seemed smart at that moment. Well, there was only one thing I could do and it was to suck it the fuck up and take my bear home. Swallow my pride and admit what had happened. After all, this happens to many hunters and obviously I am not immune.

Thankfully my son is a better person than me. He was just glad that I got a bear—and glad his was still bigger! A little fair ribbing from the guy who got the biggest is normal hunt-camp chatter. Jason just looked at me and asked what the heck happened. I shrugged and smiled!

The takeaway from my story is that it can happen to anyone. Looking back today, I am damn glad it did. To be so excited and jacked up seeing an animal that you totally lose your mind; well, that is in fact what hunting is all about. I don't ever want to lose that feeling!

Lesson – Your children learn way more from you than you know.

Devon was in diapers when he would hide behind the chair and whisper that he was hunting. His mouth never stopped when we were home, but take him across the road to hunt deer and he never made a peep. He was eight years old when I set him behind the 30-06 on a snowbank to take out a milk jug at five yards. Recoil has never meant a thing to him.

They act like they don't hear you when you try to teach them something. He heard and observed everything we did while hunting. I never got good at it until I was in my thirties. He was good at it when he was a little kid. He is by far a better hunter than I will ever be. I hope he gets the same chances I have, to do what I have done. He deserves it.

Don't ever underestimate what your kids are learning from you.

Why I Don't Care So Much About Ballistics

Gun nuts get all hung up on ballistics of the rifle round, when in all reality it means little to the animal on the other end. If riflemen had their way, we would outlaw and destroy any caliber less than .30 and if it does not have magnum in its name it is a piece of shit.

The 30-06 has killed every animal on the planet. The 30-30 was a staple in hunting for survival long ago. The measly little old .22 caliber has held its own in all types of hunting. They are now selling air rifles that drop wild boar in their tracks. But you will still hear people say that the magnums are the minimum requirement for big game. A mountain-goat outfitter proceeded to jade me on the phone saying, "7mm Remington Magnums are junk, I have seen them bounce right off goats." What an asshole!

I am not going to get in a lot of detail here because I could give a shit what you shoot. What I do care about is the people who feel they need to put down others or make them feel like they need a $3000 rifle to kill game. That is bullshit. The truth is, a few hundred feet per second change in speed or a few hundred foot-pounds of energy change is not the problem. The problem is not putting the bullet in the right spot to quickly and cleanly kill the animal.

- The problem is not getting close enough to the animal before you shoot.
- The problem is not waiting for the animal to stand in the correct position.
- The problem is not knowing where your bullet will hit at any given yardage.
- The problem is that you did not practice with the gun.

The fact is that your adrenaline spike is going to make each and every error you make ten times uglier than it would be from the bench.

If you cannot shoot a gun then it is useless. Magnum calibers kick the shit out of you and I dare say 90 percent who have them are scared shitless of the recoil. The result is bad shooting and wounded or missed animals. Use a gun that you can shoot comfortably and most of all one you love. You must have 100-percent confidence in your gun and your ability to shoot it.

I cannot stress enough that you need to love your gun. I bought a 7mm Remington Magnum when I was eighteen. This gun and I have been all over and together we have many one-shot kills. I am a gun guy too, and I always look at new rifles, but I cannot bring myself to leave this gun home. This gun is my hunting partner.

Some Typical Ballistics

		At 200 Yards	
Cartridge	bullet weight	Velocity	Energy
270	140	2561	2039
7mm Remington Magnum	140	2707	2278
30-30	150	1608	861
.308	150	2264	1707
30-06	150	2343	1828
300 Winchester Magnum	150	2636	2314
300 Weatherly Magnum	150	3005	3007

Above are some velocity and energy numbers for common rifle cartridges at 200 yards. Granted the .30-caliber guns can shoot heavier bullets than this, therefore carry a bit more energy. Magnums only really shine at long yardages because the energy does not fall off as fast as the others. The question you must ask yourself is, how far do you really want, or need to shoot? Magnums are touted for dangerous game, but close range where the animal really is dangerous, there is little difference. I would much rather shoot a charging animal with a gun I know and shoot well, than a gun that scares the crap out of me.

You should Care About Trajectory

So, I don't really give a shit about ballistics, but I do care about trajectory. I know the gravity and the ballistics are the variables that define the trajectory or path of the bullet, so don't be sending me negative comments. Whatever path that bullet takes, I want you to know what it is and how it works.

With a scoped rifle, the sights are usually one and a half inches above the barrel. So, if you stood at the target with the gun touching the paper and the crosshairs on the dot, you would hit an inch and a half lower than the spot you have the crosshairs on.

Think of an NFL quarterback throwing a football: he must throw a pretty high arc to get the ball down the field fifty yards. The gun is no different. The bullet must fly over the line of sight until it finally drops back down to hit the target. Many shooters fail to take this into account.

If you zero at 300 yards, the bullet will fly over the line of sight for most of that path until it drops down and hits the target at 300 yards. So, to make a shot on a deer inside 300 yards, you need to hold low on the spot you want to hit. How low varies depending on where you are, the bullet path will be just slightly higher for a while, rising to maybe 4 or 5" high before it starts dropping, or arcing down to the target. Knowing how much higher the bullet is per the yardage you are shooting is the key to pinpoint accuracy.

Say that a deer is 225 yards away. The deer looks very small at that distance and it can be very deceiving. Without an accurate range with a range finder, many hunters think the deer is way far away. They immediately think they should hold high, to lob that bullet in there. At 225 yards, the arc of the bullet could be flying four or five inches high at that point. Not only are they aiming high, the bullet is actually that much higher than their aim and the bullet passes right over the deer's back. They were stable, the sight picture was good, their trigger squeeze was good — so how could they miss? They missed because they don't know shit about trajectory. That hunter should have aimed four to five inches lower than the heart and it would have hit the heart with a quick and clean kill. Let me say that again: you aim low on everything up to the point you sighted your gun in, all the time. This never changes.

Yardage beyond your sight in distance, then you start to aim high. Where people fail themselves is that they don't really know what the animal looks like that far away, so they assume it is farther than it is. You will read later my struggles to kill a moose. I had never seen a moose in the wild, so how the hell would I know what it looked like 700 or more yards away? Needless to say, I missed and missed again. But then when I got my shit together, finally deciding it was a long-yardage shot, I dropped him with one shot. I had practiced 700-yard shots before I left home and that knowledge got me a moose.

Not knowing the true range is the other mistake. I had a friend that shot at multiple caribou on the opposite side of the lake and missed them all. The lake made it look like a very long shot. Later, I ranged the distance and the lake was only 225 yards wide. Aiming low on his next caribou, it folded up on the lakeshore, with a perfectly placed bullet. I shot at my moose in my sneakers, so I had left my range finder back with my boots. If I knew the range, I had a decent chance of getting him in one shot because I knew my gun and had practiced those shots.

There are two distances at which the bullet crosses the line of sight. The important one is the point of impact at the distance you sight it in for. The first one is around fifty yards; remember the bullet is an inch and a half below the scope when it leaves, so it takes a few yards to climb up, past the line of sight into its arc. This is where some will say, "Sight it in at 50 and it will be good at 200." Bullshit and bullshit. Sight it in at 200 and figure out where it crosses around 50. Cheating the sighting in process is not good for you or the animal you try to kill.

Maximum point-blank range is the piece of ballistics data you want to use to set up your rifle. Based on the speed, weight, and ballistic coefficient of the ammo you will hunt with, you can get this value from a ballistics chart. You will pick a high/low range for the trajectory, say +/- 4 inches. The program will tell you what yardage to sight your gun in to, and give you a maximum yardage. You will always be in that +/- 4-inch window up to that maximum yardage. +/- 4" is an 8" circle or kill zone. That is about right for a large deer. So, anything up to that maximum range, you simply hold center knowing that your bullet will hit that deer within the 8" kill zone. No muss, no fuss, just aim and make a good shot. You let the gun do what it was designed to do, you are just the spark that ignites it.

Anything over the maximum point-blank range, then you start to think about how much to hold over. My rifle would have a PBR of 360 yards so anything over that requires a hold over. This yardage is really pushing my capabilities of making a clean, crisp, deadly shot anyway, so my answer is to get closer.

Most people don't think this deep, but did you know that what your eyes see and brain processes is no longer there? It takes time for the reflected light that represents the animal to get to your eye. Then it takes time for your brain to process that information. Then add the time to aim and decide to shoot, plus the time of the flight of the bullet. The animal can move a lot during all this. Think about this when you decide ethically how far you are willing to shoot at an animal.

Lesson – Quit spending money on guns and go hunt

Quit spending money on new guns and go hunting. You only need one gun to hunt; you cannot carry more than one with you. You need to pick one gun that you love, one you love to shoot and can shoot well. You need to save money to go on the hunting trip of your dreams. Quit buying more fucking guns!

Arrow Trajectory Can be Vital to Success

With a bow, you have multiple pins set up for different yardages, or you move a single pin to a location based on a yardage. This is how you deal with trajectory of an arrow. Seems simple, what else is there to think about?

The arrow flies higher than the sight, in order to get to the target at a given distance. How high it flies depends on how far you are trying to shoot, the farther away the bigger the arc needs to be. This becomes very important when shooting through things like brush and branches. Most of us target practice in wide-open spaces, then try to shoot animals where there is little room for an arrow to fly. Not knowing how your arrow flies will send it into a tree limb. The clear shooting you see between the pin and the deer heart is not where the arrow flies. When I shot my mountain lion, a branch covered the spot I wanted to hit, but I knew that in that point of the trajectory my arrow would be higher and fly right over that branch. I aimed right at the branch covering the cat's heart and let the shot go.

There is a classic video of Fred Bear shooting a ram that is on the other side of the mountain. He could see the rams back, but the mountain covered the vitals. Fred Bear knew the trajectory of his arrow would fly right over the hill, dropping into the vitals of the ram. So, he aimed at the mountain and shot, killing the ram.

Practicing these kinds of shots are crucial. Putting a target behind a tree and slipping an arrow past the tree to hit the target is way harder than you think. That tree can get in your head. Concentrating on the target spot never changes and the flight of the arrow won't either, so the tree has absolutely nothing to do with it. The only way to keep it out of your head is to practice it.

My cousin didn't shoot a deer walking through the woods. When asked why, he said, "There are a lot of trees." My response was, "The slug is only three-fourths of an inch wide, you don't have any gaps between the trees wider than that?"

Lesson – Know the range and where to hold

You will always hold low on an animal that is within the range you sighted your gun at.

Lesson – We are used to a whitetail will to live.

The whitetail has an impressive will to live. I have seen them run forever with a hole in their heart or without blood. I have never seen another animal species do that. Most fold up right on the spot, or expire within a few yards. It is important to make that first shot count, and more often than not, it will be all you need.

Russian Moose

Now for The Entire Story

Diary: November 25, 2015
Last day of work. I will be off for twenty-one days. This is the longest, by far, I have ever taken off at one time. Off to Corning tonight to play with the Wilcox's. I need a distraction. My anxiety level on this trip has been peaked for days, more than any other trip. My body is not taking the adrenaline dump well and I hope I don't burn out. I am writing this after I got back home, so I will confess that I have had bad dreams and thoughts about this trip. Since most of my dreams on other hunts were good and basically came true, I have been scared that this one was going to go bad, maybe life-threateningly bad.

Diary: November 26, 2015
Thanksgiving Day with the Wilcox clan

Diary: November 27 - 28, 2015
I did my final packing. Got it figured out and it is underweight. Waiting for my girlfriend to get back here to spend the night with me and take me to the airport in the morning.

Diary: November 29 and 30, 2015 - Travel to Moscow
It is Sunday and we are on the road at 6:30 AM. I wanted to be there at 8:30 when customs opens to get a 4475-form completed. This proves that I took my gun out of the country, allowing me to bring it back. Who knew they did not open on weekends, but the one nice lady manning the office opened and did the form for me anyway. I appreciate that.

Checking in the gun went smooth. I appreciated the fact the ticket agent checked and checked again to make sure he did it right. I love it when people take the extra step.

This is the start of a thirty-hour day ending in a hotel in Moscow. First stop is Chicago. I got a little confused where to go there. I had to ask. The International terminal is a train ride away. Luckily, I got a good long layover. I had some beer and food at a bar near the gate. I talked to an older Mexican lady bartender about the trip. She was flipping out. It always amazes me who you might run into that thinks hunting is cool.

Fred and Ted finally show up at the bar across from the gate. They seemed like good guys.

So, I have to tell you about the flight across the Atlantic because I just had to laugh to myself. This plane had five seats in the middle and mine was second in. I usually prefer the aisle. Then it was in behind one of the bulkheads, so I couldn't put my airplane survival backpack under the seat in front of me. I hate getting out of a seat for anything. Then this woman sits in the aisle seat next to me. She has issues with the seat and is going to tell every flight attendant about it. Good, I thought, move and I will snag your aisle seat. She didn't move; she just bitched. The cool thing about the bulkhead was that it had spots to hang a baby basinet on the wall, so in the row there were two little babies. I will never complain about a crying baby on a flight, they must do what they have to do to keep the pressure in their ears right. Matter of fact, I have been known to threaten whiny-ass businessmen that cry about crying babies. The one thing that made me laugh was when the woman next to me whipped out her breast to breastfeed. Pretty normal and I am okay with that, but the husband and the baby were still minutes away. I had to laugh. The woman next to me then spilled her drink on my leg. I sat back in my seat and closed my eyes, laughing to myself that this was how I was going to earn my moose; only ten more hours to go!

It was just a typical airport experience and flight but it got a little crazy when we got to the baggage claim in Moscow. There we met Andre Konovalov, who would escort us the entire trip. We had to complete a few hours of paperwork to get our guns into Russia. When Russians talk to each other they sound pissed, so it was tough to tell how it was going. All we could do was stand there and sign papers when asked.

A couple-hour cab ride to the hotel and we finally can get cleaned up. A couple beers and some food at the hotel bar, and my first shot of vodka, and I am feeling much better. Now for some much-needed sleep after thirty hours of travel. Ten time zones covered today.

One thing in the hotel caught my eye, and it kind of defined the differences between Russia and what we are used to in the U.S.: the hair dryer on the wall. This is a pretty high-end hotel in Moscow, built for the Summer Olympics held in Russia in 1980. This is the same Olympics that the U.S. boycotted because Russia had invaded Afghanistan in 1979. Anyway, this is a pretty nice facility. The hair dryer was a plastic box, with a vacuum-type hose. At the end of the hose was a plastic plug with a rectangle slot cut into it. It didn't work very well either. Maybe it's just me, but this hair dryer blew my mind. Go to Walmart and you can choose between six or ten fancy-looking, bright-colored, powerful hair dryers. Granted, we get these things from China, but that even makes matters worse. Russia isn't even trading with the same people we are? The world seems like such a small place to us with our technology and money to travel, but to others it isn't. We are a million miles away and they have no clue the things that exist out there.

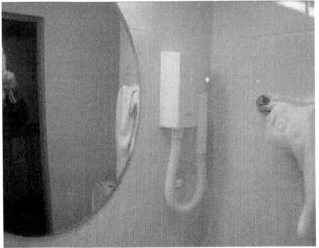

A hair dryer in a high end Moscow hotel.

Diary: December 1 and 2, 2015
Another Twenty-five-hour day of travel

This afternoon we fly to Petrovalosk. We have some time in the morning, so Andre takes us via subway to Red Square. In the station at Red Square, there are bronze statues of soldiers. One has a dog. It is good luck to rub the dog's nose, so it is all bright and shiny from everyone rubbing the tarnish off.

Not a great picture, but I need the luck of rubbing the dog's nose.

Red Square was very impressive. It was an honor to be near such a historic Communist place. I am sure Putin was running around somewhere. We walked through Lenin's tomb. He has been preserved since 1926. Of course, Fred asked, "Who is the guy in the box?" The two Cathedrals were impressive. We went inside the small cathedral, watching people come in and out praying and kissing the Jesus on the cross. They are very religious and it was a pretty awesome thing to witness.

Resurrection Gate

The wall on the right is Kremlin Wall. All the important Communist leaders are buried in this wall. Putin is running around somewhere behind there.

On the right is Lenin's Mausoleum.
On the left is the most famous building in Red Square, St. Basil's Cathedral.

Museum

The Russian version of the clock tower "Big Ben"

GUM, Russia's most famous shopping mall

The Center of Russia, (0,0) Where everything in Russia is measured from.

Off to another airport in Moscow for a couple hours of gun paperwork. We finally board a huge and full airplane. I was expecting to ride an old prop plane bouncing through the air for nine time zones. This was the best flight of them all. It had great food, our own TVs, and I was in view of the bathroom. Not bad at all.

This may sound like an easy day, but it was twenty-five hours long. After arriving in Petro, which is a tiny, little run-down place, we waited hours in a small room to get our bags and doing even more gun paperwork. One negative I noticed very quickly about the Russian people is that they have no consideration for others. They just bulldoze right through you.

We are met by Sergi, the outfitter and camp owner. He has two SUV Toyota Land Cruisers and we pack our stuff and head for Milkovo, about a five-hour drive. I ride with Andre and the other two hunters rode with Sergi. This is fun for me, because Andre can speak English, so we can talk. Sergi speaks no English, so that is a quiet ride — well except for Fred running his mouth, I am sure.

Sergi stops for beer and fish jerky. They take us to a liquor store where we load up with vodka, whiskey and beer. Drinking at camp is the last thing on my mind, as I am focused on moose hunting, but I had to have some sort of stock to celebrate with. Who knows when I might get a moose on the ground; I could be celebrating for days.

On the Internet, Petro is called the worst city in Russia. It was built up in the Cold War days because of its closeness to Alaska. At that time there was a large military presence. Once the Cold War ended, the military all but pulled out and with it went all the finances. Nothing has been upgraded since the Cold War and it showed. I am sure it would have looked better with snow cover, but it sure was a desolate, run-down place. Yet there were people walking the streets and little kids running around. Who am I to judge? Actually, I really wasn't judging them as much as I was judging myself. The money I am spending on the quest for a moose rack could support five, six, or more of these people for a year.

There is only one road that runs up through the Kamchatka Peninsula, and it runs up the valley between the two mountain ranges. The south portion of the road was paved and wide. I am sure to have lots of room to push snow back, and it piles up by the foot. The farther north we got the worse it got, ending in only a gravel road. The first part of the trip was snowing with high winds. The winds made me nervous. I was concerned the most about how bad the wind chill might be when we hunted. Andre explained that the climate changed drastically the farther north we went, and there were no guarantees the weather would be the same. We were hoping for snow because last word was that there was no snow in camp. Without snow in camp, the original and "easy" hunting plan was falling apart.

We get to this little fenced-in house and we pull the trucks behind the fence. This is our hotel for the night, a small little place with three bedrooms. It was quaint and comfortable. Sergi goes about cutting up a smorgasbord of snacks. First to hit the table was raw salmon. Then we find out his business is processing meats into sausage-type things, so we had a ton of sausages to choose from. And bread, they love their dried-up, hard loaves of bread. Then we broke out the beer and Vodka. Why not? My bed was right around the corner.

Our first stay in Milkovo

Being hungry, I ate a ton of snacks and was feeling pretty good. Next thing I know, two Russian women walk in with their arms full of groceries. Turns out these women own the little place and they are about to cook dinner for us. Oh my God, they cooked everything; it was a meal bigger than Thanksgiving Day.

We had a fun little party. I have no idea how many shots of Vodka went down and I don't remember getting into bed. Andre was busy translating questions, because they wanted to know everything about us. The woman who owned the house was a financial planner in the village. That struck me funny; I wouldn't expect them to have enough money to save for retirement. Turns out Russians retire very early. Fifty years old is considered old for them. Maybe that is why this simple life is good for them, it makes retiring early easier.

Diary: December 3, 2015
The ride into camp.

We are up and on the road at 7:00 AM. Breakfast is the same meats and cheese we had last night, with my first cup of instant coffee. They did have a tub with a handheld shower head, so I took advantage of my last—kind of—shower for the next ten days.

Sunrise is not till 9:30 in the morning, so we drove the few hours in the dark. We had the same riding arrangements as yesterday. Sergi would tear off and leave us, because Andre was a very cautious driver. It made me laugh, because he just had to sit and wait for us to catch up.

They had talked about this river crossing that we had to do. In the warm months, there was a ferry. In the cold months it was an ice crossing. The concern was that because of the unseasonably warm weather they had, they did not know what the conditions would be. What they never would talk about was if it was in between—frozen over, but not hard enough. I knew that meant the hunt was probably over before we got there. I was nervous.

Driving the dark snowy roads, Sergi pulls over, gets out and comes to my door. He opens it and reaches in to undo my seatbelt. He then pushes the door open and points to it. In my head, just like in the movies, this is where he takes me into the woods, kills me, and leaves my body. Andre finally speaks and says, "He wants you to hold the door open, and be ready to jump out. We are crossing the frozen river first."

WE ARE?

On trips like these, there are so many moments when you must do things based on blind faith. My intelligent brain is saying, *Why the hell don't I walk and you drive across?* At the same time, I am sucking it up and saying, *let's see what happens*. Off we go. You could tell the ice was on the edge of cracking just a few days ago. It was cracked and rough and others must have just made it. As we pull up to the bank on the other side, Andre confesses that was the deepest river we would cross. The Kamchatka River drains the entire valley we just drove through. If we went through, the truck would have disappeared.

"The rest of the rivers, we can drive through," says Andre. I hate rushing water. I have a phobia and it scares the shit out of me. I don't want to cross any rivers, ever. As we drive on, I laugh at myself. I have crossed so many rivers in my hunting and I never once have taken the time to stop and be scared. On horseback, on four-wheeler, in a rental car, in a truck, I have waded in with my clothes on and stripped down naked. I have tight-rope-walked giant logs, and I still sit here scared of rivers.

We drive into this village that just looked like a bunch of abandoned buildings. Your mind immediately thinks of a Zombie or *Terminator* movie. But in the mess of collapsing buildings you see wood smoke from a fire and there is life here.

We stop and sit and a few minutes later this army truck pulls up. In the truck is Sasha, the truck owner, and Barbara, soon to be our camp cook. After some Russian yelling (discussion) we are told that we will load all our gear in the truck and we humans will squeeze into one Range Rover for the next leg of the trip. We are now leaving civilization, if you could call it that. Twenty kilometers in (about twelve miles) we will come to an intermediate camp.

This sounds easy—ha!

The Range Rover has cables tied from the brush bars on the front to the roof rack. These are supposed to help push the tree branches away from the windshield. That works very well about 10 percent of the time. The trail has been rutted up by this heavy army truck over many trips in the mud. Today it is frozen and Sergi struggles to miss the ruts. Most of the time, we have one side into rut and the truck tips violently. I don't know the Russian terms for "Oh shit" and "Please God help us" but I do know Sergi used them a lot.

The less violent parts of the trail.

The rivers were wide, and I couldn't tell how deep. They were still running, but the edges were iced over. We just drove out onto the ice and it would break, dropping us into the water that was about door height. The ice buildup on the other side was challenging, you just keep running into it until it breaks away, then you hope you can get close enough to a tree to use the winch, if needed.

In the middle of one of the many river crossings

I think the twelve-mile trip took us a little over three hours. But we pulled into this awesome little camp with multiple buildings. There were other hunters there, packing to leave. Sergi would leave us and take them back to civilization.

The intermediate camp, this was the main cabin

A few outbuildings and the hunter's cabin

They whisked us into the cook cabin and pushed us to the table. We would try to be polite and I guess shy, and they wanted you to sit and eat. Because they could not talk to us, there was a lot of pushing and pulling. I am not one to be pushed around, so I found it hard to understand that they were just being nice. When I boarded the plane to come home, I remember thinking, no more Russians pushing me around. I had enough of that.

The Cook cabin, and Sergi our Outfitter on the left.

They gave us soup and plenty more snacks. Eventually the owner came in to greet us and it was time for vodka shots. I could tell he was a very proud man. He was proud of what he had built there and he loved to share it. I get that same feeling when we have parties at my ponds. I understood him. I have no issue doing shots, and I felt like you had to keep up with him, to not insult his generosity. This was the first sign that Ted was going to be like Eeyore from Winnie the Pooh—he refused to do shots and he pouted about other shit.

Nickili and Albert, our guides, showed up on snow machines.

Albert patiently waiting to go to our camp.

Nickili was a sixty-four-year-old man with no hair. His face was worn and his hands were stained and rough. Bright blue eyes shined from that worn face and they beamed when he talked. He always smiled when he talked and you knew he was a ball buster, but later in the hunt he had a few Forman fits and it was evident he was in charge. He would be the lead guide and in charge of everything in camp. All I could think when I watched him talk was that I would have loved to chase women with this guy thirty years ago. Later I learned that this camp used to be his and he sold the rights, 50,000 square miles, to Sergi. We later learned that he just came out of lung cancer surgery. This guy was tough.

Albert was a very quiet man. He said very little, but when he did speak, he meant it. I so wanted to tell him that we were very much alike. He was thirty-four years old and had a twelve-year-old daughter back home. He was just a big, tough kid, and Nickili planned to train him to take over lead guide of this camp. He eventually became my guide and we spent a lot of time together. I hated that we could not talk, because we would have become great friends. I could see what he was all about and I knew he could sense the same character and work ethic in me.

The Army truck finally caught up to us. Now we all piled in the back for the rest of the trip. This was not easy, since it was full of food and our gear. We kind of just threw ourselves on top of stuff and they shut the door.

The Russian Army truck, our ride for the rest of the day

Well, here is the bad news. We had to ride about sixty kilometers (about forty miles) this way. The Range Rover turns back, because it is too rough for it to go further. At this point, I am still in street clothes, it is cold as hell out, there is no heat in the truck, and we are sitting on frozen food. Thank God, I was drunk as hell.

Not 100 yards goes by and into a river we go. The truck is very tall and high centered, so every dip or sway is hugely exaggerated inside the truck. Gear is thrown on us and we are thrown on the gear. I am starting to get extremely cold, and for once I'm lucky that my duffle bag is thrown on my lap. I dig out my hunting clothes and put them on, finally warming up. You really couldn't do anything but sit back and relax and fly wherever the truck decided to throw you. The truck was at least two feet wider than the path, so tree branches crashed and scraped the sides of the truck, nonstop. Luckily the alcohol kicked in and I dozed on and off, getting used to much of the chaos, but waking to some of the more violent actions. Nickili and Albert were escorting us on snow machines. Four or five times the truck would come to a sudden, violent halt. Sasha would back up and crash into something, then you would hear the winch wind out and we would pull ourselves through something bad. We couldn't see out, so we really had little idea what the terrain looked like. This was no modern truck by any means. I think he stalled the motor every two or three minutes. I could not believe the starter could take such abuse.

The ride seemed to never end. We had no idea when it would, or even if we were getting closer. It was getting dark now. Nickili stopped us to see if we wanted to sight in our rifles. He did not want to do it at camp, because we hoped the camp would be surrounded by moose. I did not want to, but I had to make sure my rifle made the trip unharmed, so we dug through the pile of gear and dragged our rifle cases out into the snow.

Nickili rode a piece of cardboard out to a bush about 100 yards away. The light was fading and we could barely see him. We rested on the windshield of Albert's snow machine. Nickily took a few steps back and yelled to shoot, in Russian. I wanted to argue, but how could I, so I buckled down and in haste squeezed a round off. Oh God, I wanted that shot to be good so bad, and it was. Phew! We climb back in and continue the roller coaster ride from hell.

After shooting the guns, I made myself a better seat.

The winch came into play multiple times. In one spot they used it three times to pull us up some sort of steep incline. We were now getting used to the frequent stops, stalls with engine starts, and so on. I had given up on wishing we would get there long ago. Another deep creek crossing and the truck rolled to another stop. A couple minutes of silence and the door opened. We had finally arrived!

I was cold and tired and felt like I was a BB in a maraca. I had no idea what to expect when I crawled out that door. What I expected was to stand in the frigid cold while we set up camp, wall tents and all. To my delight, there stood a little village of cabins. They pointed to the cabin in front of the truck. That would be the hunters cabin, Andre explained. I grabbed a couple of bags and headed toward the door. Walking in, the woodstove heat struck me. It was already warm. Nothing could have made me feel better or taken away my anxiety like that warm cabin. Just maybe, I could survive this trip.

The hunter cabin was spacious and more comfortable than I could have hoped.

It was nighttime now. The sun set at 4:30, and it was much later than that. We had been locked in that truck for over five hours. The air was harshly crisp and the sky was so clear. Millions of stars blanketed us overhead. We unpacked our gear as Barbara prepared some food in the dining cabin. After a thirty-hour day, then a seventeen-hour day based on someone else's schedule, I looked forward to sitting in an outhouse and catching up on things. As I opened the door with my flashlight in hand, all I saw was a hole in the outhouse floor. Um. We were gonna have to rethink our approach to this chore.

No worries of your ass freezing to the seat in this outhouse.

An impromptu meal was nothing short of amazing. We sat and talked the best we could through Andre and celebrated our future hunt with beer and shots of Vodka. Because I was the coffee drinker, Nickili showed me how to heat the water and where the instant coffee was. We would wake up at 7:00, but we would not hunt until after the sun rose, about 10:00 AM.

Andre coaching Barbara on how to cook

Diary: December 4, 2015
Hunting Day 1

Fred gets his moose

I fell asleep hard for three or four hours, but then I was wide-awake. I am
not sure if I should laugh or kill the others in the cabin. They were snoring,
which I am very sure I did my fair share of, and the old spring cots
squeaked every time one of us moved. It was kind of funny. Then the
wood stove started just right, built to a sauna-like temperature, then died,
quickly relenting to the frigid outdoor temperature. I was not complaining;
it was far more comfortable than I ever expected. Mostly the anticipation
of the hunt kept me awake. I won't ever complain about that feeling. I live
for it.

Oh, and being older now and having to pee in the middle of the night is always a pain, but this time was damn cold. Of course, each of us with multiple trips kept us all awake. This was the last night I went out. Turns out the fear of freezing your balls off can curb the urge to have to pee in the middle of the night.

At 6:30 AM, I finally had to get up. Dressing in the dark, I headed to the cook cabin to start the coffee. Damn if I couldn't figure out how to light the stove. Turns out, there was no gas left.

The clear sky evacuated every ounce of heat from the valley. The temperature was way below zero. Now I was wondering if I had brought enough clothes.

After breakfast I had some time to take some camp pictures.

They expected to see moose near camp.

Little did I know that I was looking at my mode of transportation for the week.

Not sure what the girl on the beach was for, other than to tease us.

Our cabin is on the far left, the guides and cook slept in the peak of the center cabin, and the cook cabin was on the right.

They had one man assigned to firewood.

I love the mountains, the crisp air and the sunshine.

The main trail into camp was rutted pretty heavily by the truck.

It was close to hunting time so we started to dress. The guides tried to fasten old car bucket seats to these wooden sleds. They kept a watchful eye out for moose near camp. Nickili chose Ted to guide because he looked the biggest, I guess. He lifts weights, but only bench and curls from what I could tell. Albert chose to guide Fred, and so I would go with Sasha. We got a late start. You could tell they hoped to bag a couple moose right around camp. Sasha and I were third in line, and we did an hour and half run around the area.

Getting my ride ready. Caribou hide is the best insulator.

They decided to go back for lunch, so the train took off. Running these sleds in the tracks of the truck was a pain in the ass. My sled fell in and rolled and I was sent skipping across the snow. The funny part— well, with a few swear words—was that Sasha never, ever looked back. Off they went. I could see the camp about a mile away so I started walking, laughing, wondering what the look on their faces would be when they got there without me.

Sasha met me at camp and said he was sorry. I had calmed down by then and smiled and laughed. I was more disappointed that we were back eating again. Poor Barbara was a food pusher. I still had a poor appetite, we had just eaten breakfast, and I wanted to hunt. I was a bit short tempered. The other hunters told me to not offend the cook, but I thought fuck the cook. I couldn't eat. I am not very good at being pushed around.

Finally, we got back out hunting. We left in a train, with Sasha and I bringing up the rear. From what I could tell, we would ride out to a swamp. They would drop us off and then run the surrounding woods and bush to push moose in front of us.

The ride was interesting. I was still trying to get used to holding on to this sled, and I almost went over a few more times. Sasha never, ever looked back. As guides go, I am sure I drew the short straw. But, I thought I could read between the Russian lines and know what was going on. Guides quickly assess who their hunters are, and the others had already shown signs of wanting to get it over with. So, get them to the easy moose and get them out of the way. I cannot prove this, but the thought made me content to ride along in third place.

The Frozen swamp. This is heaven for a moose.

As we enter the swamp, Sasha and I stayed there. The others ride across the flat swamp and disappear out of sight. A few seconds later, four or five shots rang out. A few minutes of pause then a handful more. Both hunters must have run into moose. I liked my position: if any moose started running around I felt like I was in a prime spot to intercept them. Sasha got antsy, and waved to go after them. Sasha was the one who cut up the moose in the field, and he was thinking he has moose to work on. This I later figured out.

We finally found a couple of the sleds and Sasha got his ass chewed. The moose was still on the loose and the snow machine noise could have run it away. Plus, we were in prime position if the moose continued to run.

So, Fred had done the shooting. Albert found the track and sign that a moose was hit. They finally tracked it down and finished off after a total of 15 shots. Fred had never seen a rack; he just saw moose and might have shot at two different moose. I am not sure the guides were really happy about that, but they let it blow over.

Fred was the first to score on the first afternoon of hunting.

The chocolate coloring of this animal is gorgeous.

After photos in the fading light and a fire, Nickili loaded the three of us up on one sled and sleigh and dragged us back to camp. That was not a fun ride. I was on the front of the sled with nothing to hold on to, and Nickili was balls out in everything he does.

The first day was a success. Fred seemed happy with his moose. He may have been happier to not have to deal with the cold anymore. I was happy for him and happy to get one hunter out of the way. This meant Ted and I had three guides working for us. I also got to see what a moose looked like. I learned some very important things. As racks go, this moose was not like the pictures we all look at. In the field I guessed it to be less than forty-eight inches. As the size of moose racks go in this area, that size would be subpar. When we arrived at camp I measured the width at a surprising fifty-four inches, putting it into the average-plus range. I was so glad this happened, because now my expectations were in line. I did not want to pass up a moose thinking it was too small, only to find out after English translation that my guide was telling me it was huge. My guess was that Fred's moose was rather young.

Diary: December 5, 2015
Hunting Day 2

The evening was overcast which kept some of the heat in. It was still below zero, but this was the warmest morning we had. This was the kind of gloom I expected, so I was thankful of the bright sunny day yesterday. Maybe we would get some fresh snow.

The morning ritual started to sink in. I made coffee at 7:00 along with an attempt to the outhouse. Breakfast was always too early for me. When we were done, the guides would come in and eat. Then we would make the plan for the day. We would try the other direction.

I knew Ted and I would be travelling together, so I suggested we decide who gets first choice to shoot. I didn't want any hard feelings. He agreed and we flipped a coin, with me winning first choice.

We travelled a long way that morning, in and out of frozen creeks along old truck trails and in and out of the woods and brush. I was with Albert now. He was very conscientious and paid close attention to the client he was pulling through the snow. He would make wide turns to avoid the trees, and understood how the sled reacted to keep it out of the deep ruts. Nickili on the other hand went until he hit something.

Nickili and Ted are stopped a bit ahead of us. Ted was up with his gun out and Nickili was yelling for him to shoot. We slid up and I jumped off. By this time, the moose was leaving and I couldn't pick it up. The guides were mad that Ted did not shoot; Ted was waiting for me to shoot, per our deal. Well I guess that all backfired on us. We missed our first good opportunity.

We were travelling so far that we took gas with us in cans and left it at a drop off point to be used over the following days. We followed each other in a train for the morning, seeing moose tracks all over, but we were behind them.

I guess I should explain how this is supposed to work. There is supposed to be three or four feet of snow. A nice crust on top would allow the snow machines to travel fast and smooth. That same crusted snow basically traps the moose since they have to fight through it. You find a track, you drive up to the slow-moving moose, and you decide if you want to shoot him at maybe 60-70 yards. Easy! Well we have about six inches of snow. Riding is far from smooth and far from fast because we are running over everything. The moose can move freely and can hear us coming a mile or two away. Advantage moose!

About 1:30 we stopped and made a fire. Barbara made us sandwiches and candy bars, and they were frozen solid, so I just gnawed on them. They did bring Chhay. That means tea. See I did learn a Russian word.

A little frozen lunch and Chhay for a midday break.

Finally, we broke up and went our separate ways. I could tell the plan was to run in different areas, hoping one sled would kick moose out toward another. The snow proved it was working: we would run a valley with no tracks. A half hour later we ran it again and three moose had crossed. A couple hours later, even more tracks crossing it. Albert would make a little walking sign with his fingers and say "Momma and baby," pointing one direction, then say "Papa" and point the other direction. This turned out to be the story of my life.

This picture makes me feel cold.
These draws would taper steeply toward the river.

We found each other close to sundown and started the long track home. Again, Nickili and Ted were far ahead of us. We caught up to them and found Ted standing there with his rifle raised. My instinct was to watch Ted shoot, but we were so bundled up that the only place the heat could escape was around my head. Moving in the sled kept the wind on my glasses, keeping them from fogging, but as soon as we stopped, they immediately fogged up. Ted was wearing ski goggles and had trouble seeing out of them for the same reason.

So, there were two Bull Moose standing there and Ted couldn't see them because of fogged goggles, and he also must have breathed on his scope. I was trying desperately to clean off my glasses so I could watch Ted shoot. Nickili was yelling and pointing; he was actually a little too pissed for my liking. Ted yelled, "I can't see it." I really didn't know at this point if Nickili was pointing at a moose or where a moose used to be. Then Albert turned to me and I guess asked me why I did not shoot the second moose. Now I was frustrated. The Russians wanted all of us to throw lead. I wouldn't ever shoot an animal that someone else is lining up the sights on. Our morals were too far apart right now and we couldn't talk about it. Nickili yelled at Ted to sit down in the sled, and he tore off. In his mind he showed Ted three moose today and Ted failed to do his part. Luckily, we had a while to ride and I thought it through. If he had yelled at me like that we would have acted out the Rocky versus Russian fight right there in the bush. I decided it was Ted's fight to bring up.

We pulled into camp and I immediately took my glove off and shook Albert's hand, thanking him for the effort. The story escalated quickly when we got into the cabin and could speak to Andre. Through Andre, Nickili got to understand why Ted did not shoot and all was well, except for Ted's hurt pride.

I asked Andre to tell Albert that he was a very good and conscientious guide. He took care of his client very well and I appreciated it. He didn't react much, but I could sure see how that compliment made him feel the next day. He got even better. I am probably one of very few that had ever taken the effort to compliment the kid.

We had a very nice dinner of Russian food. They eat a lot of preserved things like sausages and cheese, and make a ton of dishes out of Sauerkraut. We always had a nice soup to warm us up. I stayed away from the vodka. It was time to hunt, not time to be hung over. I knew it affected my sleep because it dried me out so much. I also knew that being dehydrated was no way to tackle -30 C temperatures. Clear skies again and the thermometer was whistling as the red shit fell to the bottom.
We were told we would ride to another outpost camp twenty miles away and hunt from there. That excited me because I already had this feeling we would have to go find the moose, so I was game for a change in scenery.

Diary: December 6, 2015
Hunting Day 3

We wake up to the same morning ritual as the previous days. Today it is cold, around -30 degrees Celsius. So far, the way I've been dressing has worked pretty well. My body has stayed warm. My toes have had moments of cold, but I have been able to wiggle the toes to keep them warm; amazingly considering at this temperature the leather is concrete hard. Luckily, I bought some great Arctic Shield fingered gloves. The problem today is that I could not get the fingers dry. They last for a while, but eventually start to freeze up. Then I would change them out for my Arctic Shield Glommits. I learned very quickly that having extra gloves in a pack only meant I was changing into frozen gloves. Today I will carry all my extra gloves inside my bibs, to keep them warm.

The real issue is the fogging of my glasses, especially when we stop. Today I will try my light archery mask, my Arctic Shield beanie, and my baseball cap on top of that. This leaves out the wool facemask that I have been using. My face will have to bear the bitter cold, but I must try something new or I will never see a moose to shoot it. The baseball cap might help keep the snow off my glasses. I am only going to get one chance at a moose—it is time to suck it up and fight off the cold.

The remote camp idea got cancelled. We would go back to the same place we ran yesterday. I really couldn't argue; it was obvious the moose were there. Luckily not very far from camp the belt broke on Nickili's snow machine. Of course, the best place to keep your spare belt is camp, right? Albert went back to get belts and we waited.

Riding together sucked from a hunting point of view, but I couldn't argue it for safety reasons.

Today I was on point. I really wanted to see the moose before Albert did. My face was faring well in the bitter cold, but the worst was when we broke new trail and the fresh snow kicked up in my face. We spent a few hours in a gulley and in the woods. If felt promising, but resulted in nothing.

The trail leads us to the swamp first. The overcast from the day before is starting to move aside; you can see the end of the weather front breaking over the mountains. This is one of my favorite pictures, as the clouds unveil the mountains in front of me. The swamp extends for miles ending in brush, then turn into spruce forest, then the gradual slopes of the mountain, ending in the steep snow-covered peaks.

This picture sums up all the terrain features in one shot.

Back to the draws we ran yesterday. We pounded them hard and pushed our limits deeper and deeper. We got the sled stuck multiple times and I had to hike a few hills that it couldn't drag my ass up. We saw tracks and they were still ahead of us.

We raced to the opposite end of the hunting grounds, over where Fred shot his moose. Behind the woods where he got his was an awesome spot at the base of the mountain. It was great bedding area, but violently rough riding into it. I think Albert finally realized that I was game for anything and into it we went. There was moose sign everywhere. Tracks, beds and most of all a lot of bull shit (literally). It was exciting to see it all. I took up a watch while Albert ran around with the sled. Without me, he could move faster and often came back saying he saw moose.

We searched hard, until darkness made us go back to camp.

Diary: December 7, 2015
Hunting Day 4

The coldest day we've had. Here we go again. Ted and Nickili head for the river to walk it. Albert, Sasha, and I head a few miles down the river. Sasha and I take up a watch as Albert puts on a drive. Nothing came my way, yet Albert saw moose.

I was ecstatically excited to have two guides with snow machines with me. We planned on going back to the bedding area with all the moose sign. They would drop me off and run both sleds around. That sounded like a plan that would work.

As we quit the river watch we see Fred standing on the trail. He had hiked the trail out for something to do. He was a long way out and Sasha couldn't leave him there, so he let him ride with him. This screwed up our plans and I could tell Albert was not happy about it. So, he and I just went and repeated what we had done before. We rode hard through the rough shit and saw tracks leading away from us.

We were told in a letter from Denny that after three days the hunting would get hard. The moose would get irritated by the snow machine noise and just head to the mountains. Every track I saw today was headed to the mountains. We were no longer chasing them around, we were chasing them away.

Frustration was obvious in Albert's actions. We took off across the swamp, as fast as we could go. I was getting beat on the sled, and fighting the snow getting thrown into my face. We went miles farther than we had ever been. We came to a creek that was not frozen and simply sped right over the water. We circled up into a whole new valley. Albert was desperately trying to find a new area that had moose. At this point, my gloves were frozen solid, but I had to hold on tight. Albert finally stopped and asked if I was cold, by hugging himself and making a shivering motion. I told him to wait while I changed my gloves. We were a long way from camp, and when he said "camp" we were headed back.

As fast as we could go, we rode. A couple of the shots hurt my back pretty good. Cold was settling into my body hard. We came to that same creek and this time he stopped to ask me if he could cross. What the hell am I supposed to do now, stay here? I waved to go for it. I wondered how bad it would be if my sled didn't make it.

Before I could convince myself that we were just trying real hard for a moose. Now, I was convinced that Albert wanted me to quit. He was going to run me into the ground hoping I would give up. The thought of that just made me fight harder.

We got within a mile of camp, almost pitch dark. The guide stopped and pointed to camp, then to the swamp on the left. I pointed to the swamp. I can still see; I still want to go. My fingers did not like that decision so much. When we finally arrived at camp, I shook my guide's hand, patted him on the shoulder and said, "Tomorrow." I wanted him to know I was not done. I was going out to do it all over again, but the odds were starting to stack against me.

I didn't take any pictures today. I did nothing but hold on and try to stay warm.

Diary: December 8, 2015
Hunting Day 5 Big moose down, in my sneakers.

We are now back to where I started this book. This day's diary entry was my recollection of the day as I waited in the Moscow hotel to go home. I knew I wanted to make a significant Facebook post so that all the people who had followed me in my planning would get the story. These stories are easy for me because they're what I see when I close my eyes. It is the raw emotion that fires adrenaline through my body as a recall the steps. This is what I live for. This gives me life.

I am the first one up this morning. I drink instant coffee in the dining cabin, with my ass by the roaring fireplace. I am feeling quite emotional as I sip my coffee in the dark. I got my ass beat yesterday, beat extremely bad. I was pounded on that sled, I was frozen to the point of severe pain, but I kept going and I would not quit. We only stopped the sled once all day, and I peeled my frozen solid gloves off and put new warm ones on. We got within a mile of camp, almost pitch dark. The guide stopped and pointed to camp, then to the swamp on the left. I pointed to the swamp. I can see, I still want to go. My fingers did not like that decision so much. When we finally arrived at camp, I shook my guides hand, patted him on the shoulder and said, "tomorrow." I wanted him to know I was not done. I was going out to do it all over again, but the odds were starting to stack against me.

We were warned that if you didn't get your moose in three days, they would head to the mountain to get away from the snowmobiles. Every track I saw yesterday headed to the mountain. We rode so hard because I think Albert either wanted me to get a moose really bad, or he wanted to beat me into quitting. Either way, I knew that he knew that it was getting impossibly hard to get in front of the moose.

I was having a hard time feeling sorry for myself for wanting a "trophy", after all the hardship I had seen on the trip to camp. I felt ashamed to even feel bad about it. Plus, it is such a tough thing to come home empty handed. People shun you, like you did something stupid. "How could you spend all that money and not get anything," some say. Those people never really get why I do this. In contrast, the other hunters in camp were only focused on a rack. I hated their uniquely American attitude.

What I could say was this: I was leaving everything I had out there in that cold. Every now and then I would yell, "I am hunting in Russia" and I would suck it up. I knew one thing for sure, I was never coming back here, and I was not going home regretting not doing everything I could. The only thing that was going to stop me was a moose on the ground, or them pushing me in that army truck to go home.

On the other hand, I am fully aware how blessed and lucky I am. I never take that for granted. The greatest benefit of a trip like this is renewing my appreciation for my family back home and my life.

So, as I drank my coffee, I became very content with the fact that I would likely go home without a moose. I was proud of what I had put into it over the five days of travel and four days of hunting. You'll never take away what is in my head, and I am very grateful for that.

An hour and a half later, our cabin door is kicked in by my Russian guide, with his toothbrush in his mouth, spewing Russian and throwing his hands up like a giant moose rack. He saw a bull, turns out a half mile away, while brushing his teeth. So, out the door I went.

Luckily, I had already put my hunting pants on. I expected to shoot from camp, so I threw on my untied sneakers, grabbed my coat and on the way out grabbed my frozen gun sitting outside. Standing by the shitter, he tried to get me to see the moose. I finally picked it out and got the scope on it, but it was a million miles away.

So off we went, running through the frozen swamp. This is a bitch, because it is covered with little moguls. I slipped and stagger and fell many times. I lost my damn sneaker once and had to dig it out of the snow. We ran over a quarter-mile, stopping and trying to see if I should shoot. I had no idea the range, since my rangefinder binoculars were still in the cabin. Then I saw Albert come to a small creek and wade right through it in his rubber boots. Well, no turning back now, in the water I went with my sneakers on.

The swamp is nothing but little hidden moguls that sucked off your sneakers and dumped you on your ass.

We finally get to the last spruce tree as cover. Like a Charlie Brown Christmas tree, it is not hiding much. It is time to shoot. Now I am hot and sweaty, and trying hard not to fog up my glasses or the scope. I have nothing to rest my gun on. It is feeding, so at first I cannot even tell which way it is facing. Finally, its head comes up. The first shot did nothing, and I am not surprised. You put electrical tape on your barrel to keep the snow out, and it usually blows off. It was rock hard and I am sure deformed the first bullet. Shot two and three went off, and still nothing. When I let shot four go, I had squatted down to use my knee, but still nothing. Did I ruin my scope? Do I suck? I wanted to go home! Then it hit me: that animal is a lot farther away than I think. I raised the scope up over its back, pulled the trigger, and he dropped. It was over in seconds. One shot from my 7mm shut off a 1500-pound animal, like that!

We finished the half-mile run. Once I saw it on the ground I was psyched and relieved and thankful. A giant, eight- or nine-year-old animal with a fifty-seven-inch-wide rack was going to America with me.

I was in awe of the sheer physical size of this thing.

The rest of the crew came by snow machine from camp. They kept making camera motions, but mine was back in camp. I kept showing them my wet, untied sneaker to get them to understand that I needed to go back and get dressed. No hat, no gloves, missing bibs, and three layers under my jacket, it was still -30 degrees Celsius, my hair was soaked from sweat and I was starting to freeze. They finally caught on and we all went back for tea.

Sasha sizing up the rack.

Sasha is in charge of butchering the animal.

That is hunting, hours and hours of nothing but patience and torture for a few minutes of adrenaline rushed excitement. I love it. Sometimes it is better to be lucky than good. I am a lucky man.

Sasha and I head back out to the moose. I am dressed correctly now and it is time to take some pictures. This part I am terrible at. I hate having people wait for me, so I rush through this. The first pictures are your typical trophy pose. The problem is, I must strain to try to hold the head up at the right angle.

Tired, I sat down on the big guy to rest and Sasha got excited and took these pictures. This pose produced the best pictures. I will say this, I was very uncomfortable sitting on the animal because it is not respectful to that animal. I love the pictures, but I wish I had taken more time with a more traditional pose.

I took a few close-up shots for the taxidermy work and then these that really show the rack. Even at this point I did not fully absorb its characteristics. When Albert and I arrived at the moose, he was trying to ask me if I was happy. The only thing he could understand was me shaking my head yes, but I said, "I am happy with him because he is going to America with me."

I knew it was bigger than Fred's. I am not a competitive guy, but I won't lie, I was really happy with that fact. My reluctance was the bullshit I had engrained in my head. A seventy-two-inch-wide moose was possible here. They talked of an eighty-inch moose that a hunter had just blown an opportunity on with a frozen gun. In my head, I wanted to beat sixty inches and I secretly dreamed of breaking sixty-six inches. I knew this moose was not six feet wide. It didn't have those magnificently long points of the moose in magazines.

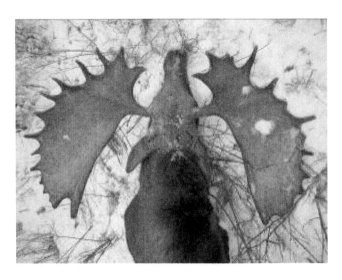

One thing I did notice, that I appreciated very much, was that this moose was a fighter. He has a couple of broken points and his right ear is torn in two places. If you look close at the bases, you can see spots polished off from rubbing trees, telling other Bulls to stay the hell away from my women. That is cool.

So, the answer is yes, I am happy with my moose, especially considering the lessening odds of getting one. All I can really ask is to take home a solid representative of the species I hunt. I couldn't take it anymore, so out came the tape measure. Plus, Devon was on my ass to send back size details. It is fifty-seven inches wide. The part I was missing was the ungodly width of these palms. This moose didn't have all those cool long points because the palms' mass was crazy wide. This moose was a stud. Later Nickili told me that it was between six and eight years old. The one thing I thought as I wrestled with the rack is that I could literally make two high-backed bar stools out of it. You could easily sit in the front tines and lean back.

Now I will say what every dipshit hunter says on TV. "Now the work starts." I hate that. I love the work: it means I was successful and this beast is going to feed a lot of people. Sasha wants me to go back to camp, but I refuse to not help skin this moose. Most hunters would be back drinking tea.

Camp is a half-mile away. How Albert saw this moose brushing his teeth is beyond me.

Skinning I could do, since I have done it for hundreds of animals. Sasha usually does this all by himself. I was very interested to see how he tied up and rolled the moose around with the snowmobile. After the skinning was done, I ran out of talent and just tried to absorb all I could from an expert. The problem was, I was no longer working and I was getting cold pretty fast. There are many ways to cheat when you break down an animal. Sasha was not cheating. As a matter of fact, he harvested everything from that huge gut pile; even the intestines were saved for sausage.

I ran out of talent after the skinning was done, but I put an order in for the inner tenderloins for dinner.

Fred hiked out to see the moose. He talked me into a few pictures of the caped animal.

Finally, Sasha yelled at me to go back to camp. I think I was interfering with his smoke breaks and he wanted to be alone. I was getting damn cold; I had been out there for more than four hours. It was time to go back and celebrate. Those beers I bought were going to get put to good use this afternoon.

This is not the coldest, but I had to get photographic evidence

At dinner, we celebrated the Russian way with nine shots of vodka. You see, it is bad luck not to do shots in groups of three!

December 9, 2015

Today I do nothing and it feels great! My moose head and antlers lie in the snow; I see them in the moonlight as I go to make coffee. What an amazing feeling! If you go back and read what my mental state was like twenty-four hours ago at coffee, you might have a chance of understanding. Yes, a day ago I said that I was okay going home without a moose, but it sure feels good not to have to. It sure feels good not to have to battle the bitter cold and the rough trails. It feels good not to have to fight off the doubt. My chest swells when I think of all I did to get to this point. I am proud of myself, and no one can ever take that away from me.

It feels good to know that all this time, effort, sacrifice, and money paid off. That sentence is a troubling one to write. In my head, even without a moose to take home, this trip would have been worth it. But without taking that trophy home, it is very hard to convince others it was. It gives people at home something to focus on, something to understand. This just hit me as I wrote that. Maybe this is why others can't bring themselves to go on a trip like this. Everything short of bringing home a big rack can seem like a failure. People are so scared to fail. I love it. Everything I am about is from learning from my mistakes or being relentless in learning everything I can so I don't ever make a mistake. Failure is not life ending, it is just a hiccup in the road.

I feel a little bad for Ted this morning. He is now all alone in his quest. He has wanted this over since the first morning. To me, I would be excited. I now have three guides working for me. I would be happy that the other two clowns are out of my way. Sadly, Ted is not like that.

Today, my only goal is to bake in the sauna, or Russian Banya. I love a sauna. To date I have just been in there to warm up and wash up. But today I am going to sweat all the evil out of me. Maybe I will get ballsy enough to jump through the ice.

The Sauna or Russian Banya

Inside of the sauna

It is customary to jump through the ice after the sauna has warmed you up. I didn't hear any takers.

I did have time to take a few more camp photos, this time coming back from the sauna.

Ted came back tonight without seeing a thing. I give him credit for sticking it out. He says he won't quit.

Diary: December 10, 2015
Today I wonder what the hell I am going to do. I don't know how Fred stood it doing nothing all week long. I think he is regretting getting his moose on day one, a little. We come back with all our hardships and things we saw and did and he did not get to experience any of that. I am so lucky I got my moose when I did. Late enough in the week to allow me to pay my dues and get the entire Siberian experience, and early enough not to kill me physically and mentally. I am such a blessed and lucky man!

Now stuck at camp, I long to get back to the mountains.

I have talked about how the guides will see moose when they are on the snow machine alone. They can go faster without us dragging behind. Ted has pissed and moaned about everything on this hunt, but he still vowed to hunt to the end. At breakfast Ted drops a verbal bomb that even I didn't expect. He asks Andre to tell the guides, "I want Albert to shoot a moose for me." My jaw dropped!

My immediate reaction was what a terrible position to put Albert in. We all know Ted is a chronic complainer and even he admits it while he bitches about things. How can Albert ever shoot a moose that Ted will approve of?

One thing I learned about the Russians is they will not answer you in a negative way. After day four, I asked Andre to ask Albert if he was having fun, or if this was becoming just a job. He just kept eating and said nothing. I have spent enough time with Albert to read him, and when Ted proposed this question, he just kept eating. There was no way Albert was going to shoot a moose for Ted. Matter of fact, I had my doubts that Albert would even try to get close to a moose from here on out.

It was all I could do to sit there and keep my mouth shut.

I have one goal in mind when I go on a hunting trip. When I leave, I want my guide to think I was the best hunter he ever guided. I want him to think of me and compare me to all other hunters. I left every guide I ever had feeling like I gained a brother. Sadly, because of the language barrier I didn't get to talk to Albert like I wanted. Guides are very client oriented. In all reality, all they really expect you to do is shoot. Not me. I look at us as a hunting team. I dig in and help. When the snow machine was buried, I got off and pushed; others would have watched. When we couldn't get up a steep bank, I guided my wooden sled back down the steep hill backwards, then hiked up while Albert raced the machine back up the hill. When my moose was down, I stayed for a few hours and helped skin and process it in the field. I knew I had earned the Russians' respect. I could see it in their faces when I pitched in to help.

Ted had done nothing all week but show that he wasn't worthy of hunting with these men. I know they couldn't hear him bitching about everything, but I was unsure how much Andre told them. But he would come to every meal with a pout-ass look on his face, wrinkling his nose up to the food and staring off into space like he was being punished by his daddy. In Nickili's mind, he had put him on three moose and he could not get the job done. In his defense, I had the same issue with fogging glasses, but Ted never tried anything different. He just bitched about it. That question he asked at breakfast just sealed his fate.

I debated whether to write any of this about Ted. It is not my style to berate someone. But, my ultimate intent is to teach others how to be successful on a hunt and Ted is the definition of what you should not do. He paid big money and expected a giant rack. That is all. He missed the experience in between.

In our cabin we all hang out while Ted dresses. "Man, it is tiring putting all these clothes on." He said. Then he dropped another bomb. Twice I wanted to grab him by the throat. This was number two. He said, "Well the good news is, if I don't get a moose I get to take my tip money home." Your tip is based on days of effort your guide puts in, it is not based on your success. This man needs to find a new hobby.

Nickili comes in and grabs Andre and says they are going for a ride. Andre is very good at his job, but he will not go out in the bush. So, I take notice. A few minutes later they return and pull Ted aside to talk. Nickili has an old moose rack stashed in the bush and he offers it to Ted, if Ted quits hunting. I get this from the Russian point of view. They are going through the same pains we are, even though they look like they are handling it better than us. They are frustrated that the moose have evacuated the valleys. And they are confident that Ted cannot get the job done if they get him on the moose. They are used to their hunters tagging out in two or three days. This has become a chore and it is not their fault that the weather is unseasonably without snow.

The rack is six inches wider than mine. It has long points and pronounced fronts. This is a textbook rack that you are looking for. Today, all they show Ted is a picture of the rack. Ted says no and that he won't quit hunting. I gained an ounce of respect.

He comes home before dark and they saw nothing. Now Ted's whiny rant turns to all the things the Russians did wrong this week. I no longer could hold my tongue and I defended them. They were busting their ass for this guy and he was loading up with excuses why he failed.

Diary: December 11, 2015

Today is the last day to hunt. We all go through the same ritual as Ted gets dressed to go. He talks about taking Nickili's rack home if he does not get a moose. I laugh to myself because I am not sure that was the deal put in front of him. This was not a consolation prize, it was a bribe to shut the fuck up and quit hunting.

Almost time to go and Nickili tears off into the woods. Back he comes with the rack on the sled. He tells Ted through Andre, "The rack is his to take home, if he agrees not to go hunting today." Ted drools over the rack and agrees.

The funniest part, because I had to force myself to laugh, is now we take trophy pictures with his rack. I joke that he will probably make the cover of the next brochure and I walk away. All I know for sure is that I can live with myself. I am proud of what I did and what I sacrificed for my moose. My moose is awesome and massive. I now can look at moose pictures and see the true size. Long points make it wider and sexier. My moose is massive, with rare wide palms, broken points and torn-up ears. Mine was a fighter. I like that character. I earned mine!

The cover of the next brochure. LOL

I get why Nickili did this. Say Ted is lucky enough to get a moose near last light. Then the guys must spend all night cutting the thing up. They had enough to do to prepare us to get out of here next day. I appreciated their strategy. I no longer gave a shit if Ted got a moose; my priority was making all these flights and getting home where I belong.

Sasha did the brunt of the field butchering, and he spent all day on mine, well into the dark. Sasha owned the army truck and was our ticket out of here. What Sasha did not do was put enough antifreeze in the truck to handle the temperatures. Our ride was frozen up, and things were broke.

Antifreeze did not hold up to -30 C

This truck was hardcore cool. It was like a camper in the back, with bench seats all around. The coolest thing was the little wood stove in the corner. We knew of the freezing issues a couple days ago, and Sasha cut out and plugged a pipe. My guess is there was a circulation system that ran through the wood stove, so they could use that as a block heater. I think one of those pipes froze. But now, there was no block heater. So, they put three handheld torches under the oil pan to try to heat the oil.

The Russian open-flame block heater

Diary: December 12, 2015
Getting out of camp

The orders are a quick breakfast at 7:00 so Barbara is free to clean and pack everything, and we will leave a couple hours later. The coffee was gone, so I had to drink tea. If there is no coffee then there was no reason for me to stay another minute.

We are up at 6:00 AM to pack. I go out to pee and the burners are still burning under the truck. Like I said, Russians won't tell you bad things. All we hear is, "We fix it."

We come out from breakfast and our block heater has now escalated to a campfire in a bucket. The American in me is getting worried. The sleds are attached to the snow machines and completely full of gear and moose racks. Literally a ton of moose meat is being thrown up on the roof of the truck for the ride out. I know we could ride out on snow machines, but there is no way all our gear could go with us on those sleds. Well, I haven't been in control of shit for the last thirteen days, so why start worrying now!

Strapping a ton of moose meat to the top of the truck.

We load all our gear in the truck. We are still told we will be leaving soon. Then Barbara makes tea. Tea time is a way to stall for time, make us warm, and keep us happy. We aren't going anywhere for a while.

A while later, the truck starts up. A sigh of relief! This truck is supposed to have some way of changing the air pressure in the tires for traction. The right front tire is down and the mechanism to do this is frozen, so now we are "fixing it." The Russians tackle that problem and all the sudden the truck shuts off and old Nickili goes into a "Nickili fit." The radiator is cracked and he is pissed.

We asked what do we do now and we get the "we fix it" response. They drain the radiator and heat the liquid on the woodstoves. Somehow, they "weld" the crack and fill it back up. The truck starts and we are told to get in, we are leaving. But what if it breaks down on the way? "We fix it," they say. Comforting!

I have been here before and I make damn sure I am the last person in so I can sit by the door and the window. This truck is top heavy and I want to know where the emergency exits are. The wood stove is burning and I am dressed warm like I was hunting. I am not getting cold anymore.

Not thirty yards from camp is the creek with probably four-foot-high steep banks. Immediately fifty-pound duffle bags and gun cases are thrown on top of us. This is going to be a long ride.

We have spent a week running this trail with snow machines and it is packed solid and polished to a shine from the sled runners. We aren't five minutes into the trip and this big ass four-wheel-drive is spinning. Five times we back up and pound through and finally you can feel it slowly creep up over the bank. Did I say this was going to be a long ride?

If everything went perfect, we are a five-hour drive to the next camp, then three-plus hours to the road. The moose meat on top was tied down, but not secured. Every time we tipped sideways you waited a few seconds for the meat to slide across and hit you once more. When we tipped forward, all the gear would launch against my back. When we tipped back, well I just wanted to puke. I fought being car sick the whole time. I dare say I could go over Niagara Falls now in a barrel and laugh at the ride.

Tree limbs scrapped and slammed against the truck. The truck was probably three feet taller with moose meat now and I really did not expect any of the meat to make it out of there. The chainsaw and the winch were well used to get us out. Again, Albert and Nickili escorted us on the sleds. Man, I wish I was being dragged behind a sled.

We pushed an 8'-wide truck through a 6'-wide hole most of the way.

Because the swamp was frozen, Sasha could cut across it, instead of going around it. Those little moguls that I couldn't walk on caused the truck to buck violently. Most of the time the truck swayed, because one side or the other would drop into a rut. In these little moguls, now each of the four tires were hitting something at different elevations at different times. Again, the bean bouncing around inside a shaking maraca comes to mind.

Cutting across the frozen swamp made for a violent ride.

The great thing about the ride was the beautiful scenery. I got to see one of the larger volcanoes in the area as we tracked through the swamps. It was a winter wonderland, with all the trees covered with snow and the sun glistening off the mountains. Brutally beautiful is the only way I could describe it. It could lure you in with its beauty and at the same time snuff your life out in an instant.

One of the larger volcanoes in the area

The last river crossing was the memorable one. The ice on the side held just long enough for the whole truck to get on it, then it gave way all at once. Pretty cool falling three feet in a Russian Army truck. The ice on the other side was just as strong and we rammed into it multiple times to break through. Sasha tried to climb the riverbank a couple times. This was the first time I really was scared. The truck rocked violently as the front tires tried to grab ground at different times. I was content with laying this truck on its side, but not in three feet of ice-cold water.

Crashing through the ice to get to the riverbank.

Out came the winch and you could hear it straining to pull the front end up on land. The truck stalled, nothing new, it stalled thousands of times. But this time, there was no starting. Luckily the door had made it to the ice. They came and told us to get out and have a rest.

Ever feel thankful about the spot you break down?

The weight of the truck on the starter wouldn't allow it to disengage. Cutting the tree down to free the winch pressure didn't help. So, under the truck Sasha goes to take off the starter.

Take the starter apart and "we fix it."

To my delight Albert points out that the camp is only 100 yards down the trail. We made it! Well, at least through the first hours of hell.

A couple shots of the river and the sun sparkling off the frost-covered bush.

Tea and snacks were quick, and as soon as they fixed the truck and it rolled up to the cabin it was time to go. More of the same torture, with one added twist. We took on two German hunters and their escort. Their escort was like Cliff Claven from the show *Cheers*. He knew all this useless information and he wanted to tell it all to me. I was doing everything I could not to throw up in his lap. Finally, Ted yelled out to Andre, "Would you tell that guy to shut the fuck up."

A couple hours in, the truck comes to a stop. The door opens and there stands Sergi. Through Andre all I hear is, "Do you want to ride in a Land Cruiser?" I pushed him out of the way and jumped out the door. He had met us on the trail and let us ride in comfort the rest of the trip. Mind you, it was still a rough ride, but at least I could look out the window and not feel like I was going to hurl.

Finally, we came to the frozen river crossing. This was the finish line. I had zero worries of it being solid enough, since it was way below freezing all week. We were now officially out of the bush and into civilization. I had made it out alive!

Sergi took us to his brother's house, which was an awkward experience. By now my sinuses were on fire. I felt like I was going to die. I was grumpy and in dirty hunting clothes. They pushed us to the table that was loaded with the usual snacks, bread, meat, cheese, and raw fish. Then they left us with a Russian couple who weas ready for bed and we had no way of talking to. They took pictures with us though, as if we were some sort of rock stars. It turned out Sergi, Andre, and Sasha were dealing with the moose meat and the gear, so Sasha could head home with his truck. When Sergi and Andre finally came back, Sergi suggested we spend the night there. There was no room for us there and luckily his brother's wife obviously did not like that idea. She immediately got on the phone and found us hotel rooms in Milkovo. The downside is we had a two-hour drive to get there. We rolled in around midnight and I went straight to bed. The others went straight to beer and vodka. They sounded like they had a pretty good time.

Diary: December 13, 2015
The ride back to Petrovalosk

I woke up to a stand-up shower and a sit-down toilet. You have no idea how awesome those two things were. I was a wreck. There was no color left in my face. I only hoped I could get on the plane before whatever I had got worse.

Milkovo from the hotel room. The Russians love their fences.

We had all day to travel. We were only going from one hotel to another. An impromptu breakfast of all the leftovers Barbara carried from camp tasted really good. No coffee though. I was having daydreams of Dunkin' Donuts.

Back into my hunting clothes to stay warm, we piled in the Land Rovers to head to Petro. The ride up was mostly in the dark, so it was awesome to see the mountains that paralleled us on both sides. Every now and then we would pass some sort of settlement, a bunch of rundown buildings with a few smoking chimneys. Each place had a bus stop on the road. I could not imagine waiting for a bus, let alone riding so far to get anywhere.

At least the ride home was in the sunshine, so I could see.

There were a few spots where they were building up the road. They were raising the road bed three or four feet and replacing culvert through the road. You must remember that most of this is swamp or wetlands, so there is no base to it.

Building up the only road.

The thing that I got a kick out of was there would just be an arrow pointing left or right, the rest was up to you on how to get around the fresh dirt and heavy equipment. I was quite sure Andre took the wrong path a couple of times since we were on dirt the bulldozers had just spread.

Once in a while there were markers, like our road cones, but they consisted of a stick stuck in a snowball with orange tape on the end.

No orange cones or barrels in Russia.

Sergi wanted to take us to a hot spring. Kamchatka is an extremely volcanic place. This little resort had a giant hot tub filled with thermally heated sulfur water. I would have done it in a minute, if I was not near death. The hot water was inviting, but I knew you'd have to dry off in -30C.

Then they took us over to the mouth of a dormant volcano. The owner showed us how he could hard-boil eggs in the 180-degree water. This was all pretty cool to see, except when you are on your death bed. I appreciated the gesture, but I just could no longer stand out in the cold.

The mouth of an ancient volcano.

Hard-boiling eggs in the 180-degree water.

Finally, we get to a little suburb of Petro and Andre needed to make a stop. I was taking pictures of the run-down dorm-style apartment buildings. The average monthly income in Russia is $500. I knew we would be in the area that brought that average down. We pass a couple of these buildings and Andre pulls in and parks at one. He had to drop his things off to his wife. This is where he lived. We talked about this at camp. He said he had a pretty good apartment. He said, "It even has hot water." I damn near fell off my feet when he said that. I assume Andre makes a decent living. It is his business that sets up all the paper work for these hunts. His wife is a schoolteacher who makes $1000 a month. The school is too small for all the kids, so she teaches two shifts, starting at 7:00 AM and ending at 6:00 PM. Many Saturdays they have school to fill in the gaps. My guess is for Petrovalosk, they are an upper-middle-class couple. I am taking pictures of these buildings to tell you how bad it is here and Andre calls that home.

A very good apartment included hot water

Finally, we arrive at the hotel. Everyone is ready to eat, drink, and celebrate but me. I climb directly into bed. The others are invited to Sergi's house to Sauna. I just needed to sleep.

Diary: December 14, 2015
The Flight back to Moscow

Damn, I feel so much better after an extra-long night's sleep. This is good because today is going to be a short nineteen-hour day. Sergi will pick us up at 10:00 AM and we will go directly to the airport for a 1:25 PM flight.

From the hotel, the volcanoes just North of Petro

The first challenge is getting the guns through customs. It takes about two hours of paperwork before they accept them. The good news is there is only one flight, so there is a great chance the bags make it on board. I think the airplane was bigger than the terminal building.

Airport at Petrovalosk

They bus you out to the plane. In the background is one of the largest and arguably most perfect volcanoes. It is a perfect cone shape and is flanked by two slightly smaller ones. You can see the one steaming at the mouth.

The volcano backdrop and our plane in the middle of the tarmac.

We take off at 1:25 and arrive in Moscow five minutes later at 1:30. Nine time zones, 4200 miles, all in five minutes of time.

Once we land it takes a couple of hours to get out of the airport and on the road. As with any city, traffic in Moscow is ridiculous. We settle in to the same hotel we stayed in on the way through. It was kind of familiar territory. I got cleaned up and hit the bar for some dinner. A beer, a salad, and a Russian pizza hit the spot.

Diary: December 15, 2015
Leaving Russia for home

We are up at 2:00 AM. This is the most nervous I have seen Andre. He must get us through hours of paperwork before we can get out of Moscow. We have a 9:05 AM flight and it takes us to about 8:00 AM before we are all set with customs, security, and ticketing. We are useless, because there is no one in Moscow that gives a shit to speak English. I can do nothing but stand and wait for Andre to talk for me.

Once the bags are on their way, we walk to passport control. It is like the point of no return. A quick shake of the hand and Andre left us to fend for ourselves. I really didn't have time to thank him enough for everything he did for us. There is no way we could have travelled through Russia, with guns, without his help. He is very good at what he does. I hope he knows how much I appreciate it.

The kid at passport control spoke a little English. He asked me where I was traveling from. I told him Kamchatka. "Why were you there?" he frowned. I said we were hunting. Even he said I was crazy.

We found the gate, and then I found some much needed coffee. I have been waiting since 2:00 AM.

Since I was flying while the earth was rotating under me, it was like magic because very little clock time passed. I physically travelled for thirty hours but the clock only showed nineteen and a half. A quick layover in Zurich, Switzerland, and I was off to the U.S.A. I could finally get a window seat so I could see another famous mountain range. The Swiss Alps were spectacular.

My time in Chicago was scheduled to be just under three hours. This is typically a long layover, but I had to go through passport control, get my bags from baggage claim, then go through customs and prove to them that my gun was mine all this time. Then I'd have to check the bags and gun on a new airline, then ride a train from the international terminal to the regular terminals and find my gate. I was nervous. If I missed my flight to Rochester, it was another whole day away. I was ready to be home.

Then to make matters worse, they had mechanical issues with the plane, so we boarded late. We sat there for some time before we pushed off, waiting for the mechanic to get all his papers signed. They had to take time to de-ice the wings and finally we were off. At the time the pilot said we would be an hour and a half late. As with most of the rest of the trip, I was not in control and there wasn't anything I could do but wait and see what happened. Luckily, the pilot must have made time in the air, because we arrived late, but not that late.

People are actually very nice when you are travelling with a gun. There are extra steps you must do, but they go out of their way to help you and no one ever says anything bad.

Often you must tell an abridged hunting story to get through. Now if you bring Russian sausage or a can of shaving cream, that is a different story. The sausage Sergi gave me was confiscated in Customs. You cannot bring meat into the country. The final kicker, after passing through security no less than twelve times, is when the TSA agents grabs my carry on and searches it. "That can of shaving cream is too big," he says and takes it away from me. I guess too much shaving cream is more dangerous than a rifle. Who knew?

Even without shaving cream, I was happy. I had made it through and arrived at my gate with time to spare. One more short hop to Rochester and I was home free.

Devon was at baggage claim waiting for me. I was glad to be home and had stories to tell. They looked through my pictures as I searched for my bags. Gun cases and oversized items are usually handled separate, but everyone I asked said they were not. I spotted my bags on the carousel, as a kid walked up with my rifle case in hand. I not only made it to Russia and back, but all my gear did too. A small miracle, I think.

Arriving home at midnight ended the last thirty-hour journey.

Diary: December 16, 2015
Home sweet home

Devon did a great job taking care of the house. I think he had fun being bachelor for a couple weeks.

There is nothing like being out in the wild and pushing yourself out of your comfort zone to make you really appreciate the comfort of home. It is a cleansing process for your heart and your soul. My chest filled with pride for what I accomplished and how I handled myself. The moose trophy was icing on the cake.

I have been on a lot of hunts, but this one generated by far the most "you're crazy" comments, a lot of them from Devon. I also know many people worried about me on this trip, and were relieved to hear I was back on U.S. soil.

Grabbing my first real cup of coffee I had a chance to sit down with the computer to really see the pictures I took. As usual, that is a disappointing time, because pictures don't ever really tell the story. But it sure is fun to pass on the moose pictures to all my friends. Even Facebook was pretty cool. There were a lot of people that followed along on my journey and I appreciate their enthusiasm. I only hope that one day they are inspired to reach for and work for their dreams.

I am not gonna lie, the bathroom was the room I wanted to see most. No more standing up to take a dump and a real hot shower were the best things in life.

Let's recap this trip to gain some perspective.

- I took 5 calendar days to get to camp and 4 to return (due to time travel)
- Going took a 30, 25 and 12 hours days
- Returning took a 17, 9, 19 and 30-hour days
- I flew 21,000 miles
- I covered 17 time zones, or ¾ the way around the world
- Russia is wider, 9 time zones, than the distance to fly to Europe
- I rode 770 miles in a vehicle
- I rode over 100 miles into the bush
- I was dragged 148 miles behind a snow mobile, in a wooden sled
- I spent 142 hours travelling
- 8 days in camp and I hunted for 5
- Lowest temperature we saw was -30 Celsius

Diary: December 19, 2015

The greatest use of a brain like mine is that I can see every detail of all my hunts. They play repeatedly in my head. Quite often I will replay moments that make me feel good, and this hunt has just added more of those moments. I am still sleeping in short intervals, so I lie awake at about 3:00 AM, the story and the emotion running through my mind. The sequence of events becomes so solid, that it starts to become words. At 4:00 AM, I cannot take it anymore and I must get up and type the story in my head. By 9:00 AM, I post the piece of this story that happened on the fifth day of the hunt, December 8th.

I get some great reactions to the post. People are really drawn into the story; they like my writing. I don't claim to be a writer; it really is just raw emotion. I am not scared to put in words the raw emotion that I feel. My success and my failures are part of me. The happiness and fulfillment, the pride and accomplishment, the adrenaline-filled rush I get from doing this can never be taken away from me. I am who I am and whatever anyone else thinks of that really doesn't matter to me. I do this for me, only me. For many reasons this is a humbling experience. I humbly want to tell stories, but don't ever want to come across as bragging. I really hope everyone can experience something like this in their lives, whatever their dream is.

Kamchatka, Russia 2015

New Jersey Black Bear – Really? Giants in Unexpected Places

There is a small pond in front of me. There is a paved county road behind me, not 100 yards away. An Interstate highway runs overhead and the tractor trailers scream by every second. Follow that interstate for an hour and you drive into New York City. I am standing by a tree, fifteen yards from a pile of corn and bread all covered in molasses. I have stood there all afternoon, waiting for dark to come and wondering why the hell a black bear would step into that little spot. A few seconds later one appears out of nowhere. A few seconds after that my arrow races through its chest and I have taken a nice New Jersey black bear with my bow.

New Jersey has a bear issue. They are all over the place, and they grow to be giant bears. We had one well over 300 and two over 200 pounds in the pickup that night. Did I mention I am an hour away from New York City? This was a short, cheap bear hunt with my son, nephew, and his friend. New Jersey started an archery hunt this year and we were glad to help. Anti-hunters and the news did everything they could to make it a bad thing. It is not a bad thing. We hardly touched a population that is nearly out of control. For some reason life is so good for bear in Jersey that they are producing three cubs at a time.

The real moral to this story is that there is awesome hunting nearly everywhere if you try hard enough to find it. Much of this hunting can be done for very cheap. I counted on my nephew and his friend to set me up, but I could have researched and done the work myself. It is all about how bad you want it and how hard you are willing to work for it.

Here is some irony for you. I went to Canada twice hunting bears. We did see lots of bears, but never the size that were prevalent in New Jersey, a tank of gas away from my home.

The Cost of Taxidermy – Taking Good Photos

We hunters love to hang animal heads on our walls. But there are two problems you need to think about. The first is time. It takes time for the taxidermist to do your mount. Six months is quick, a year is normal, and over a year is very possible. This sucks because you are dying to show off your animal when you get back home from the hunt. The second issue is that taxidermy is expensive. More hunters than you can imagine put a deposit down and never come back to get their trophy. I have seen rooms full of unclaimed trophies. Life gets in the way, or another hunt trip gets planned and the money to finish paying for a mount is just not there.

The best answer is to budget the cost into the cost of the hunt as you save. That way you have the money already. If you fail to get an animal, you can roll that money over into the savings plan for the next hunt. This is easier said than done, but it does have some merit. This also saves you from having to get the wife's permission twice.

The real answer is to learn how to take great field photos. This is a weakness of mine, so I cannot pretend to tell you how, but I can offer a couple pointers. The biggest one is to take time. Take time to set the animal up. Set it up in front of a nice natural background and clean it up properly. Then take shots from every angle. Do yourself a favor in the planning process and look at great hunting poses and photos and read how to take good pictures. Investing in a photography class would be a smart thing to do.

The camera needs to be as low as possible. A standing cameraman takes a crappy picture. Hold the camera near the ground, so you are looking up at the hunter and animal and catch the sky in the background. I carry a tiny tripod with me, so I can set the camera up and take pictures of myself. Include pictures with your guide—he will become like a brother to you and it is always nice to send him a trophy shot when you get home.

Some of the greatest trophy photos are of the scenery you get to see on the hunt. Force yourself to stop and take good scenery pictures every few minutes. You never know when one will stand out as your favorite background photo.

If you can take great photos, you might forgo the taxidermy work. I have thousands of dollars in taxidermy in my living room. I often wonder if I would have been happier spending that money on hunting and gaining more memories. This is a tough decision, but it is something to think about.

Field Data for Your Taxidermist

I think you should learn to properly cape your own trophy animal, but I say that because I was taught it in the field. My friend showed me how to cape my caribou head, and then I did the second one on my own. Guides typically do this for you, but they often don't have sharp, delicate knives and they can make a mess of a cape. A good taxidermist fixes many of these holes, but it can be a lot of extra work. In addition to my field lesson, there are many YouTube videos that show how it is done. Hell, I taught myself taxidermy by watching YouTube videos. I suggest practicing on a deer back home so the first try is not on your priceless trophy mount. To do this work properly a sharp knife is crucial. I carry scalpel blades and a scalpel handle with me. You can get these at a taxidermy supply store and once you start using them, you won't regret it.

Your taxidermist will appreciate you taking the correct measurements. There are a few measurements that allow you to pick the correct size form, or one close to the size of your animal. Three measurements are taken with the animal with the hide still on. Search out a taxidermy-form supplier and request a catalog. Then you will see how these measurements are used to pick out a form.

1. Tip of nose to the corner of the eye.
2. Tip of nose, up over the head to the back of the head, or where the skull stops.
3. For a life-size mount, you want the tip of the nose, up over the head, down the back to the base of the tail.

Once the hide is off, you need some measurements of the body of the animal without fur and skin. These measurements will translate to the size of the form before the taxidermists puts your hide over it.

4. Measure the circumference of the neck at the base of the skull.
5. Measure the circumference of the neck, near the middle of the neck.
6. Measure the circumference of the chest area.
7. Measure the circumference of the belly area if you can do it quickly before bloating starts.

Most of these measurements are used for a life-size mount, but the neck measurements insure your deer has the correct swollen neck size.

I carry a small cloth measuring tape that you might find in a store that sells material and sewing supplies, or you can order one through a taxidermy supplier.

The second thing that is helpful for the taxidermist is close-up pictures. They will use reference pictures all the time to get colors correct because a tanned hide loses it natural colors. I like to get close-up pictures of the nose, mouth, eyes, and ears. With your pictures they can paint and color it like the animal you shot, not like one in the reference books. If there are any battle scars you want to keep, take pictures of them too. My moose had torn ears from his many battles. A taxidermist might fix those tears if you don't tell them different.

Lesson – Field Preparation of Hides

I do my own taxidermy work and my plan was to mount my Manitoba bear, then mount my son's. As I test-fit the face over the head of the form, the hair pushed off the face. This is called slipping and it ruins the mount.

I saw a tip online that finally describes what I had done wrong. The hide needs to get off the animal as quick as possible and cooled. The proper thing to do is to salt it and air-dry it in a cool place. To short-circuit this procedure, we often think we should throw it in a freezer to save the work for a taxidermist. I have always rolled the face up into the hide to protect it. The issue with this is the hide around the face insulates it from the freezer and keeps it warmer longer. The result can leave the face warm enough and long enough for bacteria to cause slippage. Always keep the face on the outside and freeze (cool) it as fast as possible. Slipped spots on the body can be hidden or fixed, but if the face goes bad, the mount is ruined.

Lesson – Quit worrying about impressing others.

If you base your success on what others think, you are setting yourself up for disappointment. Do everything you do for your enjoyment, pride, and pleasure because you cannot count on others, at all. My trophies and photos are for me to enjoy, sparking all the memories that go along with it. I hardly ever tell my stories unless it comes up in conversation, because I never want to come across as bragging. I never offer tours of my living room because the reactions can be wide ranging. Most love to see my mounts, while others get so jealous and defensive it is shocking. Then of course there is always that person that simply hates the thought of killing animals, not understanding anything about conservation. Just know this passion is not for everyone and any negative reaction you get is coming from their deep-rooted insecurities. My trophy room is full of positive memories, Why would I put myself in a position to risk any negativity?

Lesson – Save money on cancelled hunts.

The outfitting business has changed drastically over the years I have hunted. Hunt prices skyrocketed with the popularity of hunting television shows and for the most part those prices have not come back down. What happens is that many hunters cannot follow through with their plans. They put a deposit down, but end up cancelling as the hunt grows near. I chalk much of that up to poor planning and discipline, but sometimes life just does get in the way of dreams.

I experienced this myself when it was finally time to pursue a divorce. I had put a 50-percent deposit down on a Newfoundland moose and caribou hunt. Retaining a lawyer was a painful cost to bare, but the thoughts of that retainer running out and needing more money to fight my battle put hunting on the back burner. The outfitter, rightfully so, had no sympathy for me, so I had to choose to lose that deposit. The bigger heartache was that I was planning to go with Dean, and he now had to make the twenty-four-hour drive by himself. I had let him down. Some hunter got a nice surprise with a hunt discounted at $3000.

What this has done has brought on an onslaught of cancellation hunts. Another hunter's deposit is typically taken off the price for an initial discount. As the hunt dates grows closer, the outfitters are forced to discount the hunt even more. Consider how much they have invested in land leases, tags, and hunting rights; they cannot afford to miss a hunt. Their income depends on it.

If you can pile up money in a hunt fund, and you can travel at a moment's notice, you can book some really awesome hunts at a discounted rate. This strategy can save you money, but takes a whole new level of discipline to pull off. You must be able to save and put away money with no real goal in mind. I don't think I will ever do it this way because I know the value and fun the planning process is to me. I just hate to miss out on that anticipation.

Lesson – Try to get a trophy fee basis

Hunt prices can be a scary thing, especially when it is one price for it all. Think about this: if you fail to get your animal, the outfitter makes a ton of money. They can walk you around an area for a week, never expecting to see an animal, and they get paid full price. I am not saying they all think this way because they don't. But I have heard some bad stories and it can happen.

Consider asking the outfitter to adjust the total cost of the hunt, allowing you to pay a trophy fee if you take your animal. This accomplished two things. It makes the risk smaller for you in that you pay less if you fail to fill your tag. Coming home empty handed is a little easier to take when you still have a few thousand in cash in your pocket. I also think it shows confidence on the part of the outfitter. He should readily agree if he thinks the odds are good that you will be successful. If they argue, I wonder if he is only in it for the money, or why he is not confident in his ability to get you on an animal.

Rifle Declarations and Customs Forms

Getting your hunting rifle through border customs has its challenges. It is something that I would suggest you research long beforehand and plan. I have done it wrong and still made out okay. I have done it right and they have ignored me anyway. It is kind of like going to the DMV: you can be as prepared as possible and still be sent away for one more thing.

We sat at the United States side of the Canadian border, trying to tell them we were armed. Well not really armed, but we had our hunting rifles and really thought they might want to know about them. Getting someone at the counter to acknowledge us was like pulling teeth. While we waited, out the window we saw agents pull a car over and empty it of its belongings. They were scattering shit all over the pavement. On the sidewalk was this very elderly couple, holding each other, shaking and looking terrified. Once an agent decided to pay attention to us, I asked what the deal was outside. He shrugged it off and said, "Searches are random, generated by a computer." I had guns in the truck, and the elderly couple were no threat, but this is how it goes at the border.

Customs form 4475 needs to be filled out. It basically says you own the gun, it is going outside the country, and you still are the owner when you come back with it. An agent will need to confirm that the serial number on the form matches the rifle. This is important to have when you come back into the United States because it proves it was yours all along. Without this form, they could think you bought the gun outside the country and are trying to sneak it in without declaring it or importing it properly.

So, you must stop on the United States side before leaving the country with your hunting rifle. When you fly over the border, this is often harder to do. Typically, you fly into a country and head straight for that country's customs area to be processed. To do it this way will take some planning, some extra layover time and likely some questions in the airport. Finding and getting to the U.S. Customs office is the issue you must figure out.

It is possible to go to a U.S. Customs department in the airport you leave from, before your flight leaves. Many but not all airports have customs. But, they only work normal, daylight hours, so an early flight out makes this impossible. I got lucky once and banging on a locked door got the attention of a night time agent who was very nice and was willing to do the extra effort to help me out.

What if you forget or cannot fill out this form? I have been there. The agent proceeded to tell me I cannot bring my gun back. Then they berate you and fill your head with all sorts of gloom and doom about you losing your gun. Be cool and be humble and beg mercy for them to help you. They will, but they will make you sweat first. Keep in mind, they must assume you are trying to break the law, and the berating is a way to feel you out and see if you might be guilty. If you don't get pissed and defensive and overreact, they will soon figure it was an honest mistake.

The next stop is the Canadian side, if that is your hunting destination. You must buy a firearm permit for $50 Canadian from their agents. A similar process applies: they need to see the gun and verify the serial number you wrote down. The worst thing that ever happened to me on the Canadian side was when I spent an hour swapping hunting stories with the agents. Canadians all seem to love to hunt.

It should go without saying, but gun safety and communications is highly important. At each location, you are whipping out and handling a firearm in a government building. I remove the rifle bolt and store it in a separate compartment in my luggage. I run a cable lock through the gun and I have a trigger lock on the trigger. When they see it, it is very evident this gun is safe. I think it makes a big deal that you show you care about safety and security.

Shipping a Trophy

So, you are off in some foreign land, and yes, Canada is a foreign land. You were successful and bagged the trophy of a lifetime. How the hell do you get it home?

The first question will be, does this animal require a CITES permit? This is proof of where the animal was taken and permission to possess it in the United States. For example, I took two wolves in Alberta, Canada. Wolves are protected in the United States and they require a CITES permit for import. Without that documentation, someone, someday might think I killed them illegally in the U.S.

The need for a CITES automatically means you are leaving your trophy in someone else's hands. Your outfitter might handle it. A taxidermist might help you. An export consultant might help you. You need to know how this works before you go. Also, everyone that touches your trophy from this point on needs to get paid. You want to plan this cost in your budget.

The skulls need to be cleaned and bleached. The hides need to be dipped or tanned. This processing makes sure all the creepy little organisms from the country of origin are nice and dead. This too takes time and money and you need to know who is doing this for you. Same goes for packaging or crating for shipment. Who is going to build you a crate or package your trophy for safe over-the-border or overseas shipment?

Now someone needs to arrange shipment, and arrange the export paperwork and the import permits. You need to talk to a Customs broker in the United States and pay them to handle this for you. They will work with the exporter and help arrange the shipment. They will work with United States Customs to make sure the package is inspected and passes Customs. They will then arrange shipment from U.S. Customs to your door. They will give you an estimate and you will agree and sign a contract of services. You may have to front the money ahead of time, or they might bill you at the end. This too takes time and money and you need to know who is doing this for you. You cannot short-circuit this process because your trophy could get trashed at Customs inspection. You need professionals to go to bat for you and insure it gets done right.

This process costs money, sometimes a lot of it. It was about $1000 to get my moose from Russia, and that was cheap since the Russian side of things was very inexpensive. The process took six months to complete and I did not have my moose mounted, only skull bleached and hide dipped.

Because there are so many people involved, the trophy often gets caught up in time with one party waiting for the other. Multiple times I had to send emails to jog everyone's memory and get them focused and talking about my shipment.

I had major issues with my two Alberta wolves because I did not plan properly. I had no idea I needed to do any of this. We ended up dropping them off at a taxidermist. Two years and two thousand dollars later I got my wolf hides. What sounded like a favor, a couple hundred bucks, and a quick drive to the border ended up me being fucked by this asshole. Every step he took, when he finally got around to doing something, required more money. I was in a hopeless position to suck it up and pay because I had no leg to stand on. At one point I considered buying a ticket to Alberta just to kick his ass. For over a year I feared he sold my hides and was just screwing me. I could have done nothing about it. I did not plan well at all and paid dearly for my mistake.

If you have your trophy mounted in the country you got the animal, then the same process applies, but you have a much bigger and heavier crate to ship, so the cost goes up.

I got a phone call from my son one afternoon. A tractor trailer was parked on the road outside my house. Devon went down to the road to see if he needed help and the driver said, "I think I have a moose for this address." There is nothing better than finally getting those packages holding your trophies. It is like Christmas morning, except Devon had the package open before I could get home from work. It may be six months or a year later, but the memories start to flow and the stories need to be retold. All your family and friends will come and see what your trophy looks like, almost like bringing a newborn home the first day. It is an awesome time!

Do-It-Yourself Hunts

I have spent a lot of words telling you how to book and enjoy a guided hunt. Truthfully, that is where my experience is, so that is what I can share with you. When people who don't think they can afford a guided hunt talk about a hunt of a lifetime they automatically jump to a self-guided hunt. They think it the best way to do a hunt on the cheap.

Do it yourself hunting surely has its place. There is a ton of state and federal land out there that can be accessed in a do-it-yourself way. Even gaining access to another person's land requires a do-it-yourself attitude. These are solid skills to develop and acquire to extend your hunting opportunities. But typically, these hunt opportunities are close to home or within a reasonable driving distance. To capitalize on the opportunity, you need to be able to spend time on that property properly scouting.

This is where the idea of a self-hunt out west or in another far-off state falls apart. Think about all the time you spend thinking about, scouting, and preparing for a deer hunt in your backyard. Now think about how successful you might be if you did none of that preparation. When you take on a do-it-yourself hunt a long distance away you are taking the chance of hunting with no preparation. Everything you must learn and do has to be done in a few days. This includes recovery of the game animal if you are successful.

Think of it this way: a guided hunt is costly, but you are paying for all the things you don't have time to do yourself. All these things are required to be successful. The guide and outfitter knows the area and the game and they have spent hours scouting it for you. They have prepared the stands and picked the best spots to ambush game. In most cases they have taken care of your lodging and comfort. If you don't own the proper gear such as tents and camping equipment, you must include that in the cost of the do-it-yourself hunt.

The biggest advantage of an outfitted hunt is that they feed you. I know it seems easy to carry your own food and cook it, but it sure is nice to come home from a hard day hunting and just eat.

What happens if you get your animal, especially if it is a large species like an elk? Field care is a lot of work, but packing that animal out will require extra help and sometimes pack animals or motor vehicles. Sure, you can suck it up and carry your own game, but sometimes the hunt comes down to the last minute of the last day. Where do you find time to do all this work then?

So be very cautious when you say a do-it-yourself hunt is cheaper. If your hunt is truly a hunt of a lifetime, then is it worth taking risks that will limit your chance of success? Yes, people do it every day and enjoy the hell out of it. I am sure there is a level of satisfaction that is far greater if you do it all yourself. But if I was planning that one dream hunt, I would want to maximize my success. The true final cost of a guided hunt was less than you think if you consider everything you get done for you.

Pushing Myself Past My Limits is What I am Most Proud of.

I have never regretted the times I have pushed myself "outside the box" or past my comfort zone. The rewards and satisfaction I have gained each time are more than I could have ever imagined. Funny, I am always surprised. I guess it is human nature not to understand the positive gains from doing more than you thought you could. That is what keeps many from ever trying. I find this sad because one thing that you always gain, and people need more of, is self-confidence. Once you figure out what you can do, you realize that you can do anything.

This parallels anything you do in life. You might become a Crossfitter and learn what your body can do and you feel great about it. But then, in another aspect of life you let doubt and procrastination take hold. Woman get through the pain of childbirth, but refuse to put in the same effort and fight to do something else they always wanted to do. If you can do it in one area of your life, the same skills, will and discipline can get you through any other aspect of your life.

I think pursuing your dream and making it happen can be the spark to change the other everyday things you need to change in your life. People hate change. Not changing is you getting stuck inside your box, inside your comfort zone. Once you prove to yourself the benefits of getting out of that comfort zone, you can do it anytime, for anything. Why not try it on something you always wanted to do, something that you have dreamt of for a very long time?

Yes, you will make mistakes during this process. You might have setbacks or unforeseen challenges. Life is not easy or smooth. I have made mistakes through my hunting career, professional career, and life, but I forged on and I learned from them. I will never make the same mistake twice. If you think about it, pushing yourself to the brink of mistakes is getting outside the box. I hope people learn from my mistakes and my journey through my big-game hunting career. If you do, it will allow you to enjoy your hunt more and get more out of it, leaving any anxiety or worry behind.

Have the will and discipline to push toward your dream!

About the Author

He has a strong belief in FREEDOM. Unquestionable LOYALTY toward the people he loves. What he does, he does FOR FAMILY, even though they see their needs of him differently. When he accepts a job to do, he is DISCIPLINED to do it at the best of his ability. He'll SELF SACRIFICE for the better of his team and friends, always THINKING OF OTHERS. He will try to TEACH others or jump in and DO IT HIMSELF if he thinks his skills can make a larger impact. He has extraordinary DECISION-MAKING capabilities. He cares nothing about other mistakes, other than to solve them, learn from them and move on. But his own FAILURES HAUNT HIM. He carries CONFIDENCE to the border line of arrogance, and this threatens the ego of others. He is HUMBLE, he doesn't do any of this for glory; it is nothing more than DOING HIS JOB. All he wants to do is FINISH THE JOB and go home.

"If I should die tomorrow,

I will have no regrets."

I grew up pumping gas and changing tires at our family owned gas station. Balancing school, sports and work throughout my high school career engrained a work ethic in me. I chose to pursue an Electrical Engineering degree to allow me to move on from the gas station life.

I always wanted to keep my hands on the technological side, but little did I know my greater skills are managing the people and the project that deliver high tech. solutions. My passion is to help people succeed and I know this book can change lives.

Made in the USA
Middletown, DE
13 September 2020